From First to Worst

From First to Worst

The New York Mets, 1973–1977

JACOB KANAREK

Foreword by JERRY KOOSMAN

McFarland & Company, Inc., Publishers
Jefferson, North Carolina, and London

LIBRARY OF CONGRESS CATALOGUING-IN-PUBLICATION DATA

Kanarek, Jacob.
    From first to worst : the New York Mets, 1973–1977 /
Jacob Kanarek ; foreword by Jerry Koosman.
        p.   cm.
    Includes bibliographical references and index.

    ISBN 978-0-7864-3466-4
    softcover : 50# alkaline paper ∞

    1. New York Mets (Baseball team)—History.   I. Title.
GV875.N45K36   2008
796.357'64097471—dc22   2008026996

British Library cataloguing data are available

©2008 Jacob Kanarek. All rights reserved

*No part of this book may be reproduced or transmitted in any form
or by any means, electronic or mechanical, including photocopying
or recording, or by any information storage and retrieval system,
without permission in writing from the publisher.*

On the cover: Rusty Staub makes one of his legendary sliding
catches (AP photo)

Manufactured in the United States of America

*McFarland & Company, Inc., Publishers
    Box 611, Jefferson, North Carolina 28640
    www.mcfarlandpub.com*

Table of Contents

Foreword by Jerry Koosman

This book brings back the day-by-day and play-by-play history of the Mets in the seventies. As I read these pages, many moments were brought back to life, some of which I had forgotten. It tells of the happenings of each day and each game and brings back the awareness of the gulf between perception and reality, between surface and substance, between words and deeds. The research behind this book makes it a baseball bible for the Met fan of that era. It takes you through our ups and downs, road trips, homestands and verbatim conversations, giving you unbelievable insight into those five seasons.

Any baseball fan would appreciate reading this book to see how "probably" the most optimistic manager in baseball, Yogi Berra, led a team to the World Series. All Mets fans will have the opportunity to have that "YA GOTTA BELIEVE!" season refreshed so thoroughly in their mind.

As a player, I was not able to be everywhere, on the field and in the clubhouse, and hear all that went on in those seasons. Jacob Kanarek has searched through the written articles of so many people that were there that those seasons have come back to life in my mind. I will carry the memories of those seasons with a better understanding of all that transpired. Yes, we as individuals and as a team made mistakes, but we also did some things that set us apart from an average team. This book will give you, the reader, an insight as to what took place for us to be called the "Amazin' Mets."

Kooz

Preface

Growing up as a Mets fan in the mid- and late seventies and seeing my team plummet to the bottom of the baseball world by the end of the 1977 season, when only five short years earlier this same franchise fell just one game short of winning a second world championship in its short existence, I was constantly nagged by a simple question: How could a franchise that reached the pinnacle in only its seventh year of existence, in the greatest city of the baseball world, sink so low in so short a time? In trying to find an in-depth and comprehensive answer, I found that no book written on the Mets adequately covered the team in the mid seventies.

Enter SABR — the Society for American Baseball Research, of which I am a member. It provided me with the necessary research material through ProQuest and Paper of Record, databases that gave me access to the vast archives of the *New York Times* and the *Sporting News*. In a nutshell, the decline of the franchise can be attributed to poor player personnel moves made by a front office that failed to face the new realities of the changing game of baseball, but beyond that, my research brought back many pleasant memories of those seasons — not just the Amazin' stretch drive of 1973, the exciting playoffs and World Series that followed, but even of the seasons that did not bring ultimate glory to Flushing. In light of the great thrill that I had in researching these seasons and my belief that all Mets fans of that era would likewise enjoy reminiscing about the Mets teams of those years, I decided to put my pen to paper and, in vivid detail, bring the day-in, day-out action of those seasons to the forefront. Not only would the household names of that era, among them Tom Seaver, Jerry Koosman, Tug McGraw, Bud Harrelson, Jerry Grote, Joe Torre, Dave Kingman, Felix Millan and Cleon Jones, once again be appearing on a daily basis, but also names long forgotten, such as Dave Schneck, Pepe Mangual, Bruce Boisclair, Leo Foster and Roy Staiger. And who could forget the immortal Paul Siebert? What Met fan wouldn't smile to see those names one more time?

Just as in baseball, in order for an idea to reach its full potential and evolve into a book, teamwork is an absolute must. To that end, this author is indebted to the many folks who helped ensure that what started off as a pipe dream became a reality. I would like to express my thanks to Kevin O'Sullivan and Joan Carroll of the Associated Press, Mary Luhrs and Kim Apley from Corbis, Michael Massman from the *New York Times*, and Patricia Kelly of the Baseball Hall of Fame for enhancing this project with the best photos available, bringing these seasons back to life as much as possible.

A special thank you to Ari Hutman, who acted as my sounding board throughout the project. Thanks to my dad, whose *New York Times* sports section I would lay out on the living room floor (as I couldn't read it any other way) so I would be able to scrutinize every box score, and to my mom, who always seemed to be chasing me into bed during the most exciting part of the game, usually when one team had the bases loaded and most likely there were two outs and a 3–2 count on the batter.

Another (last but not least) special thank you to Jerry Koosman, whose great career coincided with my childhood, for giving generously of his time to write the foreword.

Above all to God, who has given me everything I have.

Introduction

After spending their first seven seasons as the perennial doormat of the National League, in 1969 the Mets stunned the baseball world by winning one hundred games and capturing the National League East, sweeping the Atlanta Braves in the first National League Championship Series and putting the finishing touches on an amazing season by beating the Baltimore Orioles in four straight World Series games after losing the opener.

To be sure, this amazing feat was not accomplished on mirrors alone. The Mets had a no-nonsense manager, Gil Hodges, who demanded the maximum out of his players while instilling confidence at the same time, along with the best young starting pitching in the game, namely Tom Seaver, Jerry Koosman, Nolan Ryan and Gary Gentry. Additionally, the Mets were particularly solid up the middle with the best defensive catcher in the game, Jerry Grote, who aside from possessing a rifle arm was extremely adept at handling the team's greatest asset, the pitching staff; Bud Harrelson, the scrappy shortstop who anchored the infield; and Gold Glove winner Tommie Agee, who patrolled in center field. Agee, along with mid-season acquisition Donn Clendenon and Cleon Jones, fueled the offense.

Still, no one believed the Mets were ready to take on the big boys. After all, how could the Mets compete with the powerhouse of the National League East, the Chicago Cubs? Certainly the Mets had no one in the middle of their lineup who sent shivers up an opposing pitcher's spine the way Ernie Banks, Ron Santo and Billy Williams did. The only ones who believed were the Mets themselves. And believe they did. After the Mets did in fact win the division, the pundits declared the ride over. After all, even the young vaunted Mets' arms would be no match for Hank Aaron, Orlando Cepeda and Rico Carty. But again the Mets proved the pundits wrong, and the runaway train continued its wild ride by sweeping the Braves in three straight games. At last the Mets found their match, the experts proclaimed. Not only did the Orioles' starting three of Mike Cuellar, Dave McNally and Jim Palmer match up favorably to Seaver, Koosman, Gentry and Ryan, but the Mets' batters of Agee, Jones and Clendenon were Davids taking on the Goliaths of the Orioles' lineup of Brooks

Robinson, Frank Robinson and Boog Powell. And after the first game in which Don Buford, the first Oriole batter, had homered to help power the Birds to a 4–1 victory, the experts agreed that the Mets express had reached its end. But for the Mets, the first-game loss was only a minor obstacle in their ride to glory, for they went on to win the next four games and were crowned world champions.

The champagne had soon been drunk, the confetti cleaned up, the parade ended and the calendar turned from the sixties into the seventies. The emergence of a new era had begun, and it was time for the Mets to begin defending their title as reigning world champions. While repeating a title is never easy, the Mets were at a distinct disadvantage since they would be considered a force to be reckoned with from day one. In 1969 the Mets were not taken seriously until it was too late.

And for the first three seasons of the next decade, despite not capturing another title, the Mets remained a force by winning 83 games each season. Yet slowly the face of the 1969 championship team began to change. In the spring of 1971, Ron Swoboda, the right-handed side of the right-field platoon, became the first starter of the championship team to be dealt when he was sent to Montreal for slick-fielding center fielder Don Hahn. The left-handed side of the platoon, Art Shamsky, was the next to go, dealt to the St. Louis Cardinals shortly after the conclusion of the 1971 season. Two other prominent members of the 1969 cast — Donn Clendenon, the MVP of the World Series, and Ron Taylor, the relief specialist — were cut loose as well due to their diminishing production. After the winter meetings, in an attempt to close their perennial hole at third base, the Mets sent flame-throwing right-handed starter Nolan Ryan and three prospects to the California Angels in exchange for Jim Fregosi, a power-hitting shortstop who would be converted to a third baseman.

In addition, no longer was the dynamic and authoritative Gil Hodges behind the helm of the team after having tragically been felled by a fatal heart attack at the end of spring training in 1972. In its stead was Yogi Berra, whose managing style differed greatly from that of his predecessor. Whereas Hodges was a disciplinarian and an astute strategist, Yogi was more of an easygoing type without the keen perception of Hodges. While Berra got the Mets off to a great start in 1972 as they jumped out to a 25-7 record and appeared ready to run away with the division, things went awry very quickly. Rusty Staub broke a bone in his hand. Gary Gentry couldn't win, and Jim Fregosi could neither field nor hit. Tommie Agee's talents appeared to have declined considerably. Jerry Koosman suffered his worst season, Bud Harrelson missed the entire month of August with back miseries, and Jerry Grote underwent surgery for bone chips in his elbow. When the dust cleared, the Mets found themselves finishing a disappointing third place, only ten games over .500.

By the time the Mets opened their camp for the start of spring training in 1973, Tommie Agee, the leadoff batter as well as Gold Glove winner, and Gary

Gentry, the number three starter on the 1969 team, were no longer on the roster. Agee suffered two consecutive injury-plagued seasons and was sent to the Astros in November of 1972. The only starters remaining from the championship team were Jerry Grote behind the plate, Bud Harrelson at short and Cleon Jones in left field.

Despite the turnover, there was much optimism as Yogi Berra began his second season as manager. Right field was now in the hands of the very capable and popular "Le Grand Orange" Rusty Staub, who came to the Mets from the Expos on the same day of Gil Hodges' funeral in exchange for three promising young players—Ken Singleton, Mike Jorgensen and Tim Foli. The Mets were optimistic that Staub was completely recovered from his broken hand. First base now belonged to John Milner, a young and upcoming power hitter. In order to add more consistent offense and strength up the middle, the Mets sent Gary Gentry and Danny Frisella to the Atlanta Braves for Felix Millan and George Stone. For the first time in team history, the Mets had a second baseman that could adequately turn a double play. In addition, the Mets were hoping that Jim Fregosi would rebound from his dismal first season as a Met and finally give the team the long-desired production from a position that has always been characterized for its power output. If there was any concern at all entering the season, it was in center field, where Willie Mays and his gimpy 42-year-old knees would share time with Don Hahn. "My biggest problem will be coming up with a centerfielder," admitted Berra before the start of the season.

The pitching staff was still the team's greatest asset, led by the indomitable Tom Seaver and supplemented by perhaps the two best left-handed starters in the league in Jerry Koosman and Jon Matlack. Jim McAndrew and newcomer George Stone would round out the starting five, and the bullpen was once again anchored by Tug McGraw. In addition, the Mets acquired Phil Hennigan from the Cleveland Indians to be the setup man for McGraw. Hennigan filled the position held previously by Danny Frisella, since dealt to Atlanta in the Millan deal.

1

A Battle Cry Is Born

In a somber 1973 Opening Day ceremony, the Mets honored 11 returning prisoners of war who simultaneously threw out 11 first balls as the team prepared to take on the Philadelphia Phillies. An estimated crowd of 27,000 fans paid their way into a chilly Shea Stadium as two twenty-game winners from 1972, Tom Seaver and Steve Carlton, got set to hook up in what promised to be a classic pitching duel. For Seaver, who won 21 games last season, it would be his sixth consecutive Opening Day start. Carlton, who finished last season with a sparkling 27-10 record, suffered four of his 10 losses to the Mets.

The game remained scoreless until the last of the fourth inning, when the newest Met, Felix Millan, led off with a double. The first controversy of the new season developed on the next play when Willie Mays flied out to center fielder Del Unser. Millan, who got a late jump while tagging up, swerved towards left field, trying to avoid the tag by Phillies third baseman Jose Pagan. Artie Williams, a rookie umpire, called Millan safe, sending enraged Philadelphia manager Danny Ozark scurrying out of the Phillies' dugout to argue. "You're supposed to stay in one path from base to base, no more than three feet from either side," explained Ozark, of his argument after the game. "Millan went pretty far — you can still see his footmarks, and while the rookie umpire is a good one, but that's a rare play and I'll bet he'll call it differently the next time."[1]

Regretfully for Ozark, getting it right the next time was not soon enough. One batter later, Cleon Jones drove Carlton's first pitch over the 371-foot sign in left field for a two run homer and a 2–0 Mets lead. Cleon struck again in the last of the seventh inning when he drove another Carlton pitch, this one over the center field fence, giving the Mets a 3–0 lead.

In the meantime, the Phillies' offense was having no success against Tom Seaver, as he scattered five hits over the 7²⁄₃ innings he worked. Seaver, who fanned eight, had two scary moments. The first came in the top of the sixth inning, when Willie Montanez launched a deep drive to right field that Rusty Staub was able to run down as he crashed into the right-field fence. In the eighth inning, with two outs, the Phillies threatened by putting two runners on base. But Tug McGraw, who relieved Seaver, was able to end the Phillies' threat and then easily retired the Phillies in the ninth inning as the Mets picked up their fourth consecutive Opening Day win.

The Mets won again the next afternoon on a ninth-inning two-out single by Willie Mays, which snapped a 2–2 tie and lifted Jon Matlack, last season's Rookie of the Year, to his first 1973 win. After rain postponed the series finale, the Mets headed off to St. Louis for a brief two-game series with the Cardinals. Jerry Koosman, coming off two injury-plagued seasons, was relegated as the third starter behind Seaver and Matlack. He received his first assignment of the young season while facing off against Cardinals right-hander Reggie Cleveland. Four consecutive hits in the top of the first inning gave the Mets an early 2–0 lead, which was expanded to 3–0 when John Milner hit his second home run of the season in the top of the third inning. Koosman gave the Mets a solid seven innings, allowing two earned runs, and left with a 5–3 lead upon turning the ball over to McGraw. Despite McGraw's struggles, allowing six of the ten batters he faced to reach base, a great play by newly acquired Millan and clutch last-out pitching by Phil Hennigan saved the game for Koosman and the Mets. The Mets, behind Tom Seaver and Hennigan, then beat the Cardinals, 2–1, marking the first time in franchise history that the team won its first four games of the season.

From St. Louis it was back to the East with a pit stop in Philadelphia for a three-game series before returning home. It was in the Philadelphia series that the Mets lost their first game of the year. A 19-year-old rookie in his major league debut, Larry Christenson of the Phillies, halted the season-opening four-game winning streak as Philadelphia beat Matlack and the Mets, 7–1. After losing the second game of the series as well, the Mets were able to salvage the final game behind a rookie of their own. Harry Parker pitched 7⅔ innings of stellar baseball, allowing the Phillies only one run on six hits. The Mets scored two runs in the first inning when John Milner hit his third home run of the season with a runner aboard as New York prevailed, 2–1.

It was a struggling Mets offense that returned to Shea Stadium on April 17. Averaging only two runs in their last four games, the Mets took on the Chicago Cubs in a four-game series. The homecoming failed to revitalize the Mets' bats, however, as the first two games of the series saw both Tom Seaver and Jon Matlack pitch complete games while allowing only one run, yet lose as the Mets' offense couldn't muster a run in either game. A fourth-inning home run by Rick Monday off Seaver in the opener was enough to do him in as Ferguson Jenkins held the Mets scoreless on two hits. "You hate to pitch a game like that and lose," said Seaver. "Especially when you're going to go out there and 36 or 37 times a season and not always pitch that well. Those are the games you expect to win."[2]

In the second game of the series, Ray Burris, another young pitcher making his major league debut against the Mets, allowed twice as many hits as

Jenkins did. Nevertheless, it was not enough to put a run across the plate, and once again the Mets went down to defeat, 1–0, as the Cubs scored their lone run on a wild pitch by Jon Matlack in the first inning. "I pitch every day with the idea that one run might beat me," said Matlack. "I'd feel that way no matter who I was pitching for, except maybe the Cincinnati Reds or the Pittsburgh Pirates."[3] For the record, 10 games into the season, the Mets collectively were batting .181.

The series concluded with a Thursday afternoon doubleheader that saw Koosman take the mound in the first game. With Seaver and Matlack the victims of little offensive support in the first two games of the series despite exceptional pitching, Koosman continued where his predecessors left off by allowing the Cubs to score only one run as well. Yet for the first three innings it appeared that he was doomed to suffer the same fate as his teammates after the Cubs scored an unearned in the second inning. It took until the bottom of the fourth inning before the Mets finally scored a run in the series. In fact, they scored two runs, to take a 2–1 lead. An insurance run was added when John Milner, who continued to supply the Mets with the only power in the early going, hit his fourth home run in the last of the eighth inning. That run appeared to loom large after the Cubs put the tying runs on base in the top of the ninth inning. Koosman was able to steer out of trouble, however, as he picked up his second win of the season. "I haven't pitched many complete games lately and, when you see them getting guys up in the bullpen from the sixth inning on, you feel you've got to prove something," said Koosman. "This time my fastball kept getting better, and that hasn't happened in quite a while."[4]

The Mets' offense, perhaps wiped out from their initial effort, went back to sleep in the second game as they were shut out for the third time in the series. This time it was Burt Hooton with the honors as he spun a three-hitter, with the Cubs taking a 7–0 decision.

With the Cubs leaving town, the Montreal Expos were the next visitors for an unusual three-game weekend series: Friday was a scheduled off-day, and the teams played a Sunday afternoon doubleheader. Apparently tired of being on the wrong end of shutouts, the Mets, behind Harry Parker, shut out the Expos, 5–0, in the Saturday afternoon opener. John Milner supplied three runs with a single and a two-run homer — his fifth home run of the year — in the eighth inning. While on this day it didn't reflect on the scoreboard, Cleon Jones, the team's second leading hitter behind Milner, was diagnosed with a strained right wrist, putting an additional strain on an already struggling offensive attack.

The Mets split the Sunday afternoon doubleheader, losing the first game, 2–1, before coming back strong in the night cap. The offense erupted for 13 runs, as the Mets shellacked the Expos, 13–3. In the opener, Tom Seaver was on the verge of becoming a 1–0 loser for the second game in a row, having surrendered a home run to Ron Fairly in the second inning. In the bottom of the ninth inning, the Mets were still trailing by the same 1–0 deficit when Jim Fregosi drew a walk to start the frame. A wild pitch by Mike Marshall sent Fregosi to second before he moved to third on a sacrifice. Ken Boswell, batting for Tom Seaver, lined a single, scoring the tying run. With Seaver now off the hook, Phil Hennigan took over the pitching duties in the 10th inning. Hennigan, however, couldn't get out of the 10th inning before surrendering a run on a single by ex–Met Tim Foli, which gave the Expos their 2–1 victory. Jim McAndrew, who in his previous start against the Cubs lasted only one-third of an inning while getting roughed up for five runs, was the beneficiary of a rare offensive outburst that saw the Mets score 13 runs and pound out 16 hits in the second game of the doubleheader.

After an off-day, the Mets began a road trip that would take them to Houston and Atlanta to close out the month of April. After Jon Matlack was a 4–2 loser in the opener of the Houston series, the Mets took the next two games. The middle game of the series featured another strong pitching outing by Jerry Koosman, who picked up his third win without a loss. More encouraging than Koosman's outstanding pitching was the hitting of Rusty Staub, who broke out of his season-long slump with two home runs. The news wasn't all good, however, as John Milner, the team's leading hitter, pulled his right hamstring muscle while stretching for a throw from Bud Harrelson. Milner joined Cleon Jones on the sidelines, with Jones still suffering from the wrist injury he incurred in the series against the Cubs. In the finale of the series, a two-run sixth inning by the Mets and two innings of scoreless relief by Tug McGraw carried Jim McAndrew to his second victory of the season.

The next stop on the Mets' itinerary was Atlanta-Fulton County Stadium. In the stadium known as the "Launching Pad," Mets starter Tom Seaver was victimized by back-to-back home runs by Hank Aaron and Darrel Evans as the Braves took the opener, 2–0. For Hank Aaron, it was his fifth home run of the season and the 678th of his illustrious career. For Tom Seaver, it marked his third consecutive frustrating outing. Seaver had not allowed more then two runs in each of the three games, but with the Mets scoring only one run during that span, all Seaver had to show for his efforts were two losses as his record dropped to 2-2.

The Mets fared better in the Saturday afternoon game by scoring three runs in the eighth inning as Jon Matlack picked up his second win of the season and McGraw earned his fifth save of the year. The Mets also took the rubber game of the series behind Jerry Koosman, who pitched a four-hit shutout as New York squeezed out a 1–0 decision. While no longer possessing the overpowering fastball of those glorious years, Koosman had become a smarter pitcher, as witnessed in the ninth inning. With the Mets carrying a precarious 1–0 lead over the Braves, Hank Aaron stepped to the plate as the final chance for the home team. Koosman worked the count full to Aaron before delivering the slowest, most tantalizing changeup, which an overanxious Aaron popped up to end the game. "One of my goals in life has been to throw a change-up to Hank Aaron on a 3-2 count, in a 1–0 game with two outs in the ninth," said Koosman.

Equally impressed was Hank Aaron. "His fastball is good enough so that you can't sit back and wait for the slow stuff."[5]

Thus concluded the month of April, and yet despite the team's measly .207 batting average, the Mets still found themselves in first place with a 12-8 record. By far the biggest surprise of the early season was in the pitching department, where Jerry Koosman won his first four decisions while being named Player of the Month of the National League for April. In the process, Koosman showed that he had completely recovered from the various arm ailments that had plagued him over the past three seasons. "I think I'm back where I was in 1968 and 1969," said Koosman.[6]

April showers bring May flowers, but for the Mets, the rose that greeted them when they returned to Shea Stadium to face the Reds in a short two-game series was more of a thorn than a flower. Pete Rose blasted a two-run homer in the seventh inning of the opener, pacing the Reds to a 6–1 victory over the Mets. Again the anemic Mets' offense provided no support for Seaver, who had a 1–1 tie snapped in the sixth inning on a home run by Johnny Bench. Rose's home run extended the Reds' lead to 4–1, while Dave Concepcion's ninth-inning home run put the game out of reach.

With Rusty Staub hitting a grand slam home run in the first inning of the series finale and Jon Matlack on the mound, the chances for the Mets to salvage a split looked very bright indeed. But that was only until the Reds came to bat in the fourth inning. Joe Morgan led off the inning with a single, which was followed by another base hit by Johnny Bench. A double by Tony Perez plated the Reds' first run, and a single by Bobby Tolan cut the Reds' deficit in half, 4–2. A hard grounder that Felix Millan was able to turn into a fabulous double play brought home the Reds' third run. The third out that Matlack needed to emerge from the inning never came as Richie Scheinblum and Dennis Menke followed with base hits to end Matlack's day. Matlack's replacement, rookie Hank Webb, was greeted rudely by pinch-hitter Larry Stahl, an ex–Met, who hit Webb's first delivery over the 396-foot marker to put the Reds on top, 6–4. While the Mets were able to get one run back, they would come no closer, going down to a crushing 6–5 defeat. After the game Berra bemoaned the fact that the Reds had their big inning in the fourth, when it was still too early to go to his closer, Tug McGraw.

The Reds left town, the Astros came in for an early spring weekend series, and for the second game in a row, the Mets blew an early 4–0 lead and eventually lost in 14 innings. The Mets scored four runs in the last of the second inning when Astros starter Ken Forsch walked the bases loaded, setting the stage for a single off the bat of Jerry Grote, a ground out by the starting pitcher, Jerry Koosman, and a two-run double by Teddy Martinez. Koosman, still undefeated and bidding for his fifth win, kept the Astros off the scoreboard until the fourth inning when a home run by Cesar Cedeno, a triple and a single cut the Mets' lead to 4–2. Yet Koosman took a 5–2 lead into the eighth inning before he began to falter. Tommie Agee, making his first Shea Stadium appearance since being traded by the Mets at the end of the 1972 season, led off with a pinch-hit single. After Agee was forced out, singles by Jesus Alou and Cesar Cedeno loaded the bases. Exactly the situation that relief aces are hired for, Berra called on McGraw to end the threat. But McGraw had the plate jump around on him as he walked his first three batters, sending three runs across the plate to tie the game. With McGraw imploding, Berra turned to Hennigan, who was able to get out of the inning with the tie intact. The game remained tied until the top of the 14th inning. With Hennigan still on the mound, Tommie Agee, looking to prove the Mets gave up on him too quickly, singled for the second time in the game. After two more base hits followed to load the bases, Berra replaced Hennigan with Harry Parker. The long evening was ruined for the 17,000 fans in attendance when Parker walked Bob Watson to force in the go-ahead run, and Doug Rader followed with a double, driving home two more runs. The Astros won the next two games in convincing fashion to complete the series sweep, as the Mets lost their fifth consecutive game.

Happy to see the Astros leave town, the Mets welcomed Hank Aaron and the Atlanta Braves for a three-game series. Tom Seaver, ailing in the early going from a penchant for surrendering the gopher ball and from a lack of run support, appeared destined to suffer the same fate in the opener of the series after a two-run homer by Dusty Baker gave the Braves a 2–1 lead as the Mets came to bat in the last of the eighth inning. But uncharacteristically, the Mets' offense struck for six runs, and Seaver ended up on the right side of a 7–2 decision.

On May 8, in a drizzly and chilly Shea Stadium, it was the Mets holding a 3–1 lead over the Atlanta Braves as Jon Matlack took the mound in the top of the seventh inning. With the bases loaded and two outs, Braves second baseman Marty Perez stepped to the plate. Matlack ran the count to 2 and 2 when in a scene eerily reminiscent of a night nearly 19 years earlier — a drive hit by Gil McDougal of the Yankees off the face of Indians star pitcher Herb Score ruined his career — Perez smoked the next pitch through the middle, striking Matlack on his forehead before he crumbled to the ground in a heap. X-rays on Matlack, who had been carried off on a stretcher, revealed a hairline skull fracture; he would have to remain hospitalized indefinitely. In the what-else-could-go-wrong category, the Mets blew the lead and eventually lost the game, 10–8. The Mets, however, were able to win the rubber game of the series and get a measure of revenge the next night when Jerry Koosman ran his record to 5-0, as the Mets routed the Braves, 8–1.

Following the series with the Braves, the Mets flew to Pittsburgh to open a weekend series with the Pirates. Willie Mays, suffering from two aching knees and a bad shoulder while struggling along at a .105 clip, was kept home as the Mets' hierarchy played down rumors of Mays' imminent retirement. "I hope he'll play again and we think he'll play again," said Mets general manager Bob Scheffing. "He didn't tell me that he'd retire," said Berra.[7] Aside from Mays, the Mets believed they were fortunate from a medical standpoint as Jon Matlack was released from the hospital and would rejoin the club shortly. Cleon Jones was slated to make his first start in more than three weeks while John Milner was expected to return to the lineup during the weekend. Little did the Mets realize that their troubles were only beginning. The Mets took a 4–3 decision over the Pirates in the opener of the series, but what a painful victory it was. Pitches hit no less than three Mets, including Cleon Jones, Rusty Staub and Jerry Grote. While Jones suffered no lasting effects from the beaning, Jerry Grote suffered a fractured wrist and had to be placed on the disabled list. Staub, who in 1972 missed 90 games after being struck by a George Stone fastball on his right hand, was hit on his left hand by a pitch thrown by Pirates reliever Ramon Hernandez. With Staub still struggling offensively, all he needed was to have to add a painful wrist to his miseries. With Grote disabled, Duffy Dyer became the starting catcher, and the Mets called up catcher Joe Nolan to take Grote's spot on the roster.

There was more bad news to come for Yogi on the injury front the next day as he was celebrating his 48th birthday. While he did get a present in the form of a Tom Seaver shutout, a 6–0 whitewashing of the Pirates, three more Mets joined the cast of the walking wounded. Duffy Dyer was struck on the right wrist by a pitch, Felix Millan strained his left ankle, and Jim Gosger, a utility outfielder, suffered a bruised back as he crashed into the center field wall. The next day the Mets completed the sweep of the Pirates but added Willie Mays to the disabled list with his aching shoulder and two sore knees.

The victorious but bruised Mets limped into Chicago with a four-game winning streak to take on the first-place Cubs, who were carrying a six-game winning streak of their own. The Mets got a much-needed day off when the first game of the series was called on account of cold weather. While the Mets were resting their battered bodies, the same couldn't be said for general manager Bob Scheffing, who purchased the contract of veteran catcher Jerry May from the Kansas City Royals and sent Joe Nolan back down to the minors. In announcing the transaction, Scheffing made a bigger deal about the Mets hiring Dr. Pete Lamotte to a yearly contract. "By the visit it would have killed us," said Scheffing half in jest.[8] The Cubs extended their winning streak to seven games when they won the first game of the rain-shortened series, 4–3, sending Jerry Koosman to his first defeat of the season. The last leg of the road trip saw the Mets head to Montreal for a short two-game series. Rookie Harry Parker picked up his fourth win without a loss in the opener of the series, but inclement weather forced the postponement of the series finale.

The Mets returned home on May 18 to take on the Pittsburgh Pirates for a weekend series and the Cardinals for three games before heading out to the West Coast. With all the injuries, it was a makeshift lineup that Tom Seaver had playing behind him in the opener of the series. The lineup saw Teddy Martinez in center field, the "Stork," George Theodore in left field, Duffy Dyer behind the plate and Wayne Garrett at second base. It was the second baseman, Garrett, that supplied the firepower, driving home three of the Mets' four runs with a home run and a single, as the Mets and Seaver prevailed, 4–3. For Seaver, it was his fifth win of the year.

Remarkably, less than two weeks after being struck on the head by a line drive, Jon Matlack returned to the starting rotation for the second game of the series against the Pirates. Matlack, wearing a rubber foam protector, showed no ill effects from his injury as he kept the Pirates off the scoreboard, scattering nine hits while fanning six in the six innings he worked. With Matlack staked to a 1–0 lead, courtesy of a Rusty Staub home run in the sixth inning, he made way for Tug McGraw. McGraw, however, couldn't save the game for Matlack, surrendering a game-tying home run to Bob Robertson in the ninth and a game-winning three-run home run to Willie Stargell in the tenth.

With the season advancing into late May, the Mets made their first of two annual trips to the West Coast to take on the California teams. Hampered by injuries and exhausted from a cross-country trip, the Mets did not need a 19-inning, 5-hour and 42-minute affair. But that's exactly what they got in the opener of the road trip in a game against the Dodgers. After the Dodgers jumped out to a 3–1 lead against Tom Seaver, the Mets managed to tie the game with single runs in the seventh and eighth innings. It then took 11 innings for a team to push across a run when the Mets scored four times, the first coming on a Cleon Jones single and a Rusty Staub double. For Staub it was his fifth hit of the game. Two more runs crossed the plate on an Ed Kranepool double. Some of the highlights of the long evening included the Mets banging out 22 hits, with the Dodgers accumulating 18 base hits. Both teams combined to hit into nine double plays. The Dodgers Willie Davis, with six hits in nine at-bats raised his batting average by 22 points, while Manny Mota, who went 0-for-9, saw his average dip by 32 points. Tug McGraw pitched five innings of hair-raising relief, allowing 11 runners to reach, but none scored as the Dodgers hit into three double plays, two coming via home plate, with Willie Davis getting forced at the dish twice. "I can't ever remember that much trouble in a game I pitched," said McGraw after the game. The best quote from the game came from Ken Boswell, who said, "I finally found out what time I hit best. One thirty in the morning."[9]

After their exciting if not exhausting win, the Mets failed to win again until Seaver took the mound five games later against the San Francisco Giants at Candlestick Park. In the throes of a four-game losing streak, Seaver put on a one-man show as he fanned 16 batters while hitting his sixth career home run in the sixth inning. Despite Seaver's heroics, the Mets came to bat in the top of the ninth inning, trailing 2–1, courtesy of Willie McCovey's 10th home run of the year. With the Mets in danger of falling for the fifth straight game and, more importantly, falling even further in the standings, pinch-hitter Ken Boswell led off with a walk off against Giants reliever Randy Moffitt. Bud

Harrelson and Tom Seaver followed with singles. Seaver's hit was an attempted sacrifice bunt, which an indecisive Moffitt held on to when he couldn't decide which base to go to. With the bases loaded, Wayne Garrett followed with a walk, forcing home the tying run. A single by Millan drove home two more runs, and a sacrifice fly by George Theodore capped the scoring as the Mets held on for a 5–2 victory. The good news, however, was tinged with more bad news on the injury front when it was learned that Cleon Jones would miss at least a month of action due to his wrist injury that has been hampering him since he injured it diving for a ball on April 19.

The Mets concluded the California portion of the road trip winning only the three games started by Tom Seaver, including the finale in San Diego, during which the Mets lost another two players to injury. This time it was George Theodore, who was hit on his left eye by a pitch thrown by Gary Ross. Theodore, who wore glasses, suffered facial cuts and was removed on a stretcher. Additionally, Jerry May, who was acquired to back up Duffy Dyer after Grote went down, became a casualty when he strained a leg muscle running the bases in the fourth inning. Theodore was expected to miss a week with a swollen left eye, while the word on May was that he would be out for at least two weeks.

The calendar had already turned from May to June when the Mets left San Diego and headed to Cincinnati, the last leg of an already disastrous road trip. The trek became even worse when the Mets were blanked in the first game of the series, 5–0, while losing their shortstop, Bud Harrelson for at least a month. Harrelson broke some bones along his knuckles after being upended by the Reds' Bill Plummer, who successfully broke up a double play. Yet nothing prepared the Mets for the events of the next game in Cincinnati, where starters Jerry Koosman and Ross Grimsley dueled to a 2–2 tie, with Koosman giving the Mets eight solid innings before turning the game over to the bullpen. The Mets appeared to have won the game, however, when they scored three runs in the top of the tenth inning on a bases-loaded triple by Duffy Dyer off Don Gullett. The Reds had to face Tug McGraw but as Yogi was wont to say, "If you don't have a bullpen, you don't have nothing." This time the Mets got nothing, as McGraw walked the leadoff batter, Richie Scheinblum. A single by Pete Rose and a wild pitch pulled the Reds to within two runs. A walk to Joe Morgan put runners on first and second and brought Berra out to the mound, replacing McGraw with Hennigan to face the right-handed hitting Johnny Bench. Two pitches later the game was over when Bench drove a Hennigan meatball over the left-field fence.

Thus ended a calamitous road trip with the Mets winning only three of twelve games, a clear claim on fifth place and four newly injured players.

The Mets returned home on June 8 beaten and bruised to start a homestand against the California teams. Willie Mays, taking Harrelson's spot on the roster, was reactivated despite still suffering from pain in his shoulder, yet was unable to start in the opener of the series, a game the Mets and Tom Seaver lost to the Dodgers. Mays felt well enough to start the second game and looked like the Mays of old by making a tumbling circus catch in the third inning with the game tied, 2–2, and then homering in the bottom of the inning, giving the Mets a lead they would never relinquish. Jon Matlack, who coming into the game had lost five in a row and had not won since taking a line drive to his head, picked up his third win of the year. After the game the Mets continued their roster shuffling as they placed Jerry May on the disabled list and recalled center fielder Don Hahn, who was acquired in the deal that sent Ron Swoboda to Montreal. The Mets also optioned relief pitcher Tommie Moore to the minors and recalled pitcher Buzz Capra.

While Jon Matlack broke his five-game losing streak the day before, Jerry Koosman, after winning his first five decisions, saw his personal losing streak extend to five games, though through no fault of his own. In the rubber game of the series, he allowed only two runs in his eight innings of work. The Mets' beleaguered offense could offer him no support, as Claude Osteen held the New Yorkers to only three hits.

Next into town came the Giants, who took the opener of the series, 2–1, helped in large part by a spectacular catch by Gary Matthews off a ball hit by Felix Millan, saving two runs. With the Mets' offense in dire straights, and the league trading deadline just days away, Yogi Berra spoke to the press after the game regarding the Mets' need to bolster their hitting attack. "We're hurting for a hitter. I wouldn't care if he batted right-handed or left-handed as long as he could hit a long ball."[10]

The Mets failed to come up with the bat they so desperately needed as the trading deadline came and went. Nevertheless, the Mets were able to put together a five-game winning streak by taking the remaining games with the Giants and then sweeping the Padres in a three-game series. The first win came on the strength of an Ed Kranepool home run off Giants star Juan Marichal, making a winner out of rookie Harry Parker, a pleasant surprise who improved his record to 5-0. Tom Seaver, aided by home runs from Felix Millan and rookie catcher Ron Hodges, called up after Jerry May joined the overcrowded disabled list, was also a winner as the Mets took two out of three from the Giants. While Ron Hodges admitted to being nervous in his first major league start, Seaver for his part was very complimentary towards the rookie catcher. "He was very composed back there. I shook him off maybe 25 percent of the time.[11]

In the opener of the series against the Padres, the Mets used a three-run homer off the bat of Wayne Garrett in the last of the eighth inning to carry them to a 5–2 victory. Garrett's blast made a winner out of Jon Matlack, who saw his record improve to 4-8. Jerry Koosman snapped his personal five-game losing streak as the Mets trounced the Padres, 10–2, in the middle game of the series. Willie Mays, who started his seventh consecutive game, blasted his 656th home run while leading off the sixth inning. John Milner added his eighth homer of the season. The Mets completed the sweep the next afternoon, 3–1, as they touched up Padres pitching for 13 hits while making a winner out of George Stone.

With a successful homestand behind them, the Mets hit the road once again, with their first stop being Philadelphia. New York's five-game winning streak came to an abrupt halt when the Phillies smacked around Mets starter Jim McAndrew, who took the start in place of Seaver. Seaver had to be scratched after complaining of a back strain, an injury not thought to be serious enough for him to miss more than one start. The Mets lost the remaining two games with the Phillies before heading off to Three Rivers Stadium to take on the Pirates for a big four-game weekend series.

In addition to the dearth of injuries that plagued the ball club as well as a lack of offense, the Mets had another reason to be concerned — the implosion of the bullpen, resulting in numerous heart-breaking defeats. The first of the heartbreak losses occurred in the opener of the series against the Pirates. After a brilliant pitching duel between Jerry Koosman and Luke Walker brought the game to the final frame tied at 1–1, the Pirates came to bat in the last of the ninth inning against rookie right-hander Buzz Capra. Capra got into immediate trouble by loading the bases with nobody out. Rube Walker, managing for Berra, who was ejected earlier in the game, called on McGraw to bail the Mets out of a near-impossible jam. McGraw, however, almost accomplished the impossible, as the Mets nearly pulled off a miraculous triple play. His first batter, Bob Robertson, hit the ball on the ground to Millan at second. Millan went home for the easy force on Gene Clines, the lead runner. Catcher Duffy Dyer, in attempt to go for the 4-2-3 double play, threw the ball into right field, but right into the glove of Rusty Staub. Staub, noticing that Al Oliver had rounded second, fired a strike to Jim Fregosi, who tagged out Oliver. In the interim, Dave Cash, who had started the play at second base, broke for the plate. Fregosi fired to the plate in an attempt to nail Cash and complete the triple play, but Cash beat the throw. As a result, the Mets suffered their fourth consecutive loss. "It was just one of those things," said Staub. "When I called to Fregosi, Cash hadn't even reached third and I thought he had time to make the putout."[12]

Berra had been tossed in the seventh inning on the play that had given the Pirates a 1–0 lead. With Al Oliver on first and two Pirates set aside, Manny Sanguillen drilled a sinking liner to center. Willie Mays attempted a shoestring catch, but the ball broke off the tip off his glove and rolled back towards the infield. Jim Fregosi recovered the ball and fired a strike to catcher Duffy Dyer, well ahead of Oliver, who was attempting to score. Dyer applied what he thought was a tag, but home plate umpire Tom Gorman called Oliver safe. With Dyer convinced that Oliver never touched the plate, Dyer applied the tag again to no avail, prompting Berra to charge out of the dugout to argue. While kicking dirt in front of Gorman, Berra was given the good old heave-ho, his first banishment since taking over as manager of the Mets. After snapping their four-game losing streak with a 5–4 win over the Pirates behind the pitching of George

Stone and John Milner's ninth home run of the year, the Mets lost another heart-breaker with the Pirates when Manny Sanguillen singled with the bases loaded in the 10th inning off Phil Hennigan. Hennigan, the designated successor to Danny Frisella, suffered his fourth loss of the year without a win. The Mets were able to salvage a split of the series with the Pirates as Seaver picked up his ninth victory of the campaign.

Losers of five out of seven on their trip through Pennsylvania, the Mets returned to Shea on June 25, to take on the division-leading Chicago Cubs in a short two-game series. Having won five consecutive games at home before the disastrous trip, the Mets were hoping to be reinvigorated by some home cooking and positive medical news from team physician Dr. Peter Lamotte.

- X-rays of Jerry Grote's fractured wrist showed good progress and he was expected to begin batting practice shortly.
- Jerry May's wrist was improved and he was cleared to work out.
- Cleon Jones had his cast removed, but there was no timetable for his return.
- Bud Harrelson would have his cast removed the next day.
- Tom Seaver's back was fine and he could take his regular return in the rotation.

It appeared that was exactly what the doctor ordered when the Mets and Jon Matlack took a 2–0 lead into the ninth inning of the opener. Matlack got into immediate trouble, however, when he walked the leadoff batter, Glen Beckert. Billy Williams followed with an infield hit, and after Jim Hickman walked to load the bases, Tug McGraw once again found himself with the unenviable task of trying to survive a no-outs bases-loaded jam. Once again, he was unsuccessful. While in Pittsburgh McGraw nearly escaped damage with an "almost" triple play, on this night his first batter, Ron Santo, greeted the reliever instantly with a smash down the right-field line for a two-run game-tying double. Two batters later Don Kessinger singled home the tie-breaking run, sending the Mets to another one-run loss. With the loss, the Mets tumbled into the cellar, marking the first time since September of 1968 the Mets found themselves at the bottom of the National League. The Cubs won the finale handily as well as Koosman suffered his sixth loss of the season.

After completing the homestand by losing two out of three to the Phillies, the Mets ended the month of June in Chicago while taking on the Cubs. The opener of the series featured a magnificent pitchers duel between Jon Matlack and Burt Hooton. Once again Matlack found himself holding onto a precarious lead as the Cubs came to bat in the last of the ninth inning, trailing 2–1. This time Matlack was able to bear down, though, as the Mets held on to win. "I scared him," said a struggling McGraw. "When he saw me start warming up, he bore down and got them out."[13] There might have been a bit of truth in that statement. The next afternoon featured a doubleheader at Wrigley Field, with the Mets taking the first game behind Jerry Koosman and Tug McGraw, 6–5. Yet this was another affair that saw Mets fans with their hearts in their mouths, as the Cubs came to bat in the last of the ninth inning, trailing 6–4. McGraw was on the mound to start the ninth inning, and walked his first batter, Carmen Fanzone. Don Kessinger followed with a single, and Randy Hundley sacrificed the runners to second and third. Jim Hickman came within an eyelash of winning the game for the Cubs when he hit a drive that George Theodore reeled in with his back against the wall. Having already taken the opener of the doubleheader, the Mets were on the verge of a sweep by taking a 5–3 lead into the last of the ninth inning. Pitcher Phil Hennigan got into immediate trouble when both Jose Cardenal and Ron Santo singled to start the ninth. Again Berra turned to McGraw to put out the fire. McGraw retired his first two batters, but Randy Hundley, who had entered the game only two innings before, blasted McGraw's fourth pitch over the wall for the game-winning home run. The loss marked the fourth game in a ten-day stretch in which the Mets lost a game in the opposition's final at-bat.

The Mets' venue changed but not their luck as they headed to Montreal. For the second straight game the Mets lost on a walk-off home run. This day belonged to Boots Day, who took Buzz Capra deep in the last of the 10th to give the Expos a 2–1 win. Jim McAndrew took the mound for the Mets the next night against the Expos and was staked to a 5–3 lead after 4½ innings. However, McAndrew could retire only one batter in the fifth as the Expos put together a three-run inning to take a 6–5 lead. With McGraw now on the mound, the Expos lit up the left-hander, pummeling him for seven runs, with the big blow a grand slam off the bat of Bob Bailey. The Expos continued the punishment of Mets pitching when Phil Hennigan took the mound in the seventh inning. A three-run blast by ex–Met Singleton and another homer by Bailey added five more runs to the Expos' already expansive 13–5 lead. By the time the game was over, the Expos pushed across 19 runs, the most runs ever allowed by Mets pitching in a single game. The two largest culprits—McGraw the closer and Hennigan the set-up man—carried balloon-size ERAs of 6.07 and 5.88, respectively, by the time the game was over. It was clear after the game that McGraw was suffering from a loss of confidence. "I didn't have the feel for the baseball at all. I didn't have any idea how to throw the baseball. It was as if I'd never played before in my entire life. I just felt like dropping to my knees and saying, 'I don't know what to do.' I just can't hack it any more."[14]

If any Mets fan at this juncture believed that things couldn't get any worse, they were wrong. The pattern of heart-breaking, gut-wrenching losses continued and, if anything, were more profound. In the third game of the series and with no less a pitcher on the mound than Tom Seaver, the Mets took a 5–0 lead into the last of the eighth inning. Seaver walked leadoff batter Ron Hunt and then surrendered a single to Mike Jorgensen. Ron Fairly flied out, and Seaver should've been back in the dugout after Ken Singleton grounded into what looked like an inning-ending double play. But shortstop Teddy Martinez bob-bled the ball, allowing Hunt to score the Expos' first run of the game. With one out and two runners aboard, Boots Day doubled home Jorgensen, reducing the Mets' lead to 5–2. Bob Bailey drove in two more runs, and what started as a 5–0 lead was now 5–4. At that point Berra went to the bullpen to call on the culprit two nights prior, Buzz Capra, who surrendered a single to his first bat-ter, Tim Foli. After Capra got the second out of the inning, Gene Mauch, the Expos' manager, turned to Ron Woods as a pinch-hitter. Woods' lumber turned out to be deadly as he blasted Capra's third pitch into the left-center field seats, giving the Expos a stunning 7–5 lead that Mike Marshall, the Expos' closer, made stand.

Despite salvaging the final game of the series with the Expos, it was a dejected and demoralized Mets team that returned home to start a homestand against the non–California Western Division teams, starting with the Braves. The opener of the series featured a good, old-fashioned pitching duel between Jerry Koosman and Ron Schueler. While Koosman allowed the Braves just four hits, one of them was a two-run homer off the bat of Dick Dietz. Schueler was even better as he carried a 2–0 lead and a no-hitter into the ninth inning. Ron Hodges, leading off the ninth, singled to end Schueler's bid. Two outs later Millan added another single, but Schueler was able to retire Boswell on a fly out to keep the shutout intact, resulting in another undeserved loss for Koos-man.[15]

Saturday, July 7, on a hot and muggy New York summer afternoon and nearly two months to the day after Jon Matlack was carried off the field on a stretcher in a game against the Braves, tragedy struck again. With the Braves leading, 4–3, in the top of the seventh inning and a runner aboard, Ralph Garr, the Braves' right fielder, lifted a fly ball to left-center field field. Both Don Hahn and George Theodore converged on the ball and in the process collided into each other. While both players lay sprawled on the warning track, Garr circled the bases for an inside-the-park home run. Both players were removed on stretchers. Theodore suffered the more severe of the injuries, dislocating his hip, which cost him the remainder of the season. Hahn suffered minor bruises and was categorized as day-to-day. Eerily enough, two weeks previous, Theodore had a dream that he was being removed from the field on a stretcher with McGraw and Koosman holding either end.

With the rookie outfielders having been removed from the game, Berra went to the opposite extreme by calling on the 42-year-old Mays to take the place of Hahn. Cleon Jones, on his first day back from the disabled list, took over for Theodore in left. The disastrous play cost the Mets two runs, and the

Opposite: George Theodore is carried off on a stretcher after colliding with center fielder Don Hahn while chasing a ball off the bat of Ralph Garr of the Atlanta Braves (AP Images).

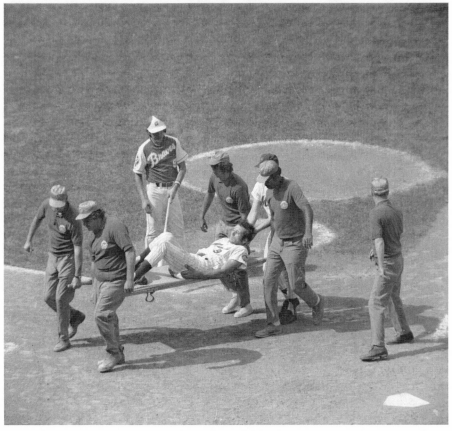

Braves carried a 6–3 lead when New York came to bat in the last of the eighth inning. Braves pitching walked the bases loaded and Willie Mays, in his first at-bat of the game, doubled home two runs. Wayne Garrett followed with a two-run double, giving the Mets an 8–7 lead as they took the field for the ninth inning. Tug McGraw, who obviously had lost his confidence in his role as closer, allowed back-to-back singles to his first three batters. A walk followed, allowing the tying run to score. McGraw was then told by Berra to take a walk, and Harry Parker was called on to halt the uprising. However, the go-ahead run scored on a ground out, and two walks later forced home the third run of the inning, giving the Braves a 9–7 lead. The Mets were able to get one run back in the ninth, but they fell again in another one-run decision.

Hank Aaron's 695th and 696th home runs of his career doomed the Mets in the series finale as the Braves took the broom to the Mets. With the loss, the Mets found themselves firmly entrenched in the basement of the National League East with a 34-46 record, a whopping twelve games out of first place.

Rumors of Berra's imminent demise were dispelled by Donald Grant, who insisted that Berra's job was safe unless public opinion demanded otherwise. With Grant basing decisions on public opinion, the New York Post decided to run a poll as to whom was responsible for the Mets' ignoble play. The list included manager Yogi Berra, general manager Bob Scheffing, and Donald Grant. When the results were in, Bob Scheffing was the landslide scapegoat, being blamed for poor trades, such as the one that sent Nolan Ryan to the Angels for Jim Fregosi. Donald Grant came in second, while Yogi Berra came out looking the best of the three.

Despite all that transpired over the course of the season, Mets management did not lose faith in the ball club. And it was to that end that on July 9, before the Mets were to take on the Astros, board chairman M. Donald Grant called a club meeting with general manager Bob Scheffing on hand to exude that message of belief. After a short but inspiring speech, Grant left the clubhouse. Coincidently, with McGraw suffering from a complete lack of confidence, he turned to some of his friends for personal advice, and it was suggested that all he had to do was to believe in himself. Having heard the same words from Grant, McGraw could hardly control himself. Just after Grant exited the clubhouse, Tug McGraw, in a moment of inspiration, yelled out at the top of his lungs, "You Gotta Believe," echoing the message he had been receiving from his friends. While many of his teammates believed McGraw was mocking Grant, his incessant chanting of "You Gotta Believe" convinced players that McGraw was quite serious, and thus exuded a new sense of confidence on the part of the players.

And while it would take time to show evidence in the standings, the Mets responded. With their newly found faith, the Mets sent their ace, Tom Seaver, to the mound to take on Don Wilson and the Houston Astros. While Seaver in his seven innings of work allowed only a solo home run by Lee May,

Don Wilson was even better as he held the Mets scoreless for the first eight innings. As a result, the Mets came to the plate in the last of the ninth inning, trailing 1–0. Rusty Staub led off the Mets' ninth with a base hit, but was forced at second on an attempted sacrifice bunt by Ed Kranepool. Kranepool then left the game in favor of pinch-runner Teddy Martinez. John Milner then struck

With the injury-plagued Mets stuck in the cellar, reliever Tug McGraw lifted the club's spirits with steady pitching and incessant chants of "Ya Gotta Believe!" (National Baseball Hall of Fame Library).

out, and the Mets were down to their last out. But Ron Hodges gave the Mets life when he singled to center, sending Martinez to third. Hodges was then lifted for another pinch-runner, Don Hahn. After some maneuvering by the Astros, during which they replaced center fielder Cesar Cedeno with Bob Gallagher, Berra sent Jim Beauchamp to bat for Harrelson. Beauchamp came through with his 10th hit of the season and the Mets had tied the game. After Willie Mays walked while pinch-hitting for reliever Buzz Capra, Wayne Garrett struck out, sending the game into extra innings.

Harry Parker kept the Astros off the board for the 10th, 11th and 12th innings. Facing Astros reliever Jim York in the last of the 12th inning, the Mets' Willie Mays singled with one out. As a result of a run-and-hit play, the grounder by Garrett could not be converted into a double play, thus allowed Mays to score with the winning run when Felix Millan followed with a single. The Mets' inspired play continued the next night when Jon Matlack took the mound against the Astros. If there was any doubt about Jon Matlack making a full recovery from the line drive that he took off his forehead on May 8, they were put to rest after he stopped the Astros on one hit in a 1–0 win. Bud Harrelson, just back from the disabled list, threw out six base runners in the first five innings and made a spectacular play in the last of the fifth inning when he moved in to grab a high bouncer off the bat of Bob Watson and threw him out on the run. In the same inning Rusty Staub leaped high against the wall to rob Lee May.

Matlack took the mound in the sixth inning with his perfect game still intact. But Tommy Helms, leading off, drilled the ball past a diving Wayne Garrett for a two-base hit, breaking up Matlack's bid. Helms remained on second base after catcher Skip Jutze grounded out to short and Matlack struck out Astros starter Jerry Reuss and former Met Tommie Agee.

Matlack had little trouble the rest of the way, as he allowed the Astros only two more walks, with one coming in the seventh and one in the eighth inning. Both runners were immediately erased on double plays. Matlack's gem marked the 10th time a Mets pitcher had thrown a one-hitter, though it was only the second thrown by a left-hander. Al Jackson tossed one in the Mets' inaugural season of 1962.

The next day came an admission from the Mets' brass that the fans knew all along. The deal that brought Fregosi to the Mets in exchange for Nolan Ryan was a colossal failure, and the team dealt Fregosi to the Texas Rangers for the proverbial player to be named later. As happy as the fans were to see Fregosi go, it appeared the infielder was just as thrilled. "Oh, I'm happy. It didn't look like I'd play here any more."[16] With the open roster space, the Mets reactivated Jerry Grote, who missed two months with a fractured wrist after being hit with a pitch. After the deal was announced, the Mets played lackluster ball, as they were pounded by the Astros, 7–1, salvaging the final game of the series. Jerry Koosman, the Mets' starter, was roughed up for six runs in five innings of work.

The Mets took to the road for a trip that would carry them to the All-Star break while visiting Cincinnati for a four-game series, including a Friday twilight doubleheader, three games in Atlanta, and a three-game weekend series in Houston.

After the Mets split the four games in Cincinnati, it was on to Atlanta, where some wild baseball took place. Jerry Koosman hooked up against Phil Niekro in the opener of the series. With the Braves leading, 1–0 in the third inning, Marty Perez, who earlier broke the skull of Jon Matlack with his line drive up the middle, lifted a long drive to deep center field. Willie Mays tracked the ball to the short center field fence, where the ball and Mays converged simultaneously. Mays reached for the ball, gloved it momentarily, then saw it pop out of his glove as he slammed into the fence and fell to the ground. Perez rounded the bases for an inside-the-park home run.

Despite some concerns for his well-being, Mays showed no ill effects from his rendezvous with the fence when he led off the fourth inning with a double and scored on a base hit by Cleon Jones. The Mets added another run in the inning and two more in both the fifth and sixth frames, giving Koosman a 6–3 lead heading into the last of the seventh inning. But Koosman began to wilt in the Georgia heat, as he surrendered back-to-back singles and a walk before Berra replaced the left-hander with a struggling Buzz Capra. Capra had no better success, and by the time the dust had cleared, the Braves had put five runs across the plate as they took the opener, 8–6. Jerry Koosman, the losing pitcher, saw his record drop to 7–9.

With Tug McGraw continuing to struggle, Yogi Berra tried to reinstall some confidence in his beleaguered reliever and moved McGraw into the starting rotation for the second game of the series. Unfortunately, McGraw fared no better in his role as a starter. He surrendered seven runs in the six innings he worked, including home runs to Marty Perez, Ralph Garr and Hank Aaron, his 698th.

Conversely, Braves starter Carl Morton, who induced Mets batters to bounce into five double plays, stifled the New York offense. As a result, the Mets came to bat in the top of the ninth inning trailing the Braves, 7–1, just three outs away from adding another game to the loss column. But the Mets' bats rose from the dead, as Garrett singled and crossed the plate when Staub cracked his eighth home run of the year. A single by Cleon Jones and another two-run homer, this one off the bat of John Milner, cut the Braves' lead to 7–5. Braves manager Eddie Matthews replaced Morton with Adrian Devine, who fared no better.

By the time Eddie Matthews came to fetch Devine, the Braves' lead was down to a single run, with the tying and go-ahead runs on base. Matthews called for left-hander Tom House to face Wayne Garrett, who was up to bat for the second time in the inning. Garrett, however, did not get the opportunity as Berra called on Willie Mays to bat for him. Mays obliged by drilling a long single to right-center, scoring both base runners to give the Mets the lead for the first time. With Garrett having been lifted from the game, and Jim Fregosi having been dealt to the Texas Rangers, Yogi Berra elected to play Jerry Grote, just recently recalled from the disabled list, to play third for the ninth inning. Grote had no opportunity to be tested, however, as Harry Parker turned in an overpowering ninth inning, saving the game for Buzz Capra.

The next night, the Mets' offense continued where it left off in the ninth inning and pummeled the Braves, 12–2. Staub belted two home runs and Milner had one while adding two singles as Seaver picked up his 10th win of the year.

After losing the opener in Houston, excellent pitching performances by Koosman and Seaver paced the Mets to victories in the final two games of the season's first half. Despite heading into the All-Star break in the cellar of the National East, the Mets were not a team in despair, having won six of their last nine. The Mets' clubhouse, which resembled a hospital ward during the first half of the season, was relatively healthy and returning to normalcy. But the best news of all was the hitting that was so inconspicuously missing in action for the bulk of the first half was now coming around. "I just hope they don't forget what they're doing right," said a relieved Berra. "Just when they're starting to get in the right groove, we've got three days off. Oh well, maybe the rest will do some good too. It's still not too late. In this division anything can happen. The big thing now is for us to get back to .500. Then maybe we can make a move."[17]

2

The Dog Days of August

The second half of the season saw the Mets open in St. Louis on the last leg of a road trip that began in Cincinnati and continued to Atlanta and Houston before the mid-season break. Yogi Berra's concern about the three-day break putting a damper into the Mets' recent fine play appeared justified as the team was swept in a doubleheader on the first day of the second half. The Cardinals pounded Jon Matlack in the first game of the doubleheader, scoring five runs in the second inning on their way to a 13–1 rout of the New Yorkers. Jerry Koosman lost a heart-breaker in the second game, victimized by his teammates' running game. Kooz, whose fastball was of the 1969 variety, allowed the Cardinals three hits and one run in the second inning but nothing else, yet was on the wrong end of a 2–1 decision.

The first base running miscue occurred with Cleon Jones on first base after leading off the second inning with a base hit. Jones then took off for second on a hit-and-run play. The batter, John Milner, executed perfectly with a clean single, but Jones failed to touch second base and had to turn back to touch the bag, where he was forced to remain. The next batter, Ed Kranepool, flied to deep right, which allowed Jones to tag up and take third, but he would've scored if not for his indiscretion. On the same play, John Milner committed the second base running mistake when he was thrown out as he tried to advance to second base.

In the fourth inning Jones ran the Mets out of another inning. After he walked to lead off the inning, he tried to go to third base on a base hit by Ed Kranepool but was gunned down by Bernie Carbo. With the double loss, the Mets started the second half of the season falling 9½ games behind the league-leading Cardinals and further entrenched themselves in the cellar of the National League East.

Tom Seaver salvaged the finale of the series and the road trip for the Mets with a 2–1 decision over Rick Wise and the Cardinals. With the Mets trailing 1–0 on a first-inning run manufactured by Lou Brock, John Milner tied the game with his 15th home run of the season in the fifth inning. The Mets went ahead to stay in the sixth inning on a base hit by Felix Millan and a double by Rusty Staub.

The Mets finally returned home on Saturday July 28 to open a series with the Expos. George Stone started the opener, pitching a complete game as the Mets clobbered the Expos, 11–3. Again the big blow offensively was struck by John Milner, who blasted a grand slam home run in the bottom of the first inning, putting the game out of reach.

The final two games of the series were in the form of a doubleheader, which for the second time in four days the Mets lost. Jon Matlack, coming off a horrific performance in his last start, was masterful in the first game of the doubleheader, holding the Expos to only one run. Unfortunately, his mound opponent, rookie Steve Rogers, was even better, keeping the Mets completely off the scoreboard, as the Expos beat the Mets, 1–0. The Mets lost the nightcap, 5–2, in 10 innings. Nevertheless, there also was encouraging news as Tug McGraw, given another start in an attempt to regain his consistency, pitched 5⅔ innings and allowed only one run and four hits, thereby earning a return to his role as the closer.

The Pittsburgh Pirates followed the Expos into Shea Stadium and once again Jerry Koosman, suffering from a lack of run support, walked off with another hard-luck loss as his record dropped to 8-11. Koosman allowed the Pirates only two earned runs over eight innings, but the Mets were able to score only once off Dock Ellis and Ramon Hernandez as New York lost, 4–1.

August 1, the date that traditionally marks the beginning of the dog days of the baseball season, saw the Mets take on the Pirates in yet another doubleheader. After losing two doubleheaders in less than a week, the Mets finally won a twinbill. Tom Seaver won the opener, 3–0, in a dominating performance in which he allowed the opposition only four hits and no walks while fanning 11 batters. Seaver improved his record to 13-5 with the win.

George Stone continued to exceed all expectations by picking up his seventh win in the nightcap as the Mets beat the Pirates, 5–2. Remarkably, the Mets came within one out of a doubleheader shutout before the Pirates scored two runs with two outs in the ninth. Had New York accomplished the feat of a doubleheader shutout sweep, it would've marked the first time Mets pitchers had accomplished the feat since Jerry Koosman and Don Cardwell turned the trick during their remarkable season of 1969. Ironically, the opposition in 1969 also was the Pittsburgh Pirates.

In the ninth with the Mets leading, 5–0, behind two more home runs by John Milner, Pittsburgh's Richie Zisk led off with a base hit. Two outs later Rennie Stennett doubled, putting runners on second and third. A single by Dal Maxvill scored both runners and chased Stone. Harry Parker relieved Stone, and after allowing a base hit to Willie Stargell, induced Dave Cash to fly out to end the game. For Parker, it marked his fourth save of the year.

In a season filled mostly with gloom and doom thus far, the pitching of Stone and Parker was one of the few bright spots. Together, the two combined for 13 wins despite having no specific role when the season began. In fact, Harry

Parker, acquired as part of the deal that sent Art Shamsky to the St. Louis Cardinals in October of 1971, was not expected to make the team when spring training began. George Stone, acquired as an afterthought in the deal with Atlanta that brought Felix Millan to the Mets in exchange for Gary Gentry and Danny Frisella, started the season in the bullpen, and didn't get his first start until the season was two months old. "I guess I was on the low end of the totem pole when the season began," said Stone. "But I made up my mind not to get discouraged. I just did my running and whatever they told me to do. I even experimented changing my grip on the ball while I worked in the bullpen. I wanted to be ready when they did need me." Yogi, however, insisted that Stone was no throw-in. "We knew he could start and relieve," said Berra. "When we made the deal and gave them Gentry and Frisella, they wanted to give us someone else. We insisted on Stone."[1]

The Mets continued their mastery over the Pirates by winning the finale of the four-game series behind Ray Sadecki and Tug McGraw. More satisfying than the win itself was the return of McGraw to the role of closer, where he saved his first game in more than two months. The next rivals, the St. Louis Cardinals, arrived at Shea for a weekend series, including a Sunday doubleheader. The Mets took the opener, 7–3, with Willie Mays striking the key blow, a three-run homer in the bottom of the seventh inning that put the game out of reach. Once again, the Mets were in the news on the injury front when it was revealed that Bud Harrelson would be out of action for a couple of weeks with a fractured sternum. Yet the Mets had to consider themselves fortunate, because the news could've been a lot worse. In the last of the first inning, John Milner drilled a ball high against the right field wall, missing a home run by inches. Milner, heading full tilt to third base, took a relay throw from Ted Sizemore flush on his right ear as he started his slide. While Milner had to leave the game, he suffered only a bruise and was not anticipated to miss any games.

The Cardinals took the second game of the series after scoring two runs off Jerry Koosman in the eighth inning, snapping a 2–2 tie, and then held off a Mets' ninth-inning rally to prevail, 4–3. The Cardinals, however, lost the services of their ace right-hander, Bob Gibson, when his knee buckled as he threw a pitch in the third inning.

Just over 40,000 fans attended the Sunday afternoon Banner Day doubleheader, but went home disappointed after the Mets lost yet another twinbill. Two runs off Tom Seaver in the seventh inning of the opener did the Mets in, 3–2. In the nightcap the Cardinals pounded out 12 hits off Jim McAndrew over five innings as the Mets lost once again, 4–1. Yogi Berra was greeted with boos when he came to the mound to pull McAndrew in the sixth inning. That marked the first time Berra was the recipient of such a negative reaction despite all that had transpired over the course of the season.

McGraw, meanwhile, showed he was back when he saved a game for Buzz Capra in a 6–5 Mets win over the Cardinals in the series finale.

On August 8, the Mets headed to the West Coast for an eight-game road trip that would take them to Los Angeles for two games and to San Francisco and San Diego for three games apiece. In Los Angeles the two teams combined to score two runs in the two games as the Mets and Dodgers split 1–0 decisions. The opener saw Jon Matlack out-pitch Andy Messersmith, with the only run scoring in the second inning when Messersmith walked Milner, who advanced to second on a wild pitch and scored on a base hit by Jerry Grote.

The Mets lost an opportunity to climb out of the cellar when Jerry Koosman lost his fourth consecutive well-pitched game, surrendering an eighth-inning run as the Dodgers avenged their 1–0 loss from the previous day. With the game scoreless, Dodgers starter Claude Osteen, a longtime Mets nemesis, led the inning off with a single, but was quickly erased when Koosman picked him off. Davey Lopes followed with a looping drive to center field, which Don Hahn hesitated on before attempting to make a diving catch. When the ball skipped past Hahn, Lopes was able to easily make it to third, where he scored on a base hit by Manny Mota.

After the short series with the Dodgers, the Mets moved on to Candlestick Park, where Tom Seaver continued his dominating pitching in the opener as the Mets beat the Giants, 7–1.

The middle game of the series saw the Mets lose another heartbreaker. George Stone, the Mets' starter, had an uncharacteristic poor performance, lasting just a third of an inning. Stone surrendered six runs, four of them earned, with three coming on a home run by Bobby Bonds to help the Giants jump out to a 6–1 lead. But the Mets, refusing to quit, were able to tie the game in the fifth inning with John Milner's 20th home run, a three-run blast, being the big blow. The Giants regained the lead by scoring a run in the last of the seventh inning, and the Mets came to bat in the ninth inning, trailing 7–6. Willie Mays, in a pinch-hitting role, led off the ninth with a double and two outs later scored on a throwing error by shortstop Chris Speier.

Tug McGraw, once again pitching like an ace, was called on to take the mound in the ninth inning. McGraw pitched a solid four innings of relief, keeping the Giants off the board through the twelfth inning while escaping a bases-loaded no-out jam. The trouble began in the last of the twelfth, when McGraw walked Willie McCovey to open the frame. Bobby Bonds followed with a check-swing grounder to third, where an inexperienced Jerry Grote was playing. Grote allowed the ball to get by him for a two-base error, putting runners at second and third with nobody out. Gary Matthews was walked intentionally to load the bases. McGraw fanned Chris Speier for the first out and then induced Chris Arnold to pop the ball into short right field, but not deep enough to allow McCovey to tag up. Dave Rader then fouled out to catcher Duffy Dyer to end the threat. McGraw wasn't able to duplicate his magic when he came out for the thirteenth inning. With one out McGraw hit Garry Maddox with a pitch. Shortstop Wayne Garrett then allowed a potential double-play grounder to get by him, putting runners on second and third. The next batter was Bruce Miller, a rookie, whom Yogi Berra elected to walk intentionally and pitch to the always dangerous Bobby Bonds. The strategy backfired when Bonds singled to left field, ending the game. For the Giants it marked their tenth extra-inning victory of the year without a defeat.

After the game, Berra explained his decision to walk Miller and pitch to Bonds. "You hate to have to walk a guy in that situation but you gotta. With first base open, they can try a squeeze play, with the bases full they won't and more importantly you don't have to have a tag play at the plate."[2]

One mistake pitch by Ray Sadecki was the difference in the Mets' 4–1 loss to the Giants in the rubber game of the series. Sadecki was cruising along with a 1–0 lead and retired the first two Giants in the last of the fifth inning before walking Giants pitcher Ron Bryant. Despite committing the cardinal sin of walking the opposing pitcher, Sadecki should've been back in the dugout after the next batter, Garry Maddox, lifted a fly ball to left field. The inning was extended, however, after Milner misplayed the ball into a double. With runners now on second and third, Sadecki worked the count to 3 and 1 to Tito Fuentes before grooving a pitch that was rerouted over the left field fence.

"It was a mistake, my mistake and that's what so frustrating," said Sadecki afterwards. "I was trying to throw the ball in the dirt, exactly the kind of pitch I struck him out with the last time out."[3]

The final leg of the road trip saw the Mets pull into San Diego, where only 2,440 fans showed up to watch the last-place Mets take on the last-place Padres. The miniscule crowd was rewarded with a thrilling 3–2 home team victory, as the Padres pulled out the game by scoring two runs in the last of the ninth inning off Mets starter Jon Matlack, who was pitching a masterpiece of a game. With the Mets taking a 2–1 lead into the ninth, Padres catcher Fred Kendall led off the inning with a base hit and was removed for pinch-runner Wayne Anderson. Dave Winfield followed with a clean single to left field. The ball was hit hard enough to hold Anderson at second base, but Cleon Jones didn't field the ball cleanly, which allowed Anderson to take third. The next batter, Rich Morales, hit a fly ball to short left field, which had Anderson tagging up. A good throw may have nailed Anderson, but Jones' throw was way off-line, and the Padres plated the tying run. Matlack then struck out the next batter, Ivan Murrell, and walked Jerry Morales intentionally, putting runners at first and second with two outs. A base hit by Derrell Thomas followed, scoring Winfield and sending Matlack to his much-undeserved 15th loss of the season.

Jerry Koosman, who undeservedly lost his previous four outings due to a lack of run support, finally lost a game he deserved to lose. The Padres touched him up for six runs in four innings and blasted the Mets, 9–0, in the middle game of the series. But the Mets were able to salvage the finale and avenge the drubbing of the previous day by blasting the Padres, 7–0, as Tom Seaver fired a two-hitter en route to his 15th win. Wayne Garrett led off the game with a home run, while Jerry Grote followed with a grand slam in the fourth inning. Cleon Jones' fifth-inning solo homer was icing on the cake.

While the Mets returned home on August 17 only 7½ games out of first place, they were still holding up the rest of the division, comfortably settled in the basement. First up were the always-tough National League champion Cincinnati Reds, who arrived for a four-game weekend series. In a matchup of left-handers, the surprising George Stone faced the ace of the Reds' staff, Don Gullett. Thanks to Willie Mays' 660th (and final) home run of his amazing career, Stone took a 1–0 lead into the ninth inning. Stone retired the first two batters in the ninth, then surrendered consecutive singles to Dan Driessen, Tony Perez and Johnny Bench. Suddenly the Reds had the game tied. Harry Parker, who in the recent past had been so successful in relief, saw his spate of good outings come to a halt when he surrendered a leadoff 10th inning home run to rookie pinch-hitter Hal King. After the game Berra had to defend his decision to leave Stone in the game to face Johnny Bench after surrendering two hits in the ninth inning. "He felt great. If he'd said he was tired, I would've taken him out."[4]

The Mets didn't let the disappointing loss get to them as they dispatched Reds starter Fred Norman in the third inning of the Saturday afternoon game by scoring four runs, three of them coming on Don Hahn's second home run of the year. Norman's successor, Roger Mason, didn't fare any better. At first the Mets played little ball, loading the bases on a single and two bunt hits. A hit batsman and a walk brought home two more runs before Sparky Anderson called on Dave Tomlin to face John Milner with the bases loaded. Milner proceeded to clear the bases but not in the manner envisioned by Anderson, unloading a 370-foot drive into the Mets' bullpen, his second grand slam of the season and his 21st home run overall. After the game, Milner commented on his blast. "It was 3 and 2 and I knew he didn't want to walk me. So I guessed that he'd throw me a fastball inside, and there it was."[5]

The last-place Mets also won the third game of the series against a Reds ball club that was playing at a .750 clip over the last two months and hadn't lost two games in a row since early July. The game took the form of an enthralling pitching duel between two veteran left-handers, Jerry Koosman for the Mets and Ross Grimsley for the Reds. The Mets struck first, when in the last of the first inning, Bud Harrelson, just off the disabled list for the second time of the season, led off with a double, moved to third on an infield out and scored on a sacrifice fly by Willie Mays. It was not until the top of the fifth inning that the Reds recouped that run. In the last of the eighth inning, Don Hahn led off with a base hit and stayed there as Teddy Martinez flied out. But Koosman sacrificed Hahn to second, and Harrelson, already with a double to his credit, drove the ball to the base of the bullpen fence, good for a double and the go-ahead run. "I couldn't believe it," said Rose. "It must have been his all-time distance shot."[6]

Koosman retired the Reds in the ninth inning with little difficulty to get credit for a long overdue win. Koosman had lost his last five decisions despite pitching well enough to win four of the outings.

It took 16 innings for the Mets to lose their magic in the series finale. After surrendering solo home runs in the second and third innings, Seaver held the powerful Reds' offense scoreless through the 12th inning. The Mets scored two runs in the last of the sixth inning, tying the game at 2–2. The game remained tied until the Reds scored a run off McGraw in the 13th inning. However, the Mets refused to quit as they scored a run of their own, sending the game onto the 14th inning. By the 16th inning, however, there was nothing left in the Mets' bag of tricks as the Reds pummeled McGraw and Parker for five runs on their way to an 8–3 win.

The Mets had no time to rest on their laurels after their grueling series with the Reds, for the first-place Los Angeles Dodgers came marching into Shea Stadium. In an apparent mismatch, the Mets sent their fifth starter, Ray Sadecki, against the ace of the Dodger staff, Don Sutton. However, by the time the Mets came to bat in the last of the eighth inning, the only difference was a Bill Russell solo home run in the fifth inning that gave the Dodgers a 1–0 lead. The Mets tied the game in the bottom of the eighth inning when they manufactured a run off Don Sutton via a walk, a bunt by Kranepool that incredibly went for a base hit, a sacrifice and a sacrifice fly. After Sadecki easily disposed of the Dodgers in the ninth, the Mets got to work in the bottom of the frame. After the first out was recorded, Wayne Garrett reached first on a walk. Yogi, pulling all the right strings, called for a run-and-hit play with Felix Millan at-bat, resulting in the Mets avoiding a double play. Staub was then walked intentionally, bringing Milner, the team's most prolific hitter, to the plate. Milner, clutch all season, came through again, as he singled home the winning run.

The middle game of the series featured more of the same flair and dramatics as its predecessor. The Dodgers scored a run in the top of the first inning, and even though the Mets loaded the bases with two outs in the fourth inning, it appeared the game would continue with the Dodgers clinging to a 1–0 lead after Teddy Martinez lifted a high pop to the mound. In a scene that could only resemble a sandlot game, Andy Messersmith, the Dodgers' pitcher, called for it as all five infielders converged towards the mound. Messersmith had the fortune (or misfortune, depending on who you were rooting for) to trip on the pitching slab when he took a step backwards, allowing the ball to fall as two runs scored, giving the Mets a 2–1 lead. The Dodgers were able to peck away at Mets starter George Stone, scoring single runs in the sixth and seventh innings. That gave the Dodgers a 3–2 lead as the Mets came to bat in the last of the ninth, trailing 3–2. Once again, the "You Gotta Believe Kids" got to work. Pinch-hitter Cleon Jones led off with a base hit off Dodgers relief ace Jim Brewer. McGraw sacrificed him to second, and Jones moved to third base on a sacrifice fly by Wayne Garrett. The Mets had the tying run 90 feet away but were also down to their last out. Millan came through with a base hit, however, scoring Jones and tying the game. Rusty Staub followed with another hit to bring John Milner to the plate. Milner needed to see only one pitch, which he smoked into center field, scoring Millan and giving the Mets another win in an incredible fashion. The win brought the Mets to within six games of the division-leading Cardinals, but even more significant was Tug McGraw picking up his first win of a long and arduous season for the left-hander. Claude Osteen brought the Mets back down to earth in the series finale, as the Dodgers were able to hold off the pesky New Yorkers in another one-run, tightly fought contest.

The always-tough Giants followed the Dodgers into New York for a weekend series. The 35,361 fans that paid their way into Shea Stadium for the opener got their money's worth as Jerry Koosman and Juan Marichal, two classy veterans, locked horns. In addition to being on top of their games, both pitchers were assisted by solid defense.

In the top of the second inning, Willie McCovey led off by drilling a Koosman pitch off the wall on a line, only to be thrown out as he headed into second base by Rusty Staub. In the last of the third inning, Jerry Grote led off with a single, and Teddy Martinez followed by scorching a hard line drive that was picked off by third baseman Mike Phillips, denying Martinez. Koosman, attempting to sacrifice Grote to second base, bunted the ball back to Marichal, who threw low to second base; Grote was ruled safe. But Marichal escaped unscathed by striking out Willie Mays and forcing Millan to pop up. The Giants threatened again in the fourth inning when Bobby Bonds led off with an infield hit. Koosman picked Bonds off first, but walked Willie McCovey. McCovey moved to third when Garry Maddox doubled. Koosman then walked Chris Speier intentionally and coaxed Mike Phillips to pop up. With two outs and the bases still loaded, Cleon Jones turned in the defensive play of the game. Dave Rader hit a sinking liner toward left field, but Jones made a spectacular tumbling catch. Jones saved Koosman again in the fifth inning when he robbed Bobby Bonds with a similar catch while Marichal was on second base. The Mets didn't threaten again until the last of the eighth inning, when Millan singled and Staub sacrificed him to second. Moments later, the Giants paid Cleon Jones back for his thievery. Jones drilled a ball toward right field that was speared by second baseman Tito Fuentes, who then doubled Millan off second base.

The Giants threatened again in the top of the ninth inning when McCovey led off with another base hit off Koosman. But Teddy Martinez robbed Garry Maddox of a sure base hit and turned it into a force play. With the speedy Maddox replacing the slow-footed McCovey as the base runner, Maddox immediately attempted to steal second base but was cut down by Grote's rifle arm. The game headed into extra innings with both starting pitchers, Koosman and Marichal, still on the mound. Koosman retired the Giants in the tenth inning, and the Mets went to work against Marichal in the bottom half. Ken Boswell, batting for Koosman, singled to start the inning. Willie Mays, owner of 660 home runs, then sacrificed Boswell to second. Moments later, Boswell came lumbering home with the only run of the game after Millan lined a single into the right-center field alley.

An exuberant Berra spoke about the team's chances despite still being mired in the cellar of the National League East. "We've got the whole month of September left, with all our games in the East. The best thing about our club now is the way the guys fight back after a tough defeat, the way they did tonight."[7]

The Giants turned the tables on the Mets the next afternoon with a little assistance from a 15-year-old fan as they downed the Mets, 1–0, behind the four-hit pitching of Tom Bradley. With two outs in the top of first inning, Garry Maddox hit a foul pop that Grote was settling under when a fan reached over in his attempt to snag a souvenir. Neither was able to come up with the ball, thereby giving Maddox new life. He quickly took advantage of the opportunity and singled home the game's lone run. Tom Seaver, the unfortunate victim, was charged with his seventh loss of the season despite another outstanding pitching performance.

The Mets lost the finale of the series as well, 5–4, as Ron Bryant picked up his 20th win of the year. While Bryant was staked to a 5–0 lead, he had to hold

Felix Millan, acquired in what undoubtedly was one of the better trades of the decade, slides safely into third base in the August 25 game against the Giants. It was the furthest a Met would advance in a game won by the Giants 1–0 (© Bettmann/Corbis).

on for dear life while the Mets scored two runs in the last of the sixth inning and two in the bottom of the ninth inning, and had the tying run on base when reliever Elias Sosa struck out Willie Mays to end the game.

Next into New York came the San Diego Padres, and home runs by Fred Kendall and Clarence Gaston off starter George Stone gave the visitors an early 2–0 lead. The Mets struck back with one run in the last of the fourth inning and came to bat in the fifth inning, trailing 2–1. George Stone, the lead-off batter, became the first Met in franchise history to be awarded first base on catcher's interference. A walk to Wayne Garrett and a sacrifice bunt that Millan was able to beat out loaded the bases with Staub coming to the plate. Staub put the Mets out in front when he hit the ball out of the park for a grand slam home run. For Staub it was his first home run in five weeks, and his first Shea Stadium home run since mid–May. With the Mets carrying a 6–3 lead into the eighth inning, George Stone's personal reliever, Harry Parker, took the mound. Parker got into immediate trouble when he sandwiched an out between a walk to lead-off batter Jerry Morales and a base hit by Dave Roberts. A two-run double by Nate Colbert, who ended up on third base after the relay throw home, cut the Mets' lead to one with the tying run only ninety feet away. But McGraw, having regained confidence and pitching as the ace of old, was called upon to extricate the Mets from the jam, and responded in splendid fashion by striking out Gaston and inducing Fred Kendall to ground out. In the ninth, McGraw struck out the side, picking up his 14th save of the year.

The second game of the series was no less pulsating, as Jon Matlack hooked up against Clay Kirby. With the game tied, 2–2, in the sixth inning, the Padres loaded the bases against Matlack with Kirby coming to the plate. Kirby laid down a suicide squeeze bunt as Clarence Gaston broke for the plate. Wayne Garrett charged the ball, barehanded it, and fired a strike to the plate, nailing Gaston. With two outs and the bases still loaded, Jerry Morales smacked a hard grounder to Garrett, who reacted perfectly and stepped on third base to end the threat and keep the tie intact. Garrett continued his one-man show when he led off the bottom half of the inning with his 10th home run of the season. The Mets continued to pour it on as they scored four more runs in the inning to take a 7–2 lead. The Mets carried that lead into the eighth inning, but Matlack began to falter as he surrendered a single and a walk. Again Berra called on Harry Parker and again he failed, yielding a pinch-hit triple to Johnny Grubb, who scored on a groundout by Leron Lee. The Mets added an all-important insurance run in the last of the eighth inning before calling on McGraw to put it in the books. While McGraw surrendered a lead-off home run to Nate Colbert, he quickly recovered to retire the side and pick up his 15th save of the year. "He lost — who knows? — his concentration, his timing for awhile," said bullpen coach Joe Pignatano, regarding the rejuvenation of McGraw. "But now McGraw is the best relief pitcher in baseball, no question about it."[8]

After spending the long, hot New York summer cooling themselves in the cellar of the National League East, the Mets finally emerged from the basement and climbed into fifth place after completing a three-game sweep of the San Diego Padres. Jerry Koosman, coming off his brilliant 10-inning shutout against the Giants, was again in spectacular form as he held the Padres scoreless for 6⅔ innings before being lifted in favor of Buzz Capra. The game, which began as a pitching duel between the crafty veteran Koosman and the Padres' rookie left-hander Rich Troedson, remained scoreless until the Mets came to bat in the last of the fifth inning. Don Hahn led off the inning with a walk and went to second on a base hit by Bud Harrelson. Koosman then beat out an attempted sacrifice bunt when nobody covered first; suddenly the Mets had the bases loaded with nobody out. After Wayne Garrett struck out, Felix Millan hit a sacrifice fly to left field, scoring Hahn. A base hit by Mays brought home Harrelson, and Koosman scored when Cleon Jones doubled to left, giving the Mets a 3–0 lead.

Koosman scattered five hits over the first six innings and retired the first two batters in the seventh inning before he began to tire. Jerry Morales lined a two-out single to bring pitching coach Rube Walker out to the mound. When Darrell Thomas followed with a base hit off Koosman's shin, it was curtains for the left-hander. Capra induced Dave Roberts to fly out and the Mets were never headed.

The Mets' trip out of the cellar was short-lived as they moved on to St. Louis to take on the first-place Cardinals for a four-game series. New York wasted a magnificent pitching performance by Tom Seaver, who held the Cardinals scoreless through the first nine innings, but for the second start came away with a 1–0 defeat when St. Louis pushed across a run in the bottom of the 10th inning.

The Mets, however, were able to even the series the next day and once again climb out of the cellar. The Mets scored three runs in the top of the 10th inning after two were out to snap a 3–3 tie. With the conclusion of the game, the month of August ended as well. While the Mets found themselves in fifth place, they also were only 5½ games behind the division-leading Cardinals as baseball entered the stretch drive.

3

The Pennant Race

Between McGraw's "You Gotta Believe" and Berra's "It ain't over till it's over," the Mets were a confident team that entered the stretch drive despite residing in fifth place. "We might be the first club to be in last place on August 20th to win a pennant," said the team's biggest cheerleader, Tug McGraw. Added Jerry Koosman, "It's beginning to feel like 1969 again. We've got that feeling." "I'll tell you one thing," said Jerry Grote. "If we continue to get this kind of pitching, we're gonna be in it for the rest of the year."[1]

All of a sudden, the Mets found numerous factors in their favor as the pennant race began in earnest. For the first time since April, Yogi was able to roll out his regular lineup on a daily basis. And while the offense was still not potent enough to instill fear in the hearts of the opposition, it was a far cry from the offense that sleep-walked through the first four months of the season. The revived hitting attack had Felix Millan and John Milner leading the way. But mostly it was the pitching. Tom Seaver, Jerry Koosman and Jon Matlack were showing why they were considered the best 1-2-3 tandem in all of base-ball. George Stone and Ray Sadecki were doing outstanding work as the fourth and fifth starters while getting exceptional relief work from Harry Parker. But perhaps most important of all was the return to form of relief ace Tug McGraw.

September 1 saw the Mets beat the Cardinals, 4–1, behind George Stone, who had already exceeded all expectations while he picked up his ninth win of the season and fifth in a row. With the win the Mets knocked the Cardinals percentage points out of first place and narrowed their own deficit to only 4½ games from the top spot.

After losing the series finale in St. Louis, the Mets returned home for a Labor Day doubleheader against the Philadelphia Phillies. The Mets missed an opportunity to advance in the standings when they split the twinbill. In the first game, Jerry Koosman zipped the Phillies, 5–0. For Koosman, it extended his streak of scoreless innings to 29⅔, earning rave reviews from catcher Jerry Grote. "He used to throw the hell out of the ball. Now he's not as fast, but he's adjusted and became a better pitcher."[2] Offensively, Teddy Martinez was the star of the game, collecting four hits, including a double and a home run. The

Just in time for the pennant race, Mets manager Yogi Berra had the middle of his lineup healthy. Clockwise from top right: John Milner, Cleon Jones, Felix Millan and Rusty Staub (National Baseball Hall of Fame Library).

. Mets, however, couldn't grab the nightcap, as the Phillies downed Craig Swan, who was called from the minors after the rosters expanded to 40 players on September 1.

An overpowering performance by Tom Seaver in the third game of the series led the Mets to a 7–1 victory over the Phillies. The seven runs scored by the Mets was a breath of fresh air for Seaver, who had lost his previous two games by identical 1–0 scores. Seaver, who picked up his 16th win of the season, had 13 strikeouts to increase his league-leading total to 218, while lowering his league-leading ERA to a microscopic 1.69. The series with the Phillies culminated with Ray Sadecki and Tug McGraw combining to shut out the Phillies, 4–0, as Rusty Staub connected for his 12th home run of the season. With the victory, the Mets leap-frogged the Chicago Cubs into fourth place.

Next it was on to Montreal, where the Mets sent their left-handed aces, Matlack and Koosman, to the mound against the Expos for yet another doubleheader. In the opener, Matlack shut the Expos out on five hits, enabling Wayne Garrett's 12th home run, a solo blast, to stand up in the 1–0 victory. Matlack needed last-out assistance from Tug McGraw after walking Pepe Mangual and Mike Jorgensen.

In the nightcap, Koosman held the Expos off the scoreboard for the first 2⅓ innings, extending his scoreless inning streak to 32, before the Expos finally broke through to score a run to take a 1–0 lead. The Expos, behind their starter Mike Torrez, were able to maintain that lead until the Mets tied the game on an unearned run in the seventh inning. With the game tied after nine innings, it became a battle of the relief aces: McGraw for the Mets and Mike Marshall for the Expos. The game remained tied until the Mets came to bat in the top of the 15th inning. John Milner led off with a single and moved to third on a double by Ed Kranepool. A sacrifice fly by Don Hahn broke the tie, and then McGraw helped his cause by driving home a couple of runs. When the Expos were able to score only one run off McGraw in the last of the 15th, eight hours and eight minutes of baseball concluded with two more victories for the Mets.

Both the Mets' pennant hopes and Tom Seaver's lofty goal of winning 20 games were put on hold as New York lost the series finale in Montreal, stopped by the Expos' sensational rookie, Steve Rogers, a 23-year-old right-hander. In a frigid Canadian evening, Seaver surrendered a two-run homer to ex–Met Ken Singleton and a solo blast to Ron Fairly, which accounted for all of Montreal's runs. The win for the Expos, who far and away were having their best season in their short history, closed their gap to within 2½ games of the division-leading Cardinals. The Mets, meanwhile, still resided in fourth place and ended the day's action trailing the Cardinals by four games.

With the series in Montreal complete, the Mets headed to Veterans Stadium for a three-game series with the Phillies. Jerry Koosman, who entered the game having allowed only one run in his last 38 innings, saw his string of outstanding performances come to a halt. With the long ball being his undoing, he surrendered six runs in eight innings of work despite being spotted to a 4–0 lead. The Mets got back on the winning track a day later, with Matlack and McGraw combining to hold off the Phillies, 3–2. The Mets took the finale as well, a 12-inning affair, with Tom Seaver picking up his 17th win of the year while going 11 innings and striking out 10. McGraw pitched the bottom of the 12th inning and collected his 20th save.

September 14 brought the Mets back home for a big three-game weekend series with the Chicago Cubs. A Friday evening rainout forced the Mets to play yet another doubleheader the next afternoon. Berra tabbed his second-line left-handers, George Stone and Ray Sadecki, as his starters. While Stone was masterful in winning his seventh consecutive decision, Sadecki was not as fortunate in the nightcap, as the Cubs roughed him up in a 7–0 drubbing of the New Yorkers. The split left the Mets 3½ games out of first with 14 left to play. The Mets then took off for Pittsburgh trailing the Pirates by only 2½ games after defeating the Cubs in the final game of the series, 4–3, while the division-leading Pirates lost.

The moment of truth arrived as the Mets' next five games would be against the Pirates, with two games at Three Rivers Stadium before the clubs came back to New York for three more games.

The Mets sent their best, Tom Seaver, to the mound against Bruce Kison. But Seaver was far from being his best, as Willie Stargell and the rest of the Pirates' lineup smacked the pitcher around for five runs in the three innings he lasted as Pittsburgh blasted the Mets, 10–3. Stargell teed off against Seaver with a triple and a home run and then added two more doubles against the bullpen. The Mets were able to salvage the final game of the series in Pittsburgh, leaving no worse than when they arrived.

The opener of the three-game series at Shea saw George Stone continue his remarkable pitching, while a suddenly very hot Cleon Jones hit two home runs as the Mets stopped the Pirates. Stone went the first six innings and McGraw went the last three to pick up his 22nd save of the year. With the win, only 1½ games separated the Mets from the Pirates.

What three weeks earlier could only be considered a pipe dream was now close to becoming reality. The Mets pulled out a miraculous victory in 13 innings over Pittsburgh in the second game to move into second place, only one-half game behind the division-leading Pirates.

Jerry Koosman, pitching his best baseball since 1969, hooked up against the Pirates' Jim Rooker in the middle of the three-game series against the division leaders. The Pirates scored first when they touched Koosman for a run in the fourth inning, but the Mets got that run back in the last of the sixth inning on a two-out single by Cleon Jones. Fate seemed to be against the Mets when Richie Hebner, who replaced Rennie Stennett after pulling a muscle, homered off Koosman in the seventh, putting Pittsburgh up ahead again. The Mets knotted the game again in the last of the eighth inning when Jim Beauchamp, batting for Koosman, singled, was sacrificed to second, and scored on a base hit by Millan. The Pirates regained the lead again in the ninth inning off reliever Harry Parker. But the Mets, refusing to die, still had some tricks left in their bag as they came to bat in the last of the ninth inning, trailing 3–2. The first trick was pinch-hitter Ken Boswell, who started the frame with a base hit. Boswell was sacrificed to second, and stayed there as George Theodore struck out. With the Mets down to their last out, Berra pulled out his final trick in the form of Duffy Dyer, who was called on to pinch-hit. Dyer, whose last hit came 27 days ago, doubled home Boswell for the tying run.

Ray Sadecki gave Tug McGraw a rare day off and took over the pitching as the game headed into extra innings. Sadecki got through his first three innings without difficulty. However, Sadecki ran into trouble in the 13th inning and was saved only by a miracle. With Richie Zisk on first, Dave Augustine drilled a ball that appeared to be heading out of the park. As fate would have it, the ball hit at the top of the fence and bounced into the glove of Cleon Jones. A perfect relay to Garrett, who fired a strike to the catcher Ron Hodges, was just in time to tag a sliding Zisk and thwart the threat.

The rejuvenated Mets came to bat in the last of the 13th inning against Pirates reliever Luke Walker, who walked the first two batters he faced. Moments later, Ron Hodges, already a hero after successfully blocking the plate and making a great tag on Richie Zisk only a half-inning earlier, provided the coup de grace with a single to left-center, scoring John Milner.

A raucous crowd of over 50,000 fans showed up at Shea Stadium to watch Tom Seaver lead the Mets to their fourth straight win over the fading Pittsburgh Pirates. Seaver, who in his previous start was pasted by the Pirates, was in vintage form. The Mets' offense pounded out 13 hits and scored 10 runs against Pirates pitching. First place, which the Mets vacated on May 3, belonged to them once again.

The Mets got off to a quick start against Pirates starter and 1971 World Series hero Steve Blass when they touched up the right-hander for four runs in the bottom of the first inning. Wayne Garrett got the Mets started when he led off with a single. A single by Staub and a double by Cleon Jones brought home two runs, and later in the inning Jerry Grote drove in two more runs with a bases-loaded double, giving the Mets a 4–0 lead. The Pirates cut the Mets' lead in half in the top of the second inning on a walk, a triple by Richie Zisk, and a sacrifice fly.

The Mets got those runs back, however, in the last of the third inning when John Milner slugged his 23rd home run of the year with a man on. The Mets continued their power display when Wayne Garrett hit his 14th home run of the season in the sixth inning and Staub clubbed his 15th in the eighth inning as the Mets romped, 10–2.

It was bedlam in the stands during the game and in the Mets' clubhouse after the contest as New York had come full circle. Fans jammed the aisles and danced on the dugout roof, chanting, "We're No. 1!" "It brings back memories of 1969," said Jerry Koosman. "But it's as though it's the first time all over again."[3]

There was no stopping the marauding Mets as they swept the Cardinals in a two-game weekend series at Shea. The opener saw just over 24,000 fans attend the game on a cool and cloudy early autumn day. The weather didn't matter to Wayne Garrett, who hit his fifth home run in September, a two-run job in the third inning, and to Jon Matlack, who made those runs stand up with a nifty four-hitter, as the Mets beat the Cardinals, 2–0. For Matlack it was his seventh win in his last eight decisions, as he picked up his 14th victory. With the end of play on September 22, 1973, the incredibly tight standings were as follows:

Team	W	L	PCT	GB	Games Left
New York Mets	78	77	.503	-	7
Pittsburgh Pirates	75	76	.497	1	11
Montreal Expos	75	78	.490	2	9
St. Louis Cardinals	76	79	.490	2	7
Chicago Cubs	75	79	.487	2½	8

Pennant fever in New York ratcheted up a notch after the Mets completed a sweep of the Cardinals, 5–2, in front of a sellout crowd of over 50,000 fans.

The Mets took a momentary break from the tight pennant race to pay tribute to Willie Mays before the regularly scheduled game with the Expos. Mays, who had previously announced that he would retire at the end of the season, was introduced by Lindsey Nelson and received a six-minute standing ovation from the overflow crowd. An emotional Mays, with tears in his eyes, strode to the podium to deliver his farewell speech. "I hope that with my farewell tonight, you'll understand what I'm going through right now.

In an emotional ceremony Willie Mays and his 660 home runs say goodbye to his fans and teammates (AP Images).

Something that I never thought: that I would never quit baseball. But, as you know, there always comes a time for someone to get out. And I look at those kids over there, the way they are playing, and the way they are fighting for themselves, and it tells me one thing.... Willie, say good-bye to America. Thank you very much."[4]

With the ceremonies over, it was time to get to the business of the pennant race, with the Mets entering action having won six games in a row to lead the National League East by just one-half game over the Pirates. The Mets sent veteran left-hander Koosman and his 12-15 record to the mound against Montreal's rookie sensation Steve Rogers, who had won nine games.

The game remained scoreless for the first 4½ innings, with both sides receiving tremendous defensive plays from their respective shortstops—Harrelson for the Mets and the ex–Met Tim Foli for the Expos. It was Harrelson, however, who got the Mets started when they batted in the last of the fifth inning. Harrelson hit a ball that glanced off Steve Rogers for a single. Jerry Koosman then sacrificed Harrelson to second. The shortstop moved to third on a bad-hop single that bounced over the out-stretched glove of Tim Foli. Harrelson then was able to tag up and score the game's first run when Felix Millan flied out to left field.

The Expos immediately recouped that run in the top half of the sixth inning when Ron Woods singled with one out. Woods then stole second and Bob Bailey followed with a walk, putting runners on first and second. The Expos then tried to pull off a double steal, but Grote threw out Bob Bailey on the back-end of the attempted play. Hal Breeden followed with a smash that Garrett couldn't handle on the backhand to score Woods. The Mets went ahead again in the last of the sixth inning, when Cleon Jones launched his ninth home run of the year with one out and nobody on.

The Expos made a bid to tie the game again in the seventh inning, when with two outs, Koosman surrendered singles to Pepe Frias and Jose Morales. Berra then called on McGraw to face Felipe Alou. Alou lashed the ball into left-center field, but Cleon Jones, the offensive hero, became the defensive savior by making a nice one-handed running catch. The Expos didn't give up, however, mounting another threat in the top of the eighth inning. Again, Ron Woods led off with a base hit and Bob Bailey followed with a walk. After the Mets held a hasty conference at the mound, the next batter, Hal Breeden, put down a bunt toward first. McGraw pounced on the ball and fired a strike to Garrett, forcing Woods. McGraw was then able to get Singleton to pop out to short, and John Bocabella grounded to short, and the Mets were able to escape with their 2–1 lead still intact. McGraw retired the Expos in the ninth as well to save the win for Koosman. For McGraw, it was his 24th save of the year; for Koosman, it was his 13th win.

Meanwhile, in Pittsburgh, Steve Carlton and the Phillies downed the Pirates by the same 2–1 score. As a result of the Mets' win and Pirates' loss, the

Mets extended their lead to 1½ games with only five games left in a season that had suddenly become very exciting. The Mets' lead was slashed back to just a half-game after the Expos roughed up Tom Seaver by scoring four runs in the top of the first inning and adding another run in the second. With the Mets trailing 5–0 after 1½ innings, Berra elected to hit for Seaver. "I took Seaver out after two innings because Seaver didn't have his control, we were five runs behind, and I needed a pinch-hitter," said Berra.[5] In a season in which adversity was a constant companion, the Mets also climbed out of this hole, scoring four runs in the last of the second inning and then tying the game in the fifth inning. However, they could not overcome the deficit after Bob Bailey blasted a two-run homer off Harry Parker in the seventh inning.

As a result, the Mets entered the last weekend of the season with a half-game lead over the Pirates and four games left to play with the Cubs in Chicago, and an uncooperative weatherman. The first three games were postponed by rain, forcing the Mets to play a doubleheader on the final day of the season and, if need be, another doubleheader on the day after the season was officially slated to end. When the Mets finally resumed play, all they needed was one win to clinch a tie for the division championship.

Yogi Berra sent Jon Matlack to the mound in the opener of the doubleheader against the Cubs' Rick Reuschel. Matlack, who hadn't pitched in eight days, did not appear to be perturbed by the long layoff as he kept the Cubs off the scoreboard for the first seven innings. Unfortunately for Matlack, his mound opponent was just as tough as Reuschel allowed the Mets no runs on seven hits and was greatly assisted by three double plays turned by his defense.

Reuschel was forced to leave the scene in the top of the eighth inning with a blister to his right index finger, but Cubs manager Whitey Lockman, pulling all the right strings, made a double switch, calling on Dave Rosello to take over at second base while batting ninth and bringing in Bob Locker to face the Mets. Locker was able to dispose of the Mets in the eighth inning, and Lockman's strategy hit paydirt when Dave Rosello, leading off the last of the eighth, singled past third base. The next batter, Don Kessinger, laid down a bunt, which was fielded by Matlack. Matlack turned and fired to second in an attempt to force Rosello, who beat the throw, putting Cubs on first and second. Rick Monday then struck out for the fourth time and Billy Williams flied out, leaving Matlack with only Ron Santo to retire in order to return to the dugout unscathed. But Ron Santo, hitless for the past week, played the role of spoiler, as he singled into left field, scoring the first and only run of the game.

The Mets threatened in the ninth inning when John Milner singled and Cleon Jones sacrificed him to second. Dave Schneck then went down on strikes for the second out, and after Ken Boswell walked, Ed Kranepool grounded out, ending the game and prolonging the agony.

The Mets, however, wasted no time in the second game as they scored three runs off Ferguson Jenkins in the first inning, with two runs coming on a throwing error by Ron Santo. The Cubs responded with two runs of their own in the last of the second, courtesy of a couple of errors by Wayne Garrett and Cleon Jones. But some clutch pitching by Jerry Koosman and great defense enabled the Mets to cling to their 3–2 lead until the sixth inning. In the second inning, Cleon Jones misjudged a fly ball to the wall and fell on the wet grass before finally grabbing the ball while flat on his stomach. The next inning Jones made another great catch while sliding past a tumbling Bud Harrelson. Rusty Staub added two great plays of his own, one a diving catch and another by hauling in a long fly ball in the ivy vines.

The Mets extended their tenuous lead in the sixth inning, when Cleon Jones blasted his 10th home run of the year with a man on. Rusty Staub drove home a run in the seventh and then put the game out of reach with a two-run double in the ninth inning.

Jerry Koosman, who picked up his 14th win of the season, scattered six hits while striking out seven as the Mets clinched at least a tie for the National League East championship. With the season officially over, the Mets still had a makeup doubleheader to play with the Cubs, while the Pirates still had a makeup date with the San Diego Padres. All the Mets had to do was win one of the games to take the division outright. If the Mets lost both games and the Pirates won their game, the Mets, Cardinals and Pirates would be tied, forcing a sudden-death playoff the next day.

Only 1,913 fans showed up to Wrigley Field on this day after the season was officially scheduled to end as the Mets needed to win one of two games in order to once again reign as the champions of the National League East after spending most of the summer at the bottom of the division. Yogi went with his ace, Tom Seaver, in the opener, but there was little drama as the Mets led from the second inning on when Cleon Jones hit his second home run in as many days for a 1–0 lead. The Mets extended their lead in the fourth inning after loading the bases with nobody out. Rusty Staub singled and John Milner and Cleon Jones followed with walks. Jerry Grote then delivered a two-run single, and the Mets now had a 3–0 lead. John Milner increased the lead to 5–0 when in the next inning a Wayne Garrett double was followed with singles by Millan and Staub and Milner's sacrifice fly.

The Cubs finally got to Seaver in the last of the fifth inning when they scored two runs and narrowed the gap to 5–2. The Mets, however, got one run back the next inning and took a 6–2 lead going into the last of the sixth inning. A two-run homer by Rick Monday narrowed the gap to 6–4, thus prompting Berra to call on the hero of September, Tug McGraw, to wrap things up. McGraw didn't disappoint as he allowed only one hit and the Mets went on to a 6–4 victory. When the Mets reached their clubhouse after their win, they were cheering and shaking hands with one another but conscious that another game was scheduled to be played. Five minutes later, however, word arrived that the second game, now meaningless, was canceled. Only then did the real celebration begin, led by Tug McGraw, who played the most pivotal role during the Mets' revitalization during the home stretch. While the Mets won 23 of their last 32 games, McGraw, who was winless through the end of August, won four games and saved 12 in his last 17 appearances. McGraw stood atop an equipment trunk, yelling at the top of his lungs, "One, two, three, you got to believe," and the champagne began to flow. There was no question about it that when the Mets began pouring champagne all over one another, each and every soaked player deserved it. Their victory was definitely a team effort.

The Post-Season

The surprising National League East champions found themselves in Cincinnati a to take on Sparky Anderson's Big Red Machine as the 1973 National League Championship Series got underway. In a series that was touted as the Mets' arms against the Reds' bats, the pundits gave New York just about no chance against the powerful Cincinnati lineup that started with Pete Rose and continued with Joe Morgan, Dan Driessen, Johnny Bench, Tony Perez and Ken Griffey. Not even the arms of Seaver, Koosman and Matlack could stop the Reds' powerful machine over a five-game series, said the experts. In fact, over the course of the regular season, the Reds had beaten the Mets in eight out of 12 games.

Over 53,000 fans piled into Riverfront Stadium as Tom Seaver squared off against Reds right-hander Jack Billingham. While the Mets' hopes were riding on the right arm of Seaver, it was the pitcher's bat that struck the first blow of the series. With two outs in the second inning, Bud Harrelson drew a walk and Tom Seaver followed with a double, driving home Harrelson with the first run of the playoffs. While the Mets couldn't do anything more against Billingham, Seaver held the powerful Reds' offense completely at bay. He kept the Reds off the scoreboard through the first seven innings while striking out ten batters in the process.

Despite adding three more strikeouts over the last two innings to establish a playoff record, Seaver's effort went for naught when Pete Rose blasted a home run off the right-hander with one out in the eighth inning, tying the game. One inning later it was a dejected Tom Seaver who walked off the mound after Johnny Bench touched the pitcher for a home run in the bottom of the ninth, giving the Reds a stunning victory and a 1–0 lead in the championship series.

In a game dominated by pitching, there were precious few scoring opportunities for both ball clubs over the course of the afternoon. The Mets squandered their best scoring opportunity in the first inning when they loaded the bases with only one out. However, Billingham induced Jones to ground into a double play to choke off a potential rally. The Reds threatened in the last of the second inning when Bench doubled and Ken Griffey was hit by a pitch. But Seaver was able to escape when he struck out Cesar Geronimo and Darrel Chaney.

The Reds threatened again in the fourth inning when Dan Driessen led off with a pop fly double, but Seaver emerged unscathed when Tony Perez flied out and both Bench and Griffey struck out. Neither team was able to do anything offensively until Rose's blast in the eighth inning. In the ninth the Mets made some noise when Tom Hall, in relief of Jack Billingham, walked Staub to lead off the inning. After falling behind John Milner, 2–0, Sparky Anderson went to his ace, Pedro Borbon, who was able to retire Milner after the count went to 3–0. Borbon then retired Cleon Jones and Jerry Grote to send the tied game to the last of the ninth inning. Two batters into the inning and one swing by Johnny Bench broke the tie and ended the game in heart-breaking fashion for the Mets.

"Rose hit a pretty good pitch," a disappointed Seaver said after the game. Sparky Anderson praised Seaver's performance. "It looked like it was going to be enough," referring to the Mets' 1–0 lead.[1]

Nearly five months to the day that Jon Matlack was felled by a line drive off the bat of Marty Perez that nearly decapitated the pitcher, he sparkled in what to date was the most significant start of his career. Matlack stymied the powerful Reds' bats by holding them to just two hits as the Mets evened the series, beating Cincinnati, 5–0.

"It was probably the best game I ever pitched," said Matlack. "I wasn't overly strong, but that seemed to help me, because they were off stride."[2] The Mets scored first when Rusty Staub hit a fourth-inning home run off Reds starter and ace Don Gullett. But the New York offense could do could nothing more against the Reds' pitching until the Mets came to bat in the top of the ninth inning. Still clinging to a 1–0 lead with one out, Felix Millan singled to right field. Rusty Staub then walked, and Cleon Jones followed with a single, giving the Mets a much-needed insurance run. But the Mets didn't stop there. With Hall then falling behind John Milner, 2-0, Sparky Anderson pulled Hall and called on Pedro Borbon. Borbon intentionally walked Milner to load the bases with the hope of inducing the slow-footed Jerry Grote to bounce into an inning-ending double play. Grote foiled the strategy when he grounded a single up the middle, bringing home two more runs. When the inning finally ended, the Mets found themselves with an insurmountable 5–0 lead.

Despite the overwhelming Reds' firepower, only Andy Kosco, a reserve outfielder, troubled Matlack. Kosco singled in the second inning and then again in the seventh inning, but both times Matlack was able to emerge from the frame with no further trouble. The Reds mounted their biggest threat in the fifth inning after Matlack sandwiched walks to Kosco and Chaney in between strikeouts of Driessen and Geronimo. However, Matlack fanned pinch-hitter Ed Armbrister, ending the threat. In fact, the biggest threat to Matlack was not the Reds' lineup, but a blister that cropped up on the middle finger of his pitching hand in the seventh inning, which trainer Tom McKenna was able to treat effectively.

With the series deadlocked at one game apiece, the combatants headed to New York for the final three games. Close to 54,000 Mets fans piled into Shea Stadium as Jerry Koosman squared off against fellow left-hander Ross Grimsley. The Mets, who struck first in the initial two games of the playoffs, scored first again in the third game. For the second straight game, a Rusty Staub home run in the bottom of the first inning gave the Mets a 1–0 lead. But unlike the previous two contests, where the Mets failed to score again in the first game, or waited until the ninth inning to score four more runs in the second outing, the Mets' offense immediately went back to work in the second inning. Jerry Grote started the inning by drawing a walk. Don Hahn followed with another walk, and after Harrelson flied out, Koosman attempted to advance the runners with a sacrifice. Koosman bunted toward the mound, but when Grimsley attempted to field the ball, he slipped and fell to load the bases for the Mets. A sacrifice fly by Wayne Garrett brought home Grote, and a base hit by Millan scored Hahn, giving the Mets a 3–0 lead. With Sparky Anderson having seen enough of Grimsley, Tom Hall was called on for the third consecutive day. Hall's first batter was Rusty Staub, who made Anderson regret his decision. Staub redirected a Hall pitch into the right-field stands, increasing the Mets lead to 6–0.

In the top of the third inning, the Reds matched their scoring total for the first two games of the series when they scored two runs off Koosman. Denis Menke homered off the left-hander, and one out later pinch-hitter Larry Stahl followed with a base hit. Base hits by Rose and Morgan followed and Stahl scored. But the unflappable Mets responded by pouring it on. A single by Koosman in the third drove home the Mets' seventh run, and in the fourth inning a walk, a double by Cleon Jones, an outfield error, and singles by Milner and Hahn brought home two more runs.

With the Mets now comfortably ahead 9–2, it was a downcast Reds team that came to bat in the top of the fifth inning. After Koosman retired the lead-off batter, Pete Rose followed with a base hit. Joe Morgan then hit a grounder to first baseman John Milner. Milner threw to shortstop Bud Harrelson, covering second for the force, and then fired the ball back to Milner to complete the double play. Rose, in an attempt to fire up his flat team, came into second with a particularly hard slide, upending Harrelson as he tried to break up the double play. Harrelson took exception and came up swinging. Since Rose was close to twice the size of Harrelson, it wasn't a particularly clever move on the shortstop's part, but it succeeded in having both dugouts and bullpens clear. After Rose and Harrelson were separated, there was a lot of milling around but no additional punches thrown with the exception of Buzz Capra and Pedro Borbon, who went head-to-head with each other.

Bud Harrelson takes exception to Pete Rose's hard slide into second base while attempting to break up a fifth-inning double play, and squares off against the Reds star (© Bettmann/Corbis).

When a semblance of order was restored, the Reds took the field for the bottom of the fifth inning under a deluge of boos. But the New York fans, not satisfied with some plain old-fashioned booing, began to pelt Rose in left field with debris, beginning with cups and programs and culminating with bottles of whiskey being heaved. With the situation becoming dangerous, Sparky Anderson pulled his team off the field. "We'll get this straightened out," said umpire Chris Pelekoudas. "Let me know when," responded Anderson as he walked into the dugout with his players.[3]

Order could not be restored until the Mets were threatened with a forfeit by National League president Charlie Feeney and commissioner Bowie Kuhn should the team fail to control the crowd. As a result, out of the Mets' dugout emerged Yogi Berra, elder statesman Willie Mays, Tom Seaver, Rusty Staub and Cleon Jones, who appealed directly to the crowd to halt the object throwing. The delegation was successful in assuaging the fans' emotions, and play was able to continue unimpeded.

With the game resuming, Jerry Koosman continued his mastery over the Reds, allowing only two more hits the rest of the way and striking out nine in the process, as the Mets coasted to a 9–2 victory.

The Mets needed only one more victory to conclude part two of their remarkable climb toward the top of the baseball world. Despite being heavy

Moments after Rose and Harrelson's altercation, both dugouts cleared and the largest brawl in playoff history ensued (© Bettmann/Corbis).

underdogs against the Reds, the Mets' pitching proved to be the story of the playoffs. The three Mets' starters — Seaver, Matlack and Koosman — all pitched complete games and limited the Reds to only three runs over the three games while striking out 31 batters.

The Mets turned to George Stone, who had a remarkable season in his own right, to hopefully close out the series. His mound opponent was another left-hander, as the Reds pinned their hopes on Fred Norman. Once again the Mets struck first, scoring a lone run in the third inning after Norman walked both Don Hahn and George Stone before Felix Millan singled home a run. Stone was able to maintain the Mets' razor-thin lead until the seventh inning, when Tony Perez, carrying a 0-for-14 albatross on his shoulders, smoked Stone's first pitch into the Reds' bullpen to tie the game.

With the Mets unable to do anything against Don Gullett, who was pitching in relief of Fred Norman, the Reds continued to generate scoring opportunities, only to see the Mets barely escape. In the ninth inning Rose singled off McGraw, who was making his first appearance of the series. Joe Morgan followed by reaching on an error, marking the first time in the series that Rose and Morgan reached base in the same inning. McGraw got the first out of the inning when Tony Perez popped up. Johnny Bench then walked to load the bases. But McGraw, walking a tight rope, escaped damage when Andy Kosco struck out and Denis Menke bunted right into the glove of Wayne Garrett.

In the tenth inning the Reds had McGraw on the ropes again when they loaded the bases after two were out. Again McGraw was able to escape, however, when Tony Perez flied out. McGraw emerged from trouble again in the eleventh inning, this time assisted by a great play by Rusty Staub. With one out, Kosco and Menke singled. While the next batter, Cesar Geronimo, struck out, Dan Driessen drilled a ball deep to right field. Staub, running to the fence, made a great over-the-shoulder catch while slamming into the wall. Staub, who momentarily lay motionless, was able to walk off the field on his own power to the roaring delight of the more than 50,000 fans that assembled.

The Mets' luck ran out, however, in the twelfth inning after Pete Rose, who was hearing catcalls all day from the Shea faithful, drilled a 2–2 fastball from Harry Parker, who had taken over the pitching from Tug McGraw, over the right-field fence to give the Reds a 2–1 win, sending the series to a deciding fifth game. "It was a fastball too high," lamented Berra after the game. "Grote just got done telling him to get it down."[4] Rose, for his part, was sucked in the moment for all its worth as he rounded the bases with his right fist clenched high.

The journey from cellar dwellers to National League champions ended after the Mets clubbed the Reds in the finale of a hard-fought playoff series. The game started on a crisp fall afternoon, as again over 50,000 poured into Shea Stadium for the deciding game. The pitching matchup was the same as the opener, with Jack Billingham twirling for the Reds and the Mets countering with their ace, Tom Seaver.

The Reds immediately had Seaver on the ropes in the top of the first inning when they loaded the bases, but Seaver was able to escape unscathed. Seaver's first-inning travails began when he walked Joe Morgan with one out. Dan Driessen then singled, and a subsequent wild pitch put runners on second and third. Seaver then struck out Tony Perez after running the count to 3–0. With two outs, Seaver walked Bench intentionally to load the bases, but Ken Griffey flied out, ending the Reds' first-inning threat.

Billingham was not as fortunate in his first inning of work as the Mets touched him for two runs. With one out Felix Millan singled. With Staub out of the lineup due to the ailing shoulder he injured while smashing into the wall the previous game, Cleon Jones was inserted into Staub's usual spot in the lineup. Jones singled, and Milner followed with a walk to load the bases. Ed Kranepool, starting in left field, wasted no time by delivering Billingham's first pitch into left field for a two-run single and a 2–0 Mets lead.

The Mets couldn't hold the lead for long, with the Reds getting the first run back in the third inning. Joe Morgan doubled, took third when Cleon Jones juggled the ball, in right field and scored on a sacrifice fly by Dan Driessen. The Reds then tied the game in the top of the fifth inning on a double by Pete Rose and a single by Tony Perez.

With the game tied and four and one-half innings left in the championship series, the Mets came to bat with Wayne Garrett as their leadoff hitter. Garrett, who singled in his first at-bat of the playoffs and had gone hitless since, broke his streak of futility with a two-base hit. Felix Millan, attempting to sacrifice, laid down a bunt toward the mound. Billingham pounced on the ball and fired a strike to Driessen at third base. However, Driessen, forgetting that it was not a force play, failed to tag Garrett, giving the Mets runners at the corners and nobody out. Cleon Jones, continuing his hot hitting, doubled off the left-center field fence to score Garrett and give the Mets a 3–2 lead. That was it for Billingham, and Anderson once again turned to Don Gullett to face Milner. Gullett walked Milner, loading the bases and bringing Kranepool up to the plate. Playing the percentages, Berra called Kranepool back, and to the delight of the crowd, sent Mays up to the plate. Anderson countered by bringing in right-hander Clay Carroll. While Mays didn't hit the ball more then twenty feet from home plate, the Reds had no play as Millan scored, giving the Mets a 4–2 lead. A grounder by Jerry Grote forced Cleon Jones for the first out of the inning, but Don Hahn singled home Milner. After Grote was forced at second base for the second out, a base hit by Harrelson brought home Mays, giving the Mets a 6–2 lead.

The Mets added an additional run in the seventh inning when Seaver doubled and scored on a base hit by Cleon Jones. With the Mets now ahead by a comfortable 7–2 margin, they needed only six more outs in order to accomplish the impossible. While Seaver had no problems in the eighth inning, the Reds put a scare into the Mets when they loaded the bases in the ninth inning. One more base runner and the tying run would come to the plate. Not taking any chances, Berra called on McGraw to get the final two outs. He almost failed to accomplish that, but not due to any poor pitching. Instead, fans were already trying to storm the field, even before the final out was recorded. With the crowd going from tumultuous to riotous, the wives of the Reds were escorted to the safety of the Cincinnati dugout before play was resumed. McGraw retired the final two batters, and while the Mets scurried to the clubhouse to celebrate, the crowd surged onto the field, destroying everything and anything that it could get its hands on.

The 70th World Series kicked off with the Mets as the underdogs as they faced the defending world champion Oakland A's. Again it would be the arms of Seaver, Koosman and Matlack trying to stop the overwhelming firepower of the A's lineup, which included Bert Campaneris, Joe Rudi, Sal Bando, Reggie Jackson and Gene Tenace. Injuries were also a factor as the A's would be without the services of their speedy center fielder, Bill North, who was injured in the playoffs and would miss the entire series. In his stead, Reggie Jackson was moved to center field, while Jesus Alou would slide into the right field position. For the Mets, Rusty Staub was listed as day-to-day. He would miss the opener while still suffering from a sore shoulder, the consequences of his run-in with the Shea Stadium right field wall after robbing Dan Driessen of an extra-base hit in the 11th inning of the fourth game of the playoffs. With Staub out of the opener, Willie Mays was given the start in center field, while Don Hahn was moved to right field.

The pitching matchup for the opener featured a battle of left-handers, with Jon Matlack pitching for the Mets and veteran Ken Holtzman taking the mound for the Oakland A's. Fittingly enough, Willie Mays, who was ending his career as a winner regardless of the outcome, got the first hit of the series when he singled in the first inning. The Mets were unable to do anything else in the inning and the game remained scoreless until the A's came to bat in the third.

With one out, second baseman Dick Green draw a walk, bringing pitcher Ken Holtzman to the plate. Due to the American League inaugurating the designated hitter rule at the start of the season, Holtzman, with one plate appearance all year, was called on to sacrifice Green to second. Holtzman never got the opportunity, as Green was thrown out trying to take second base after a pitch bounded away from catcher Jerry Grote. With the bunt now off, Holtzman, with his one at-bat behind him, lined a Matlack pitch down the third base line for a two-base hit. Matlack appeared to be out of trouble, however, when the next batter, Bert Campaneris, bounced a ball to Millan at second. Unfortunately for Millan and the Mets, the ball never took the anticipated hop, getting by Millan and allowing Holtzman to score the game's first run. Matlack again appeared to be out of trouble when he apparently had Campaneris picked off first. Matlack's pickoff throw to Milner was high and Campaneris took off for second, beating Milner's peg. A single by Joe Rudi scored Campaneris, giving the A's an early 2–0 lead.

The Mets came right back in the fourth inning to get one run back when Cleon Jones doubled with one out and scored on a base hit by John Milner. The Mets were deprived of any additional runs when Reggie Jackson made a spectacular running catch of a ball hit by Jerry Grote that carried about 375 feet. While the Mets continued to claw away at the A's pitching, they consistently fell short of bringing the tying run home. In the fifth inning, Matlack led off with a walk, but Garrett's attempt at a sacrifice was turned into a double play when Holtzman caught the ball on the fly and trapped Matlack off first. Felix Millan then followed with a triple but died there when Mays flied out. More noise was made in the sixth inning when Rollie Fingers was called on to take over the pitching duties for the A's. Cleon Jones led off the sixth with a single. With two outs and Jones on second, Don Hahn struck out but was able to reach base when the ball got by Ray Fosse. Fingers escaped, though, when he fanned Harrelson.

With the A's taking a 2–1 lead into the ninth, the Mets threatened again as Yogi turned to his bench. Ed Kranepool was sent up to bat for Hahn and lined out hard to short. Next up was Ron Hodges, batting for Bud Harrelson and drawing a walk. Teddy Martinez was then called on to run for Hodges, while Staub was inserted as a pinch-hitter for Tug McGraw. A's manager Dick Williams then countered by replacing Fingers with left-hander Darold Knowles. "I know Rusty Staub," Williams said in discussing his strategy for bringing Knowles in. "I know he can drill a hit to left field, even with a sore shoulder."[5] Playing the percentages, Berra called Staub back and sent up Jim Beauchamp to bat for Staub. Beauchamp nearly tied the game when he hit a soft liner that looked like it would drop in. Dick Green had other ideas in mind as he ran into short right field to make a spectacular over-the-shoulder running catch. It was now all up to Garrett, who ended the game by flying out.

It was a sun-drenched field that greeted the combatants in the second game. Again it would be a battle of left-handers, with Vida Blue facing off against Jerry Koosman. The sun was an immediate factor, as Cleon Jones lost sight of a long drive off the bat of Joe Rudi that fell in for a double in the bottom half of the first inning. Sal Bando followed with a triple to score Rudi, and after Gene Tenace draw a walk with two outs, Jesus Alou doubled Bando home to give the A's a 2–0 lead after one inning.

The two clubs played see-saw over the next inning and a half as Cleon Jones hit Vida Blue's first pitch of the second inning into the right field stands, cutting the Mets' deficit in half. The A's regained their two-run lead in the bottom half of the inning when Bert Campaneris tripled and scored on a base hit by Joe Rudi. However, Wayne Garrett's home run in the top of the third inning again cut the A's lead back down to one run.

Jerry Koosman, who sparkled in his two World Series starts in 1969, lasted only into the third inning of his first start in the 1973 World Series. Oakland loaded the bases in the last of the third inning and Koosman was replaced by Ray Sadecki. The Mets escaped damage, however, when Dick Green botched a suicide squeeze play, trapping Gene Tenace off third base. Green then struck out to end the threat. The game continued with the A's still clinging to their 3–2 lead until the Mets came to bat in the sixth inning. With one out, Vida Blue walked Cleon Jones, and John Milner followed with a base hit to chase Blue and bring on reliever Horacio Pena. Pena immediately hit his first batter, Jerry Grote, with a pitch to load the bases. Don Hahn beat out a squib to third for an infield hit, and the Mets finally tied the game. The next batter, Bud Harrelson, followed with a solid single to right field, scoring Milner for the Mets' second run of the inning. For the first time in the series, the Mets carried a lead, 4–3. Pena was then lifted for reliever Darold Knowles, who appeared to be out of trouble when he induced pinch-hitter Jim Beauchamp to bounce the ball back to the mound for an apparent double play ball. Knowles threw wildly to the plate for a two-run error, giving the Mets a 6–3 lead. The A's were able to score a run off McGraw in the seventh inning. Oakland came to bat in the last of the ninth inning facing McGraw and needing two runs to tie the game. A walk to Sal Bando and singles by Reggie Jackson and Gene Tenace followed a double by Deron Johnson that Willie Mays lost in the sun. That gave the A's the two runs they needed to send the game into extra innings.

The Mets thought they had scored the go-ahead run in the tenth inning when Bud Harrelson attempted to score on a fly ball hit by Felix Millan. While replays seem to indicate that A's catcher Ray Fosse missed the tag, home plate umpire Augie Donatelli saw it otherwise, calling Harrelson out and creating a storm from the Mets' dugout. Willie Mays, in the on-deck circle, had the closest look at the play, and from a begging position on the ground argued long and hard but in vain. Arguments by Harrelson and Berra went unheeded as well, and when the dust finally cleared, the Mets were fortunate they didn't lose any players to ejection.

The game continued to the twelfth inning with the game still tied at six.

While this sequence appears to show Bud Harrelson evading the tag of A's catcher Ray Fosse as he attempts to score the tie-breaking run in the 12th inning of Game 2 of the World Series, home plate umpire Augie Donatelli saw it differently and called Harrelson out. Even a pleading Willie Mays, who was as close to the play as was the umpire and had a great view, could not get Donatelli to change his call (AP Images).

Bud Harrelson led off with a double, his third hit of the day. Tug McGraw then laid down a bunt that popped over Sal Bando's head and went for a base hit, putting runners at first and third with nobody out. Two outs later, the runners were still at the corners as Wayne Garrett struck out and Millan popped out. But, fittingly enough, Willie Mays came through with a ground single, scoring Harrelson, and once again the Mets were on top. Cleon Jones then singled to load the bases and end the afternoon for Rollie Fingers. Paul Linblad, a left-hander, came in to face John Milner. The inning was prolonged when Mike Andrews let a grounder roll through his legs, allowing two more runs to cross the plate. Mike Andrews committed another error when the next batter, Jerry Grote, hit a grounder that Andrews stopped, yet threw wildly to first as the fourth run of the inning scored.

With a four-run lead, and the Mets' best reliever on the mound needing only three more outs, it appeared a cinch that New York had Game 2 in the bag. McGraw, however, yielded a lead-off triple to Reggie Jackson and walked Gene Tenace, putting runners on the corners. An alarmed Berra immediately scurried out to the mound for a conference with his pitcher. With the entire infield gathering around the mound, McGraw surprisingly admitted to being arm weary and was lifted in favor of George Stone. Stone's first batter, Jesus Alou, singled home a run, narrowing the Mets' lead to 10–7 and bringing the tying run to the plate. Stone was able to get a force play on the next batter, but walked Mike Andrews to load the bases. Stone buckled down as Vic Davillio popped up to the infield and Bert Campaneris grounded out, finally putting an end to the marathon.

The scene shifted from the warm sunny climate of California to the frigid autumn air of New York. While the first two games featured pitching matchups between quality left-handers, Game 3 saw the right-handed aces of the respective teams take the mound as Tom Seaver squared off against Catfish Hunter.

For the first time in the series the Mets scored first when Wayne Garrett led off the bottom of the first inning with a home run. Felix Millan then singled, moved to third on a hit-and-run single by Rusty Staub, and scored on a wild pitch. Hunter was able to bear down and get out of the inning, trailing just 2–0.

Tom Seaver, who had a week of rest, was dominant going into the sixth inning by fanning nine batters while protecting his 2–0 lead. But in the sixth inning, the A's started to get around on Seaver's heat as Joe Rudi, leading off, hit a drive to deep right-center field that Don Hahn was able to grab with a great leaping catch. Sal Bando hit a drive that Hahn couldn't get to that went for a double. Reggie Jackson then struck out, but Gene Tenace lashed another double to score Bando and cut the Mets' lead to 2–1. Seaver worked an easy seventh inning, but ran into trouble in the eighth when Campy Campaneris, the A's sparkplug, led off the inning with a base hit. Campaneris promptly stole second despite a strong throw by Grote that barely missed nailing the runner.

A single by Rudi scored Campaneris to tie the game, putting a damper on Seaver's marvelous effort, which netted him a total of 12 strikeouts before he was lifted for a pinch-hitter in the bottom half of the inning.

Ray Sadecki entered the fray in the ninth inning and got into immediate trouble on an infield error and a base hit before Berra turned to McGraw, who already had eight innings of work behind him through the first two games. McGraw, who's been stellar since early September, was able to get out of the jam without the A's scoring. In the meantime, after the Mets scored two runs in the first inning, a plethora of A's pitchers were able to shut down the Mets' attack and send the game into extra innings for the second consecutive game, a World Series record.

McGraw pitched a scoreless tenth, and the Mets failed to score in the bottom half of the inning. In the 11th inning, Harry Parker replaced McGraw on the mound. With one out, Parker walked Ted Kubiak and struck out Angel Mangual. However, the third strike got by Grote, and while Mangual wasn't able to run first since it was occupied, Kubiak advanced to second. Bert Campaneris continued his assault on Mets pitching when he singled to center field, driving home Kubiak. The inning ended on the same play, though, as Campaneris was thrown out trying to take second on the throw.

The Mets came into the bottom of the 11th inning trailing by one, 3–2, but refused to go down without a fight. Wayne Garrett led off with a single, bringing Felix Millan to the plate and Dick Williams to the mound, where he called on his ace, Rollie Fingers, to slam the door. Millan did his job as he sacrificed Garrett to second base, but Staub flied out and Jones grounded out to end the game. Once again the Mets found themselves down one game in the series.

The day did not go without controversy. A's owner Charlie Finley, never one to shy away from controversy, placed Mike Andrews on the injured list after the second baseman committed two consecutive errors in the second game. The move enraged both Dick Williams and Andrews' teammates to the point that Williams announced he would not return to manage the A's next season. Commissioner Bowie Kuhn took exception as well and ordered Mike Andrews immediately reinstated to the active roster.

A crowd of more than 54,000 showed up to Shea on a cold wintry evening for the fourth game of the World Series. The pitching matchup was a rematch of the first game, when Jon Matlack and Ken Holtzman hooked up against each other. Unlike the first game, where Holtzman shackled the Mets over five innings while allowing only one run, on this day Holtzman showed up without his stuff, as he admitted after the game. "I didn't have it. No control, no speed, no nothing."[6]

Garrett, who led off the third game with a home run, began this game with a single. With the Mets trying to get at least one run early, Felix Millan laid down a bunt, which he beat out. Staub was asked to sacrifice, but after getting down in the count, the bunt was taken off. One pitch later, the Mets had three runs after Staub deposited a Holtzman pitch over the left field wall. A walk to Milner and a single to Grote ended the night for Holtzman, who was replaced by Blue Moon Odom. Odom was able to stem the bleeding, and the inning ended with the Mets leading, 3–0.

The A's bats were silent until the fourth inning when a grounder by Sal Bando bounced off Garrett's glove for an error. Reggie Jackson followed with the A's first hit, putting runners at the corners. Bando then scored on an infield single by Gene Tenace. That was all Matlack allowed, and when the Mets came to bat in the last of the inning, they recouped that run threefold.

After loading the bases in the bottom of the fourth inning, a grounder by Millan was booted by Dick Green for one run, and Staub, injured shoulder and all, singled for his fourth and fifth runs batted in of the evening, giving the Mets a 6–1 lead.

Neither team was able to do anything more offensively; Jon Matlack was in complete control, and the A's bullpen held the Mets in check. The biggest excitement late in the game came when Mike Andrews, forcibly reinstated by commissioner Bowie Kuhn, was asked to pinch-hit to the delight of the crowd. Andrews received an additional standing ovation after grounding out.

For the third consecutive evening, the crowd of more than 50,000 fans was greeted by wintry weather as the two clubs got set to start the fifth game of the series that was tied at two games apiece. Once again it would be a battle of left-handers, a rematch of the Game 2 starters. Koosman took the mound for the Mets, while Vida Blue served as his opposition.

Cleon Jones, in the starting lineup despite suffering from the flu, got the Mets started in the last of the second inning when he doubled over the head of Joe Rudi in left field. A base hit by John Milner scored Jones, and the Mets took a 1–0 lead. The Mets added to their lead in the sixth inning on a single by Jerry Grote and a triple by Don Hahn, but not before Joe Rudi robbed Cleon Jones of another extra-base hit with a spectacular catch as he crashed into the left field fence. For Don Hahn, the hit was the biggest of his young career, while for Blue it was his last pitch, with the lefty being replaced by Rollie Fingers.

In the meantime, masterful pitching by Jerry Koosman and clutch defense kept the A's offense at bay. Koosman, a native of Minnesota, thrived pitching in cool weather. "I like cool weather and I hate hot weather; I tend to get tired," said Koosman. "The only problem with cool weather was that the ball was so dry I couldn't keep any perspiration on my fingers for my breaking ball."[7] Koosman helped himself out when he picked off Campaneris, who had recorded the A's first hit, in the third inning. After a couple of pick-off attempts, Koosman finally caught Campy leaning the wrong way and he was a dead duck. Koosman helped himself even further when he induced Reggie Jackson to hit into an inning-ending double play. In the sixth inning, Koosman was assisted by a tremendous running over-the-shoulder catch by Felix Millan with a runner on base.

It wasn't until the seventh inning that the A's mounted their first serious threat of the game. Gene Tenace led the inning off with a walk, and one out later Ray Fosse doubled past Wayne Garrett, putting runners on second and third. Despite Koosman's outstanding performance, Berra turned to his fireman, Tug McGraw. Dick Williams sent Deron Johnson to the plate to bat for Dick Green, who walked on a 3–2 pitch. With the bases now loaded, McGraw was able to get Angel Mangual on an infield popup, and when he struck out Campaneris looking, the crowd, which had been waving orange handkerchiefs all night while yelling, "Goodbye Charlie," in reference to the embattled owner of the A's, broke into a frenzy. Even the mayor of New York, John Lindsey, got into the act as he unfurled a banner with the inscription "Ya Gotta Believe." An exuberant McGraw pumped his fist in the air and headed to the dugout with his trademark habit of slapping his glove against his hip. McGraw got into trouble in the eighth inning when he walked two batters, but was able to escape damage when Jesus Alou lined out to Garrett at third base. McGraw had a 1-2-3 ninth inning while striking out the last two batters, giving the Mets a thrilling 2–0 victory.

The World Series now shifted to Oakland, where the Mets would need only one more victory to accomplish the seemingly impossible. Needing one more win to reign once again as world champions, Yogi Berra was in a quandary

The Shea Stadium scoreboard tells the story. The Mets need just one more victory for the miracle to repeat itself. The victory never came (AP Images).

as to whom he would start for the sixth game. With the A's pitching their ace, Catfish Hunter, Berra had the luxury of turning to his fourth starter, George Stone, who was 12-3 during the regular season, and save Seaver for a Game 7, if necessary, or going with his ace on just three days' rest, hoping Seaver could close it out. After conferring with Seaver, Berra elected to go with the right-hander in hopes that Seaver could in fact shut the door.

While Seaver didn't have the great command he had in the third game, ultimately it was the failure of the offense that cost the Mets in the sixth game. Reggie Jackson, whose powerful bat was held in check by the Mets' pitching staff in New York, came to life in the first inning when he doubled home Joe Rudi, giving the A's a 1–0 lead. In the third inning Jackson struck again when he doubled home Bando. While Seaver settled down, allowing the A's nothing further through the seventh inning, Oakland starter Catfish Hunter was dominant by holding the Mets off the scoreboard through seven innings. The Mets made some noise in the seventh inning with one out when John Milner singled and Jerry Grote came within inches of tying the game when he drove Joe Rudi to the wall before the outfielder hauled in his long drive.

The Mets were finally able to get on the scoreboard in the eighth inning. With one out, Ken Boswell, pinch-hitting for Seaver, singled to right field. Dick Williams decided to replace Hunter, and for a World Series record sixth consecutive game called on left-hander Darold Knowles. Wayne Garrett greeted Knowles with a base hit, putting runners at the corners with only one out. A single by Millan cut the A's lead to 2–1, with the tying run only 90 feet away. But while bearing down, Knowles struck out Staub, leaving the situation up to Cleon Jones. Playing the percentages, Dick Williams turned to Rollie Fingers to pitch to Jones. The move worked perfectly for Williams as Jones flied out to center field.

With Seaver leaving for a pinch-hitter, McGraw took over the pitching, hoping to hold Oakland to just a one-run lead. But the Mets' chief tormentor, Reggie Jackson, led off by lining the ball to center field. Don Hahn, trying for a shoestring catch, allowed the ball to get by him, enabling Jackson to make it all the way to third base. A fly ball by Jesus Alou brought Jackson home, giving the A's an insurance run that proved to be unnecessary. With the Mets' loss, it marked the 25th time in baseball history that a seventh game of the World Series would be required.

The Mets' magnificent miracle drive came to an abrupt halt, falling just one game short of winning their second championship in the short history of the franchise, when the A's defeated the Mets, 5–2, in the seventh game of the World Series.

A crowd of just fewer than 50,000 poured into the Oakland Alameda County Coliseum for the final game of the 1973 season. For the third time in a week, Jon Matlack and Ken Holtzman faced off against each other. While Matlack had given the Mets two outstanding performances, Holtzman was looking for redemption after his poor showing in Game 4, during which he failed to get out of the first inning.

For the first two and a half innings, it appeared that the scoreless game would be another nail-biter. But in the last of the third inning, Ken Holtzman, who started the damage in the opener of the first game with a double, struck again as he doubled down the left field line. And then it happened. The powerful A's bats, which in the first six games could not take Mets pitching deep, found their power stroke. Bert Campaneris, the most unlikely of candidates after hitting only four home runs during the course of the regular season, swatted Matlack's first pitch over the right field fence. Joe Rudi followed with a base hit, and one out later, Reggie Jackson followed with an even deeper drive. Suddenly the miracle workers found themselves four runs behind and their starting pitcher out of the game.

The A's made a miracle even less likely when in the fifth inning Campaneris singled and took second after Cleon Jones let the ball get by him. A single by Joe Rudi brought Campy home, and now the Mets were trailing, 5–0. In the sixth inning the Mets finally broke through and scored a run on consecutive doubles by Felix Millan and Rusty Staub. But Rollie Fingers, the man with a curveball as big as his handle-bar moustache, was called on, and very quickly the Mets threat was halted.

The game continued onto the ninth inning with the A's still leading, 5–1. The Mets were down to their last three outs and needed four runs to tie. But the team with the battle cry of "You Gotta Believe" would not go down without a fight. John Milner led off the inning with a walk off Rollie Fingers. One out later Don Hahn singled, putting runners on first and second. Bud Harrelson then tried to take the A's infield by surprise and bunt for a base hit, but was thrown out. With runners at second and third, the Mets had just one out to play with. Up came pinch-hitter Ed Kranepool, who hit a grounder to first, which should've ended the World Series there and then. But Gene Tenace booted the ball, scoring Milner and bringing the tying run in the form of Wayne Garrett to the plate. Was there another miracle in the offing? Darold Knowles, who set a World Series record by appearing in all seven games, was called in to prevent another Mets miracle from occurring. Garrett looped a ball that was caught by Campaneris, and the Mets, as incredible as their stretch drive was, had to settle for the title of National League champions.

The team as a whole accepted their defeat with pride and gratitude. "It's really something to be proud of," said Rusty Staub. "To be able to come back from last place in our division, like we did, then win the playoffs and get to the seventh game, I'm really proud of what we did."[8]

5

Déjà Vu All Over Again

If ever an Opening Day game would be a harbinger of how a season would progress, one would have to look no further than the results of the Mets' 1974 opener in Philadelphia. The team was essentially the same club that fell one game short of the 1973 world championship — with the notable exception of Willie Mays, who retired — that occupied the Mets' dugout on Opening Day 1974. From the onset of the hot stove season, Mets manager Yogi Berra, rewarded with a three-year contract and a say on future personnel decisions, made it clear that the Mets' coveting Joe Torre and Paul Blair would not be at the price of his prize pitching. "I'll take Joe Torre," said Berra. "But not for Jerry Koosman. I'm not giving up one of my top three pitchers or Tug McGraw. I got other guys I'll deal, but not those four pitchers. We won with them and we're gonna keep 'em."[1] The Mets were also in hot pursuit of Astros center fielder Jimmy Wynn, but refused to part with George Stone, who exceeded all expectations as the number four starter, and either Craig Swan or Hank Webb. "I could've made a deal," said general manager Bob Scheffing. "I could have had Jimmy Wynn at the winter meetings but we turned the deal down. Both Yogi and I felt that Houston's asking price was too high. They wanted George Stone, plus one of our younger pitchers, and we weren't about to weaken ourselves there."[2]

Despite the inability or unwillingness to make a deal for a proven slugger or a center fielder, Yogi had confidence in the ball club that headed to Philadelphia to open the 1974 season. "We can get enough hitting if we stay healthy. We got some good hitters in our lineup. We just haven't had them together at the same time often enough. When we did, we did pretty good. You give us Jonesy and Rusty and Milner playing the full season and hitting the way they can and I'll take my chances. I won't need another hitter if they play everyday." Yogi was willing to take his chances platooning Dave Schneck and Don Hahn in center field. "We won with pitching," said Berra. "That's our strongest department. I wasn't going to weaken myself over there. I know what I got. I'm not sure what I'm getting when I make a deal."[3]

After all, not only did the Mets have the best front-line pitching in all of baseball with Seaver, Koosman and Matlack, along with arguably the best reliever in Tug McGraw, but the Mets' second-line starters were considered a strength as well. "When you realize what Sadecki, Parker and Stone did, you have to give them as much credit for us winning as you do to the others on the staff," said Mets GM Bob Scheffing. "The great thing about Sadecki is that he can sit around for 10 days or two weeks and then come in and throw strikes. Ray gives you one solid pitcher on the staff who you know is there when you need him. That's his value. In addition he's good for the club. He keeps morale up, he keeps the guys loose and he takes care of himself."[4] In addition the Mets had penciled in Craig Swan, a promising rookie, as their fifth starter. "Just what they needed," bemoaned Cardinals manager Red Schoendienst. "It's amazing; they keep coming up with new ones every year. Somebody must be doing something right in that organization." Schoendienst's grudging admiration was directed at Craig Swan.[5] The last two pitching slots belonged to rookie Bob Apodaca, whose role was to be the right-handed setup man to Tug McGraw, and to Bob Miller, an original Met who was reacquired at the end of the 1973 season. "He can still throw, never has a sore arm, and we need a right-hander like him in the bullpen," said pitching coach Rube Walker. "He's experienced and he's been with winning clubs for a long time. We expect Bob to be a big help."[6]

For the sixth year in a row the Mets sent their ace, Tom Seaver, to the mound, and for the second straight season faced the ace of the Phillies' staff, Steve Carlton. And for the fourth consecutive year it appeared that Seaver would walk off a winner, having left the game after seven innings carrying a 4–3 lead, despite not being his usual overpowering self. Tug McGraw replaced Seaver for the eighth inning. McGraw was dominant as he struck out the side, and the Mets were only three outs from remaining undefeated for the decade on Opening Day. The momentum of the game was broken, however, before the Mets came to bat in the ninth inning when the inevitable streaker, a somewhat portly male wearing nothing but brown boots, emerged from the right field stands while Wayne Garrett prepared to lead off the inning. While the streaker was caught and wrapped in a raincoat, a fully dressed fellow ran on the field, followed by another. During the uncalled-for delay, Tug McGraw went into the clubhouse to keep warm, but the wait proved long before he returned to the mound on the cold day. Annoyed, McGraw took the mound in the last of the ninth inning and allowed a base hit by the leadoff batter and a sacrifice bunt to bring a young infielder with a .196 lifetime batting average by the name of Mike Schmidt to the plate. Just as suddenly as acrobat Hugo Zachini was catapulted out of a cannon behind second base into a net as part of the Opening Day ceremonies to begin the season, McGraw's second pitch was launched over the wall, sending the Mets to a shocking 5–4 loss.

The Mets recovered in the second game against the Phillies by scoring nine runs in the last two innings, three of them coming on a Jerry Grote home run.

Jon Matlack came away with a 9–2 decision to send the Mets to New York for the home opener with a .500 record.

The last game played at Shea Stadium was on a frigid October evening, and when that game was complete, the Mets were just 27 outs from winning their second World Series. Unfortunately, those 27 outs never came, and as a result the Mets were now returning to their home park on a frigid April afternoon as National League champions and not world champions to take on the St. Louis Cardinals. After the grounds crew raked the snow off the tarpaulin and the Opening Day ceremonies were held, during which the National League championship flag was raised and the National League championship rings were distributed to the players, it was time to start a new decade of play at Shea Stadium, which opened in 1964.

Jerry Koosman, the Mets' starter, was splendid for the first eight innings, while Jerry Grote sparked the offense with a home run and a single as New York took a 3–1 lead into the ninth inning. Reggie Smith led off the ninth inning for the Cardinals with a fly ball to center field that turned into a triple when Don Hahn slipped in the mud. One out later a single by Ted Simmons scored Smith, narrowing the Mets' lead to 3–2. After Bake McBride followed with an infield single, it was time to go to the pen. With McGraw unavailable due to a fever, Berra turned to Bob Apodaca to save the game. Apodaca's arrival caused Cardinals manager Red Schoendienst to turn to Tim McCarver to bat for Ken Reitz. McCarver bounced Apodaca's second pitch back to the mound, which he turned into a 1-6-3 double play, ending the game while he picked up his first big league save.

Apodaca's quest to become a prominent relief ace took a detour the next day when he failed to hold a 3–2 lead in the nightcap of a doubleheader, resulting in a 4–3 Mets loss. Craig Swan had already blown a 7–6 lead in the opener, a game in which the Mets lost, 8–7, after coming back from a 6–0 deficit. After the Cardinals left town on the heels of their doubleheader sweep, the Phillies came calling. Inclement weather forced New York to play another doubleheader, which again the Mets lost, and again it was the bullpen that let the team down. In the opener Jon Matlack gave the Mets a solid seven innings, allowing only one run on five hits while fanning ten before leaving with the game tied at one. While Matlack's immediate successor, Bob Miller, was able to keep the Phillies off the scoreboard, Tug McGraw, back from his bout with the flu, could not keep Philadelphia from scoring. McGraw surrendered a run on a suicide squeeze off the bat of Bill Robinson in the 11th inning as the Mets went down to defeat, 2–1. In the nightcap the Mets saw a masterpiece by Jerry Koosman go by the wayside as Bob Miller could not hold the 3–1 lead he inherited in the top of the eighth inning. A three-run ninth inning by the Phillies off Miller gave Philadelphia a 5–3 win, ending a long and miserable day for both the Mets and their fans. All five Mets losses in the early season were direct results of the failures of the bullpen. "We coulda been 7–0 instead of what we are," complained

Berra. "That's our bread and butter (referring to the bullpen). We ain' goin' anywhere until they start doin' their job."[7]

With the 1–4 homestand behind them, the Mets took a brief trip up to Montreal to take on the Expos for a three-game series before returning home to face the Pittsburgh Pirates. The Mets' woes continued in Montreal as the Expos swept three straight from the Mets, who now returned to Shea Stadium with a seven-game losing streak. Most disconcerting to the New York brass was the pitching of Tom Seaver, who had yet to win a game and whose fastball seemed to have lost some of its zip. "I think I can still pitch," said Seaver. "I looked at some movies after the second game and I think I found what was wrong. I was rushing my delivery too much. I wasn't being deliberate enough."[8]

The seven-game losing streak came to a halt on April 20, as the Mets beat the Pirates behind the pitching of Jerry Koosman and the power of Wayne Garrett. With the Pirates leading 2–1 in the last of the seventh inning and Wayne Garrett batting eighth in the order, Berra sent Ken Boswell to the on-deck circle to bat for Koosman. Koosman begged Garrett to hit it out so the pitcher could remain in the game. Garrett obliged and thus reprieved Koosman, who remained in the game and picked up the win when the Mets scored three runs in the last of the eighth inning.

Seaver followed Koosman to the mound the next day, with the right-hander still seeking his first win of his season. Seaver, however, suffered his worst outing of the season, as the Pirates shelled him for six runs in five-plus innings. The Pirates reached Seaver for 12 hits, including home runs by Manny Sanguillen and Richie Hebner, in

The refusal of the Mets brass to accept Wayne Garrett as the regular third baseman resulted in the Mets making two of the worst trades in club history. The first sent All-Star outfielder Amos Otis to the Royals and the second saw future Hall of Famer Nolan Ryan dealt to the Angels (National Baseball Hall of Fame Library).

a 7–0 beating of the hapless New Yorkers. When Berra lifted Seaver in the sixth inning with no outs, Seaver walked off the mound with his head bowed and the Bronx cheer reverberating in his ears. "I don't think his pitching motion is right," said Berra of his ace starter. "That right leg ain't getting dirty."[9]

If the Mets thought they would benefit from a change of scenery, they were wrong as they headed out to San Diego to start a swing that would take them to San Francisco and Los Angeles as well. The Mets got crushed in the opener of the series by the Padres, 10–2, and then lost a heart-breaker, 4–3, when the Padres scored a ninth-inning run off Bob Apodaca. Apodaca got the ninth-inning call because Tug McGraw developed a shoulder problem and was not available. Exactly what was bugging Tug was unclear, but he was complaining of a pulled muscle and a fatty lump around his left shoulder blade. The loss gave the Mets sole possession of last place, a position not unfamiliar to them, considering the fact they spent the bulk of the 1973 season in the same position.

Jerry Koosman, who acted as the stopper in the Mets' previous seven-game losing streak, played the role again as New York downed the Padres, 5–2, by scoring three runs in the top of the ninth inning. Despite an outstanding performance by Koosman, who allowed two unearned runs on six hits while striking out 12, a win was very much in doubt for the visitors. The Mets came to bat in the top of the ninth with the game tied 2–2 and Koosman scheduled to lead off. With the bullpen in tatters, Berra allowed Koosman to bat for himself and he responded with an infield hit. Bud Harrelson followed with a bunt, which Padres starter Bill Greif threw away, allowing Koosman to take third base. A single by Millan scored Koosman, giving the Mets a 3–2 lead. Another bunt, an intentional walk, and a two-run single by John Milner added a couple of insurance runs, as the Mets went on to victory.

The real Tom Seaver finally showed up when the Mets moved on to a frigid and chilly Candlestick Park. Seaver shut down San Francisco on only four hits, walking none and striking out seven, as the Mets shut out the Giants, 6–0. For Seaver it was his 25th career shutout. Before the game Seaver spoke to the press about his uncharacteristic poor start. "I feel fine and that's the problem. If only I didn't, then I'd have something specific to worry about."[10]

The two-game mini winning streak came to an unglamorous halt the next day when the Giants smacked around Craig Swan, knocking him out in the fifth inning and scoring six runs off the rookie right-hander in his four-plus innings of work. His successors didn't fare any better, as the Giants pounded Mets pitching for 11 runs on 11 hits in an 11–3 decision. Most glaring, however, on this afternoon was the poor defensive play of center fielder Dave Schneck. Schneck's defensive woes began in the bottom of the third inning of what until then was a scoreless game. With two outs and the Giants' Ken Rudolph on second base, Giants second baseman Bruce Miller lined a ball toward center field. Dave Schneck, wearing regular spikes as opposed to rubber soles, had trouble with the footing on the synthetic turf of Candlestick Park. Ultimately Schneck found himself on the ground, the ball at the wall, Miller on third base, and the Giants with a 1–0 lead. A single by Garry Maddox moments later made the score 2–0, but the worst was still to come. Bobby Bonds followed with a fly ball to right-center field, which Staub called for. As Staub was settling under it, Schneck came over and reached for it, and the ball fell between the fielders, resulting in an inside-the-park home run. Schneck, upon questioning by reporters after the game regarding his adventures in the outfield, elected to plead the fifth. "I have nothing to say about that, to tell you the honest truth."[11]

With baseball being a game of redeeming features, the next day brought redemption to both Schneck and the Mets as New York swept the Giants in a doubleheader. Schneck blasted two home runs and Jon Matlack in a spectacular effort shut out the Giants on four hits as the Mets won, 6–0, in the first game. The second game saw the Giants take an early 3–1 lead off Harry Parker, who was making his first start of the year in the nightcap. John Milner's second home run in two days brought the Mets to within one run in the fourth inning before New York tied the game in the sixth inning on a single by Rusty Staub. The Mets went ahead to stay when Ron Hodges hit his second home run in two years, a two-run blast in the seventh inning.

The Mets moved on to Los Angeles, where they exchanged 8–7 decisions in the first two games of the series. In the opener the Dodgers shellacked George Stone as they knocked him out after an inning and roared off to an 8–0 lead after two innings. The Dodgers had to hold off a Mets onslaught when they scored two runs in the fourth and three in the fifth, with Felix Millan's first-ever home run in Dodger Stadium serving as the big blow. New York added a solo run in the seventh to narrow the gap to 8–6. In the ninth the Mets were able to get one more run across against Mike Marshall, the Dodgers' relief ace, but could not push through with the tying run. Aside from the Mets refusing to go quietly, the good news from the game was the two innings of scoreless relief thrown by Tug McGraw, who had been struggling since Opening Day.

The situation was reversed in the second game of the series as the Mets blew a 6–0 lead, only to score two runs in the ninth inning and hold off the Dodgers for an exciting 8–7 victory. New York starter Jerry Koosman breezed through the first five innings, surrendered two runs in the sixth and another run in the seventh, and was obviously laboring when he took to the mound in the eighth inning. Yogi, yet to get any satisfaction from his bullpen, elected to stick with Koosman, who promptly yielded a three-run homer to Steve Garvey to tie the game. Koosman was replaced by Bob Miller, who was the beneficiary of the Mets' two-run ninth inning and picked up his first win as a Met in 12 years.

Miller tried to recall his first Met victory twelve years earlier on the next to last day of the season after 21 starts and 12 losses. "That's so damn long ago. I do remember there weren't any people in the stands and there weren't any writers in the clubhouse after the game."[12] The only other real memory Miller had of that season was the fact that his manager, Casey Stengel, could never get a name straight. "He never called me Miller, or Bob or anything close to my right name. He called me Nelson. Don't ask me why. One day the phone rang in the bullpen and Joe Pignatano answered it. I kept hearing Piggy ask, 'Who? Who?' Then he hung up. But he picked up a ball, took it to the mound in the bullpen and placed it on the rubber. 'Casey says he wants Nelson to warm up and I know we ain't got no Nelson.' I knew he wanted me, so I got up."[13]

But the clubhouse wasn't all cheery after the game, as Tom Seaver and Jon Matlack were offended by Berra's handling of Koosman by leaving him in the game despite obviously being out of gas. "He was losing something in the sixth and he didn't bounce back," said Jon Matlack. "He should never have been left in to pitch to the tying run."[14] The conclusion of the game ended the dismal month of April for the defending National League champions.

Tom Seaver, who had his best outing of the season in his last start while shutting out the Giants, was in vintage form in the series finale against the Dodgers. Seaver went 12 innings, allowed one run and fanned 16, but was not around for the decision, a 2–1 Mets loss. "I feel I'm all back," said Seaver. "If I had come here and gotten rocked, I'd asked what was wrong. I'm in good shape."[15]

The Mets returned home on May 3 to take on the San Diego Padres for a three-game weekend series. Rain forced a postponement of the Friday evening game, which was rescheduled for a Sunday afternoon doubleheader. Once the series got under way, there was more encouraging news after Tug McGraw pitched two scoreless innings in relief while striking out four. McGraw saved the game for Jon Matlack, who was the beneficiary of a five-run seventh inning, as the Mets downed the Padres, 6–3. McGraw's good fortune didn't last more than one day, however, as he was called on to hold a 4–3 lead for Koosman in the ninth inning of the first game of the Sunday afternoon doubleheader. McGraw surrendered two runs instead as the Mets fell, 5–4. The bullpen also blew a 3–0 lead in the second game, and only a two-run 10th-inning home run by John Milner saved the Mets from yet another doubleheader sweep.

The weather continued to play havoc with the schedule as the series opener with the Giants was called on account of rain, forcing the Mets to play yet another doubleheader. Tom Seaver, who felt he was all the way back in his last start against the Dodgers, surrendered a three-run homer to Gary Matthews in the eighth inning, eclipsing a 3–1 Met lead, as the Giants held on to win, 4–3. Seaver was so distraught after the game he refused to speak to reporters. In the nightcap, George Stone held the Giants off the scoreboard for eight innings, but was equally matched by his counterpart, Jim Barr. The Giants scored three runs in the top ninth inning to send the Mets to their third doubleheader sweep of the season. The Mets salvaged the final game of the series and the homestand finale behind a masterpiece thrown by Jon Matlack, as the

Mets downed the Giants, 4–2. Matlack allowed just four hits while fanning 12. "Matlack displayed as good a fastball as I've ever seen him throw," said a pleased Berra.[16]

With the homestand complete, the Mets headed to the Midwest for six games against the Cubs and the Cardinals. Jerry Koosman opened the series against the Cubs and won his fourth consecutive game without a loss as the Mets pummeled Chicago, 7–2. "I've become the complete pitcher," said Koosman. "I use the fastball only when I need to. I'm throwing the slider this year for the first time. It's a pitch that pitching coach Rube Walker doesn't like too much, but I've shown him I can use it on occasion just to be effective and he lets me throw it. I've also got a better curve than I had in '68 and '69 and I could change up on it.... Fast, slow ... they never know what's coming."[17]

Home runs by Don Hahn, Cleon Jones and Rusty Staub paced Craig Swan to his first major league win in the middle game of the series. While Jones and Hahn hit their first home run of the year, Staub clubbed his team-leading sixth home run. Tom Seaver took the mound in the series finale as the Mets went for the sweep. While the Mets took an early 1–0 lead when they scored a run in the top of the first inning, Seaver was victimized one more time by the long ball when Jose Cardenal blasted a two-run homer in the bottom of the first frame. With the Cubs leading 3–1, the Mets came to bat in the top of the eighth inning. After Eddie Kranepool singled for his 1,000th career hit, Staub tied the game with his seventh homer. As a result, Seaver came out to pitch the last of the ninth inning with the game still tied, 3–3. Seaver started the ninth in grand fashion by striking out Jerry Morales, but walked Carmen Fanzone on a 3–2 pitch. Fanzone was replaced on the base path by Matt Alexander, who promptly stole second. George Mitterwald then blooped a single, scoring Alexander with the winning run. Once again Seaver found himself saddled with a late-inning loss and the frustrated pitcher refused to talk with the media. The Mets were recipients of more bad news when it was learned that Matlack would miss his next start, scheduled for the opener of the series in St. Louis, with a strained thigh muscle. As a result, Bob Apodaca was called out of the bullpen to take Matlack's start and face grizzled veteran and certain future Hall of Famer Bob Gibson. Yet at the end of the day it was the rookie that prevailed after Apodaca gave the Mets five solid innings and Cleon Jones and Jerry Grote hit two-run homers as the Mets beat the Cardinals, 5–3.

Jerry Koosman lost his first game of the year when the Cardinals pummeled him for six runs in 6⅔ innings in St. Louis' 10–1 victory in the middle game of the series. The Mets, however, were able to take the rubber game of the series with the Cardinals before heading home to start a weekend series with the Montreal Expos. George Stone, last year's 12-game winner, picked up his first win of the year and improved his record to 1-3.

Tom Seaver, struggling with a 1-4 record, opened the four-game weekend series against the Expos with his fastball hopping once again, striking out 13 as the Mets rolled to a 5–0 victory. But Tug McGraw, who had been hampered all season with shoulder problems, was finally placed on the 21-day disabled list.

More than 45,000 fans attended the middle game of the series at Shea Stadium and were rewarded by another super pitching performance by a member of the staff's big three. Jon Matlack shut the Expos out on four hits and the

Ed Kranepool, an original Met, played a valuable role on the club as a backup outfielder, first baseman and prolific pinch-hitter (National Baseball Hall of Fame Library).

Mets scored four first-inning runs on their way to a 6–0 victory. With the win the Mets were now just two games under .500, with a chance to reach the break-even mark if they could sweep the Expos in a Sunday afternoon doubleheader.

Unfortunately, it was the Expos who did the sweeping as the Mets lost their fourth doubleheader of the season, the latest in front of 40,461 fans. Despite the double setback, the Mets found themselves only four games under .500 and four games out of first place, with the Chicago Cubs coming into Shea to spend the week playing four single games.

Controversy came to the forefront of the opener in the series, a tough 2–1 loss, when home plate umpire Bruce Froemming accused Mets catcher Jerry Grote of deliberately missing a pitch so it would hit the umpire. "He let it go by on purpose and you can print that," fumed Froemming. "It was a class D act." Berra was quick to come to Grote's defense. "He doesn't know what he's talking about. Grote was crossed up on the pitch. He called for a curve, and Parker had trouble seeing the signs. He threw him a fastball. Besides, why didn't Froemming answer when he asked where the previous pitch was?" "Bull," responded Froemming. "There were two keys to the play. First, he never moved his glove. Second, he never went out to the pitcher to tell him he crossed him up. I tell you he let it go by on purpose."[18]

While the Mets behind George Stone were able to win the second game of the series, 10–5, Tom Seaver's Dr. Jekyll-and-Mr. Hyde season continued in the third game. The Cubs roughed Seaver up for six runs in five innings, and he left the mound once again with a flurry of boos emanating from the 16,196 fans in attendance. Yet Seaver was not the loser as Bob Apodaca, back in the bullpen, surrendered a three-run homer in the ninth inning to Jerry Morales, sending the Mets to a 9–6 defeat.

The next road trip sent the Mets to Pittsburgh, where they won two games, and to Cincinnati, where they were swept by the Reds in a three-game series. Jerry Koosman picked up his fifth win of the season in the opener against the Pirates, and a four-run ninth inning in the middle game led the Mets to a 5–3 win against the Pirates. After the finale in Pittsburgh was rained out, the Mets moved on to Cincinnati, where once again Tom Seaver struggled, losing his fifth game of the year in New York's 4–2 defeat. The finale of the series was another heart-breaking loss when Tony Perez took Harry Parker deep in the 10th inning to beat the Mets, 3–2, despite another splendid outing by Matlack.

Back home, the Mets closed out the month of May getting pounded by the Astros, 7–1. Jerry Koosman, the starter and loser, saw his record drop to 5–3 after starting off the season with a 4–0 record. The month of June started on a more optimistic note as the Mets, behind Tom Seaver, beat the Astros, 3–1. For the first time since the Mets knocked off Cincinnati in the playoffs the previous October did the Reds come calling at Shea Stadium. Except for Pete Rose being roundly booed every time he stepped up to the plate, there was none of the acrimony and tension that permeated the stadium during the NLCS. "They were like the old Met fans — noisy but no problems," said Reds manager Sparky Anderson.[19] For the fourth consecutive game against the Reds, the Mets went down to defeat as Cincinnati pinned a 5–2 loss on Jon Matlack.

The next evening saw for the umpteenth time that season the bullpen fail to hold a lead for Jerry Koosman. Koosman was removed from the game in the seventh inning with the Reds at-bat and the bases loaded with two outs. Koosman's replacement, Harry Parker, surrendered a two-run single to tie the game — one in which the Mets would eventually lose in 10 innings. The Mets were able to salvage the finale of the series, though, courtesy of John Milner's ninth home run of the year in the eighth inning, which broke a 3–3 tie. The blast came too late, however, for Tom Seaver, who pitched seven decent innings but left trailing 3–1. A two-run, two-out rally in the seventh inning tied the game before Milner's blast decided it. Ray Sadecki, the loser in the 10th inning of the middle game, was the winner in relief to raise his record to 3-2. A happy Yogi imparted his wisdom after the game, "Chances are we needed a victory like this to put us back on the track. We really had to sweat this one out."[20]

The Mets hit the road again for a trip that would take them to Houston and Atlanta. The only reprieve Yogi received from one-run games on this road trip was an 11–1 beating at the hands of the Astros. Otherwise, the Mets lost two 1–0 games, with Harry Parker the tough-luck losing pitcher in both games and a 4–3 11-inning setback, and notched a 6–5 14-inning win. The Mets returned home without the services of Buddy Harrelson, who was put on the disabled list with a fractured right wrist suffered when he was hit by a pitch from Braves starter Carl Morton while leading off the final game of the road trip. They also were without Craig Swan, who was disabled with an inflamed right elbow. The roster spots were filled with Tug McGraw, who hadn't pitched in over a month, and veteran journeyman right-hand relief pitcher Jack Aker, who was purchased from the Atlanta Braves.

The Mets returned home on Friday, June 14, to start a homestand against the Dodgers and Braves. To no one's surprise, the Mets lost the opener by one run, 3–2, despite another good effort by Jon Matlack, who allowed only two runs in his eight innings of work. With the Dodgers leading, 2–0, and the Mets unable to do anything against Dodgers starter Tommy John for the first eight innings, Tug McGraw made his first appearance in more than a month and surrendered one run and three hits in the inning. The run turned out to be very costly after Cleon Jones hit his fifth home run of the year with a runner aboard in the bottom of the ninth.

Jerry Koosman snapped the Mets' four-game losing streak with a complete game five-hitter, and Rusty Staub hit his ninth home run of the year in the Mets' 4–1 win over the Dodgers. Koosman played the role of stopper again after the Mets lost the series finale with the Dodgers and then were swept by the Braves. Koosman beat the Phillies, 2–1, in the opener of a five-game series in

Philadelphia. More bad news followed the next day when Tom Seaver had to leave the game because of pain in his left hip after pitching five solid innings. The Mets won the game on two home runs by John Milner and one by Rusty Staub. Any ground the Mets made up in their first two days in Philadelphia went by the wayside the next day as they lost yet another doubleheader. To add insult to injury, the Mets' bullpen had to be vacated after some over-exuberant Phillies fans began tossing fireworks into the bullpen. Left fielder Ed Kranepool had to wear a batting helmet in the outfield after being pelted with golf balls. When the dust settled, the Mets found themselves in last place, 10 games out of first, and the makings of a long summer ahead of them.

After the doubleheader, Yogi Berra made a decision to drop the center field platoon of Don Hahn and Dave Schneck, and installed Hahn as his regular center fielder. While Schneck was having trouble defensively all season, a play in the first inning of the first game, when he failed to catch a long drive off the bat of Mike Schmidt that eventually led to three first-inning runs, was the trigger that led to Berra's ultimate decision. What was killing the Mets as much as Schneck's fielding was his failure to hit. He went an entire month without driving in a run and had only one hit in 30 at-bats.

The season continued to take on the form of a seesaw, as any ground and momentum seemingly gained by the team was immediately reversed. After sweeping the Cubs, the Mets returned home and lost three out of four, including another doubleheader to the Cardinals. The one win in the series went to Jon Matlack, who entered the game with four losses and three no-decisions since his last victory, fired a one-hitter in a 4–0 Mets win. "Today was one of those days you have once in a great while where everything falls into place," said Matlack. "You make mistakes and they take them or they swing and they miss. The biggest thing to me was the stuff I had on the ball. I've got to put everything together to pitch well. The leg muscles, the back muscles all have to go towards the plate. When those things are together my ball explodes at the hitter. It rushes at him the last ten feet."[21]

The Mets also believed they were robbed of a win in the second game of the Sunday afternoon doubleheader on a controversial call by the umpire. After losing the first game despite another fine pitching performance by Jerry Koosman, the Mets went into the last of the ninth inning of the nightcap trailing 3–1. Four hits and an infield out produced the tying runs. Then with two outs and two runners aboard, Cleon Jones hit a sinking line drive to right field, which right fielder Reggie Smith dove for in an attempt to make the catch. Smith rolled over to one side, and after making a complete turn, faced the plate with the ball triumphantly held in his right hand. Chris Pelekoudas called the ball in play, allowing what appeared to be the winning run to cross the plate. After Cardinals manager Red Schoendienst rushed out to argue, the four umpires got together, and after a short conference reversed their decision, calling Jones out and sending the game into extra innings. The Mets went on to lose when Tug McGraw surrendered two runs in the 10th inning. "We've been robbed by those guys (the umpires) at least four times this year," complained Berra. "Every time I ask an umpire to ask the other guy what he saw, they refuse to do it. But other clubs ask and they get the decision reversed."[22]

The Phillies followed the first-place Cardinals into Shea for a big four-game series, including a Fourth of July doubleheader. Tom Seaver, making his first start since June 21, opened the series by stopping the Phillies on three hits in the 7⅓ innings he worked as the Mets beat the Phillies, 4–2. Seaver, allowing only one unearned run, picked up his fifth win of the season. Cleon Jones wielded the big bat for the Mets, hitting his seventh home run of the year with Rusty Staub on base in the first inning. Cleon Jones' eighth home run of the year came the next day, along with Staub's 12th, as the Mets again beat the Phillies in the middle game of the series.

Having already lost six doubleheaders, the Mets found themselves in a position to finally win one after Jon Matlack came up with another dominating performance, striking out 10, as the Mets won the opener. The Mets, however, never came close to sweeping the doubleheader, as the Phillies opened up the nightcap by scoring two runs off starter Ray Sadecki on their way to a 6–2 victory. Cleon Jones continued his red-hot hitting, delivering five hits over the course of the doubleheader, but also delivered some July 4th fireworks of his own with a scathing attack on his critics, who accused him of dogging it. "You know, they always say that black people are lazy. When I first came up they said I was lackadaisical, but that's only saying the same thing in a different way, isn't it?"[23] The lazy tag started when the late Gil Hodges, thinking Jones hadn't hustled on a base hit during a game the Mets were being demolished in, came out of the dugout and replaced Jones.

The San Francisco Giants were next into Shea Stadium, where the Mets took two out of three from the Giants. Dave Schneck, getting a rare start, was the hitting star in the opener of the series, driving home two runs, as the Mets downed the Giants, 3–2. Schneck, relied on by the Mets as the left-handed part of the center field platoon, was benched after struggling mightily offensively, posting only one hit in his last 31 games, none in his last 16 contests, and no runs batted in since May 21.

Jerry Koosman was the beneficiary of Schneck's new-found hitting prowess, holding the Giants at bay while picking up his team-leading ninth victory. "I don't consider myself a fastball pitcher anymore, although I would say I had an overpowering fastball today," said Koosman. "I'd categorize myself more as a pitcher than a thrower.[24]

After losing the middle game of the series, there was both good news and bad news in the rubber game. The good news was Tom Seaver improved his record to 6–6 after the Mets beat the Giants, 6–0. The bad news was that Seaver had to leave the game after five innings with his hip acting up again. "It's an inflammation of the sciatic nerve," was the diagnosis of team physician Dr.

James Parkes. "We're hoping we've got it enough under control so that we don't have to sit him down for a couple of weeks."[25]

Despite ending the homestand by losing two out of three to the Padres in a weekend series, the Mets still found themselves playing their best ball of the year, having won nine out of their last 14 games. The Mets almost made it 11 out of their last 16 games before falling just one run short in the finale of the homestand. New York scored three runs in the last of the ninth inning on a three-run homer by Ron Hodges after entering the inning trailing 5–1.

With a successful homestand behind them, the Mets headed back to California, where they split eight games between Los Angeles, San Francisco and San Diego before breaking for the annual All-Star Game.

With Tom Seaver ailing, a struggling Bob Apodaca was once again called out of the bullpen for a spot start in the opener of the road trip against the Dodgers. Apodaca responded with six scoreless innings, and the Mets scored four runs in the seventh inning on their way to a 5–2 victory. Newly acquired Jack Aker pitched the last three innings, allowed two runs, but was still able to save the game for Apodaca. After Harry Parker lost another tough one-run decision in the middle game of the series, Jon Matlack came back in the rubber game with a six-hitter as the Mets prevailed, 4–1.

The Mets lost both games in San Francisco to the Giants. In the opener the Giants ambushed Jerry Koosman, roughing him up for six runs in the fifth inning after he allowed only three hits over the first four innings, and went on to a 9–4 victory. Bob Apodaca, who was impressive in his start against the Dodgers, was anything but in his next start, as the Giants smacked him around for five runs in three-plus innings.

The Mets had better luck with the Padres while winning the first two games of the series. Jon Matlack fired a five-hitter and picked up his ninth win while winning himself a trip to the All-Star Game. Jerry Koosman, despite winning his 10th game and earning his 1,000th career strikeout in a 10–2 drubbing of the Padres, was surprisingly not selected by National League manager Yogi Berra as one of his starters. After the Mets lost the final game of the series, the first half of the season came to a close. Just as the 1973 season, when the Mets found themselves in the cellar of the N.L. East at the All Star break, New York again found itself in last place with a disappointing 40–52 record, 7½ games behind the league-leading Phillies. Yet it was an upbeat Berra who addressed the press before heading off to manage the National League All-Stars. "I'm just hoping for a healthy team the rest of the season," said the eternal optimist. "We've had our shares of troubles, but I'm not complaining. What I like is that we got a lot of games left with the teams in our own division — Montreal and Pittsburgh. We ain't played them at all. We've got a lot with both of them. I think it's possible for a team to win again with 82 victories, 84 ... maybe even with a .500 record."[26] Last year's National League East champion Mets won only 81 games. As Yogi Berra was wont to say, "It's déjà vu all over again."

Lightning Doesn't Strike Twice

The second half of the 1974 season began exactly the same way that the second half of the 1973 season did — by losing a doubleheader to the Cardinals in St. Louis. Ironically enough, as they did in 1973, Jerry Koosman and Jon Matlack started for the Mets, and Bob Gibson and Alan Foster started for the Cardinals. "If we had known that," said Jerry Koosman, "we could have just given them the two and showed up tomorrow."[1] Of greater concern to the Mets than the double loss, which left them nine games out of first, was the continued ineffectiveness of Tug McGraw, who couldn't hold a 3–2 lead for Jerry Koosman in the ninth inning of the first game.

Nineteen days after Tom Seaver last pitched in a game, he returned to the starting rotation to take on the Cardinals in the series finale. And what a performance it was, as Seaver shut out the Cardinals on four hits. John Milner added his 14th home run and the Mets won, 3–0. "I needed that one," said Seaver. "We all did."[2]

After more than a two-week hiatus, the Mets returned home to Shea Stadium on July 27 to start an eight-game homestand against the Expos, Pirates and Cubs. Buoyed by the resurgence of Tom Seaver, the Mets completed an impressive sweep of the Expos, including winning the last two games of the series with eighth-inning rallies. The middle game of the series saw Tug McGraw pick up his first win of the season, while John Milner swatted his 15th home run of the year that was the deciding blow in the series finale.

The Pirates followed the Expos into Shea Stadium for a three-game series, including a make-up doubleheader, which the Mets split. Jon Matlack was roughed up in the opener, a game in which the Mets lost, 6–0. Jerry Koosman, however, saved the day when he pitched the Mets to a 4–3 complete-game victory in the nightcap. The month of July ended the next day on a down note for both the Mets and Tom Seaver as the Pirates pounded the right-hander for eight runs on 12 hits in less than five innings, dispelling any notion of a Seaver renaissance.

The Mets ushered in the month of August with a doubleheader against the Cubs that they wasted no time in losing. The first game ended in 10 innings with Tug McGraw walking in what proved to be the winning run after surrendering the game-tying run in the eighth inning, eclipsing a 4–3 Mets lead. The big bat for the Mets in the first game was Wayne Garrett, who hit his eighth home run of the year and had four hits overall, and John Milner, who hit his 16th home run. Cleon Jones' eighth home run of the year was the only run scored by the Mets in the second game of the doubleheader, as they went down to defeat, 3–1.

After the finale of the series with the Cubs was rained out, the Mets embarked to Montreal to start a key road trip, which would then take them to Pittsburgh before returning home to meet the elite of the National League West. Jon Matlack opened the series in vintage form as he hurled his fourth shutout of the season, with the Mets blanking the Expos, 3–0. Once again Cleon Jones and Wayne Garrett starred offensively. Garrett slammed his ninth home run of the year, while Jones, with three hits, drove home the other two Met runs.

After another rainout washed away the middle game of the series, Tom Seaver's enigmatic season continued in the finale, with the right-hander surrendering four runs in the first four innings. Trailing 4–2 in the seventh inning, Seaver was taken off the hook when Ken Boswell, batting for the pitcher, hit a game-tying two-run homer. Tug McGraw, fighting through an enigmatic season of his own, was on top of his game, however, throwing three shutout innings of relief. But the big story of the game on this night was not what McGraw did on the mound, but rather what he did with the bat. With the Mets loading the bases in the eighth inning, Tug McGraw was allowed to hit for himself because Berra had no one to go to in the bullpen. McGraw responded by smashing a double to right-center field, clearing the bases. "I haven't had a hit all year," said McGraw, "and the kid on the mound (Expos starter Dennis Blair) knew it. He threw it straight down the middle, but I surprised everyone including myself by getting a good piece of wood on it."[3] The Mets scored three more runs in the ninth inning on their way to a 10–4 romp over the Expos.

McGraw's up and down (but mostly down) season continued as the Mets opened a key series with the Pirates at Three Rivers Stadium. A day after winning a game with his bat, McGraw lost a game with his fielding. Mets starter Jerry Koosman, victimized all season by relievers failing to hold leads for him, was victimized once again after the bullpen failed to hold an 8–3 lead. The Pirates scored five runs in the last two innings to send the game into extra innings. With McGraw on the mound in the last of the eleventh inning, Gene Clines led off with a grounder to short that was booted by Bud Harrelson for an error. Poor fundamental play continued when the next batter, Ed Kirkpatrick, laid down a sacrifice bunt that was handled by McGraw, who threw to second base in an attempt to nail Clines despite having no chance to nail the speedy outfielder. Mario Mendoza, a weak-hitting infielder, followed with a bunt of his own that was once again handled, or better yet mishandled, by McGraw. McGraw, with plenty of time, once again went for the force play on

Clines. This time McGraw unleashed a throw that sailed over Garrett's head, allowing Clines to cruise home with the winning run.

After surrendering nine runs in the opener of the series, the Mets went one better in the middle game as Harry Parker, Bob Miller and Jack Aker combined to allow the Pirates 10 tallies, as Pittsburgh routed New York, 10–1. The Mets were held to only three hits by Pirates rookie pitcher Larry Demery.

On August 8, the night that President Richard Nixon shocked the nation with the announcement of his resignation, Richie Zisk put a shock into the Mets' pennant hopes when he smashed a one-out home run in the last of the ninth inning to send the Mets to a stunning 4–3 defeat after leading 3–0 after 4½ innings. Jon Matlack was the victim of another hard-luck one-run defeat. With the loss the Mets fell 9½ games behind the league-leading Pirates as New York headed home to take on the Reds for a three-game weekend series.

The series with the Reds was a microcosm of the season thus far. For every step forward the Mets took, they followed by taking two steps backwards. New York lost the final two games of the series after winning the opener, 4–1, behind the pitching of Bob Apodaca and the power of Don Hahn. In addition to losing two out of three over the weekend, the Mets received more bad news when George Stone, struggling along with a 2-7 record, was put on the disabled list with an aching shoulder that's been bugging him the entire season.

With the second-best team in the National League, the Cincinnati Reds, departing the scene, the circuit's best team, the Los Angeles Dodgers, came calling. In a season where nothing seemingly went right for the New Yorkers, the Mets pulled off the unthinkable by sweeping the Dodgers. In the opener, Harry Parker, powered by John Milner's 18th home run of the year, picked up his fourth win and first career complete game.

Jon Matlack's league-leading fifth shutout and Jerry Grote's fifth home run of the year was the story of the middle game of the series as the Mets silenced the Dodgers, 3–0. With the win, Matlack tied Koosman for the team lead in victories with 11. The Mets completed the sweep of the Dodgers, the first time since 1971 they had accomplished the feat, in dramatic fashion, scoring two runs in the last of the ninth inning after trailing 2–1 since the fourth inning. Despite a fine performance by Seaver, who allowed only two runs in seven innings, he was on the hook as the Mets came to bat in the final frame. Mike Marshall, who had displaced McGraw as the league's top fireman, walked Ken Boswell to start the ninth inning. McGraw, once again allowed to bat for himself, successfully sacrificed Boswell over to second. Ron Hodges, batting for Bud Harrelson, drove a ball that center fielder Tom Paciorek misplayed into a two-base error, scoring Boswell with the tying run. A base hit by Millan followed, which sent Hodges to third. A drive by Staub over the drawn-in outfield drove home Hodges with the game-winning run. The win was especially gratifying after the Mets squandered a first-and-third, nobody-out situation in the eighth inning.

It was an elated and optimistic ball club that headed on to Cincinnati as the Mets prepared to take on the Reds for a three-game weekend series. The optimism continued to grow as the Mets took the opener of the series in 12 innings, defeating the Reds, 2–1. The Mets had won four games in a row, during which the New York pitchers allowed the opposition only four runs. Jerry

Though it is not reflected by his record, Jon Matlack had what may have been the best season of his career in 1974, throwing seven shutouts (National Baseball Hall of Fame Library).

Koosman, the Met starter, more than made up for his poor start against the Reds in his last outing by holding Cincinnati to only one run in his eight innings of work. For the second straight game it was the bat of Rusty Staub that drove in the winning run when he doubled home Bud Harrelson in the top of the 12th inning. Tug McGraw, with two solid innings of relief work, picked up his fourth win of the year.

Two days later there was nothing left of the burst of optimism after the Mets were hit hard in the final two games of the series, losing both. More disturbing, however, was the voice of dissension appearing in the clubhouse after the Mets' latest debacle. The voice was that of Jon Matlack, the losing pitcher in the series finale. "The maximum potential is not being obtained from the guys in the room," charged Matlack. "I'm not saying anyone is dogging it, but we're not playing as good as we're capable of. Some guys are capable and don't need anything. Some guys are capable and need a pat on the back. Some guys are capable and need a kick in the ass. I don't know where the pat or the kick should come from — the manager, the players themselves or the general manager. I know it's not coming. We're not a machine; we're not programmed to do things every time. It really helps to have that constructive criticism. Maybe it helps to have somebody tear you down from time to time. I don't think there's anybody here with the driving ambition to be a Pete Rose, a team leader. If I were in a position of more seniority or experience, I would try to lead more. There have been instances where I could've spoken out, but I don't think that's my place. I'm relatively a baby."[4] Matlack had been a regular with the Mets only since 1972.

If Matlack's tirade was intended to light a fire under the bottoms of his teammates, it apparently had the opposite effect as the Mets headed on to Houston, where they lost the first two games of a three-game series while scoring a total of three runs. In a season where good performances were hard to come by for Tom Seaver, a masterful performance in the opener went for naught when Milt May singled off Seaver with two outs in the last of the eleventh inning, sending home Greg Gross with the game-winning run as the Mets fell, 2–1. The loss was Seaver's eighth of the year and dropped his record to a disappointing 7–8. The game started off as a scoreless pitching duel between Tom Seaver and Tom Wilson for the first eight innings. In the ninth inning an error by second baseman Tommy Helms allowed Wayne Garrett to reach base. Garrett moved over to third base on an off-the-wall single by Jerry Grote. Rusty Staub was then called on to pinch-hit and came through with a base hit to bring home the first run of the game. A walk to Bud Harrelson loaded the bases, but reliever Ken Forsch was able to retire the Mets without any further damage. As a result, Seaver took the mound only three outs away from picking up his eighth win of the season. But Seaver walked Cesar Cedeno, the lead-off batter, who one out later was standing on third base after Bob Watson doubled just over the edge of Ed Kranepool's outstretched glove. The game's hero, Milt May, followed with a sacrifice fly to tie the contest and send it into extra innings.

After the Mets lost the middle game of the series in a lackluster effort, Jon Matlack denied a report that he wanted to be traded, and at the same time apologized for his earlier tirade. "That's nonsense," said Matlack, when asked to confirm the report. "All I said was that I wouldn't mind playing for a team as aggressive as the Reds."[5]

The Mets' sputtering offense came alive in the final game of the series, as they thumped the Astros, 10–2. Jerry Koosman fired a six-hitter as he picked up his 12th win of the season to regain the team lead in victories.

The final leg of the road trip brought the Mets to Atlanta for a four-game series, beginning with a Friday night twilight doubleheader. Doubleheaders and Tug McGraw, the source of much anguish for the Mets during the season, combined to add to the overflowing cup of woes. A painful evening hurt even more after Tug McGraw couldn't hold a 3–2 lead handed to him by Jon Matlack. Matlack, taking a 3–2 lead with him into the ninth inning, surrendered a leadoff base hit to Davey Johnson and was immediately lifted by Berra in favor of McGraw. McGraw's first batter, Leo Foster, laid down a bunt in front of the mound. McGraw once again found he had difficulties fielding bunts and threw high to first base as both runners were safe. The runners moved up to second and third base on a groundout. Craig Robinson, running for Davey Johnson, then scored the tying run on a fly ball off the bat of Paul Casanova. McGraw was able to end the inning with the tie intact but couldn't escape the Braves' attack in the 10th inning. Marty Perez led off the 10th inning with a base hit and was sacrificed to second by Darrel Evans. McGraw was just one out away from ending the threat by striking out Rowland Office, but a base hit by Mike Lum scored Perez with the winning run, sending the Mets to another bitter defeat and banging another nail into the Mets' 1974 coffin. The Mets remained comatose in the second game of the doubleheader, losing 6–0. Harry Parker's season of being consistently inconsistent continued as the Braves pounded him for five runs in less than four innings. For Parker it was his 12th loss of the year.

The agony for the Mets continued in the third game of the series, as 34,000 Brave fans showed up to Atlanta Fulton County Stadium to watch Bob Miller walk in the winning run in the last of the 10th inning as the Braves beat the Mets, 4–3. With the Mets trailing 3–2 as they came to bat in the ninth inning, Tom Seaver, struggling through his most distressing season, was only one out away from suffering his ninth loss when Wayne Garrett singled home Cleon Jones to tie the game and take Seaver off the hook.

Ray Sadecki single-handedly played the role of stopper, salvaging the final game of the series by throwing a five-hit shutout and driving in the game's only run in the fifth inning. "He was absolutely great," said catcher Duffy Dyer. "His fastball seemed to do the best job, but he also had those Braves guessing on his change-up and curve."[6]

With two outs and nobody on in the ninth inning, the Braves sent Hank Aaron out as a pinch-hitter, which immediately sent pitching coach Rube Walker scurrying to the mound as quickly as his portly form would allow. Sadecki, the consummate joker, asked Walker, "Where did they get this guy? Do you know anything about him?" "No. But you're not going to let him beat us," responded Walker.[7]

Despite being sixteen games below the .500 mark and their dream of repeating as National League East champions in need of divine intervention, the Mets were an inspired team that returned to Shea Stadium on August 26. In a homestand beginning with a four-game series against the Astros, the opener saw the Mets score three runs in the last of the ninth inning to come from behind for a 5–4 win. Jerry Koosman, who pitched his 11th complete game of the year, picked up his 13th win. The thrilling victory was slightly dampened by injuries to Jerry Grote, who was hit on the right hand by a foul tip, and to Cleon Jones, who injured his left knee chasing a ball in the seventh inning. Both players were removed from the game and were listed as day-to-day.

With neither Grote nor Jones available, the Mets dipped into their Tidewater affiliate and recalled Benny Ayala, who was in the lineup the next day. The Mets' mystique continued when Benny Ayala became the 40th player in history to hit a home run in his first at-bat. Ayala's home run in the second inning was the first of three runs to cross the plate in the inning as the Mets took the second game of the series, 4–2. Just as he did in 1973 in an attempt to get McGraw straightened out, Berra gave him the start. The move paid off handsomely as McGraw went six solid innings, allowing the Astros only one run in a 4–2 Mets win.

The Mets, however, ran out of magic in the third game of the series as they lost in 10 innings despite scoring two runs in the last of the ninth to overcome a 2–0 deficit. A pinch-hit home run by Cliff Johnson off rookie pitcher Jerry Cram did the Mets in. A fine pitching performance by Matlack and Rusty Staub's 16th home run went to waste.

The Mets completed the series with the Astros by winning three out of four games after shutting out the Astros, 7–0. Tom Seaver picked up his first win since shutting out the Cardinals on July 26.

In came the Braves for a weekend series and the Mets' dream for another miracle became more realistic after they swept Atlanta. Ray Sadecki pitched another complete game for his second win in less than a week over the Braves. A two-run eighth-inning single by Rusty Staub paced the Mets to a 6–5 victory in the middle game, while Tug McGraw pitched his first major league shutout, enabling the Mets to complete the sweep. The big story in the finale was the farewell to Hank Aaron, baseball's all-time home run leader who made what was most probably his final Shea Stadium at-bat.[8] Aaron, who was greeted lustily each time he came to the plate, had only one hit in his four plate appearances of the afternoon. "I was tickled that he only got a single off me," said

McGraw. "Henry hit the first home run that I gave up in the major leagues and three more over the years."[9]

The Mets headed off to Chicago, where they extended their winning streak to six consecutive games after sweeping the Cubs in a doubleheader behind Jon Matlack and Tom Seaver. John Milner was responsible for all of the scoring in the opening game with a first-inning single and his 19th home run in the sixth inning. Jon Matlack threw his sixth shutout of the year and picked up his 12th win. Five-run seventh- and eighth-inning outbursts spurred the Mets on to an 11–4 drubbing of the Cubs in the nightcap. The winning streak reached seven after the Mets completed a sweep of the Cubs as Ray Sadecki won his third consecutive start.

Despite the seven-game winning streak, the Mets' pennant hopes were hanging by a thread as they headed to St. Louis for a weekend series with the Cardinals. If there was anyone clinging to the hope of another miracle, it was Yogi. "You never know what's going to happen," said the indomitable optimist. "We're getting the pitchin' now and the hittin' at the right time."[10] Barely were the words out of Yogi's mouth when the hitting headed south one more time, as both Koosman and Matlack saw dynamic pitching performances wasted while the Cardinals won the first two games of the series. Both talented left-handers were losing pitchers despite allowing only two runs in their outings. Tom Seaver salvaged the final game of the series as the Mets beat the Cardinals, 5–3. For Seaver it marked his third consecutive win of the season. The bigger story of the series was Lou Brock, who stole three bases to pull within one of tying the single-season record for stolen bases by Maury Wills.

By the time the Mets returned to Shea Stadium on September 9, Yogi may have been the only one who still believed the Mets had a fighting chance. Only 9,960 fans, the smallest crowd of the season, showed up as the Mets took on the Montreal Expos. Once again Ray Sadecki was on top of his game, pitching a complete game as the Mets trounced the Expos, 7–1. For Sadecki, it was his fourth consecutive outstanding pitching performance, earning the raves of general manager Bob Scheffing. "The amazing thing about the guy is that he's ready whenever you want him. Never has a sore arm, never complains. Just goes out and does his job. And the sonofagun's control is amazing."[11]

September 11 saw the St. Louis Cardinals come into Shea Stadium for the start of a short two-game series. With New York too far behind in the standings, and the Cardinals and Pirates locked in a bruising battle for first place, the Mets found themselves playing only for pride and for the opportunity to play the role of spoiler. The opener appeared to be an easy Mets win, as Koosman took the mound in the ninth cruising along with a three-hitter and a 3–1 lead, courtesy of Cleon Jones' two-run homer in the fifth inning. Nobody was prepared for what happened next. Koosman, in search of his team-leading 14th win, was denied when Ken Reitz blasted a two-run homer with two outs in the ninth inning to tie the game. When the Mets failed to score in the bottom of

Shea Stadium, September 12, 1974, 3:20 A.M. and moments after the Mets lost a 25-inning, 4–3 decision to the St. Louis Cardinals (AP Images).

the ninth inning, the game headed into extra innings. The two teams then played and played and played some more. By the time the game ended 16 innings later, it was 3:13 A.M., seven hours and four minutes after the game started. In all 50 players saw action, including seven Cardinal pitchers, while the Mets used six of their own. When the dust settled, the Mets found themselves saddled with another one-run loss after Bake McBride raced all the way home from first base on an errant Hank Webb pickoff throw. When Ron Hodges dropped the throw to the plate from John Milner, the go-ahead and eventual winning run scored.

The best line of the long evening came from the Mets' dugout and Tom Seaver. After Met rookie Brock Pemberton singled in the 25th inning for his first major league hit and the Met bench called for the ball, Seaver yelled, "Don't give it to him, it's the last ball we got."[12] However, the best overall line during the game came from the Cardinals' dugout. When Cardinals manager Red Schoendienst called for a bunt in the 20th inning, pitcher Alan Foster told his manager, "We've been playing for one run for five hours; let's play for the big inning. Let him hit away."[13]

"The Endurance of the Night" award, however, had to go to Ed Sudol, the home-plate umpire, who stood straight without sitting down for seven hours and four minutes. For Sudol, it was hardly anything new. The umpire was behind the plate on May 31, 1964, when the Mets and Giants played a 23-inning,

Jerry Koosman led the Mets staff in victories in 1974 with 15 (National Baseball Hall of Fame Library).

seven-hour 23-minute game at Shea Stadium. Sudol also had the good fortune to be the home-plate umpire when the Mets played a 24-inning game in Houston on April 15, 1968. "Why does it always happen to me?" wondered Sudol.[14]

Despite being a foregone conclusion, official elimination for the Mets didn't come until September 18, after the Expos swept a doubleheader in Montreal. Of more concern, however, to the team was the health of Tom Seaver, who once again found himself having problems with the sciatic nerve in his left hip and had to be removed in the sixth inning. Before leaving because of the discomfort, Seaver was on cruise control, not allowing a hit through the first five innings while fanning eight. In the sixth inning, Seaver surrendered three runs on three hits before signaling to Berra to come get him.

With the Cardinals and Pirates locked in a dead heat for the National League Eastern Division championship, the Mets, despite being out of contention, were still an integral part of the pennant race with seven games left against the Pirates in the last week and a half of the season. The first of the games began on September 20, as the Mets and Pirates began a three-game weekend series in Pittsburgh. The opener was a microcosm of the Mets' season as a whole, as Ray Sadecki, working on a five-hitter, took a 3–1 lead into the ninth inning. After Sadecki walked Art Howe, the leadoff batter, Berra once again turned to McGraw, who once again could not get the job done. A wild pitch and two base hits later, McGraw was out of the game, and Harry Parker was in. With one run in and runners at second and third, Parker induced Manny Sanguillen to ground a ball to the shortstop Martinez. Martinez, who had a play at the plate to cut off the potential tying run, instead elected to go to third, where he had no play. Al Oliver was then walked intentionally to set up either a play at the plate or a double play. Parker got what he wanted when Willie Stargell bounced the ball to first baseman John Milner, who had an easy play at the plate. Milner, however, elected to take the out at first as the winning run crossed the plate. With the win the Pirates ended the evening a half-game behind the Cardinals.

The Pirates remained a half-game out after Koosman stymied Pittsburgh on six hits while striking out nine, as he picked up his 14th win of the season in the middle game of the series. A three-run homer by Wayne Garrett in the seventh inning was the big blow for the Mets, who prevailed, 4–2. "I have to admit being with a club at this time of the year that is out of the running sort of keeps a player from having his whole heart in a game before he gets to the ballpark," said Koosman. "But once I get to the mound and find myself facing a contending team, I automatically find myself giving the game my all."[15] Apparently Jon Matlack had no problem getting himself psyched for a meaningless game this late in the season. Matlack spun a three-hit shutout as the Mets took the rubber game of the series.

After stopping in Philadelphia for a three-game series, including another doubleheader that the Mets lost, it was time to return home for the final seven games of the season. First in were the Pirates, who tattooed Mets pitching as they romped, 11–5. Jerry Koosman, who was masterful in his last outing, lasted only two innings, surrendering six runs. With the win the Pirates finally caught the Cardinals, tying them for first place. Each team had identical 83-73 records.

While Jon Matlack fared better than his left-handed counterpart did the day before, the two runs he surrendered to the Pirates in the sixth inning were enough to do him in as the Mets lost, 2–1. With the loss Matlack saw his record drop to 13-14. By winning the third game of the series as well, the Pirates were able to leapfrog the Cardinals into first place by one game. However, the Mets, behind Bob Apodaca, who once more was thrown into a starting role, were able to salvage the finale of the series. With the Cardinals winning, the Pirates left New York in a tie for first place.

With the conclusion of the big series with the Pirates, the Phillies came in for three games to conclude a long and disappointing season. Jerry Koosman concluded his finest season in five years when he pitched the Mets to a 5–2 victory over the Phillies in the opener of the series. It was Koosman's 15th win of the season to lead the team. Wayne Garrett supplied Koosman with the margin of victory by once again hitting a three-run homer in the sixth inning.

Tom Seaver, sciatic hip and all, made one last start in the middle game of the series. Only 5,341 fans, the smallest crowd of the season, showed up. While Seaver showed no ill effects from his hip injury while pitching a complete game and striking out fourteen, he received no offensive support as the Mets went down to a 2–1 loss. The loss for Seaver dropped his won-lost record to 11-11, the worst showing of his stellar career. Seaver's 14 strikeouts gave him a total of 201, marking the seventh consecutive season that he fanned 200 or more batters. Seaver went into the season sharing the National League record with Sandy Koufax of six straight seasons with 200 strikeouts. Now Seaver held the record by himself. Seaver also tied the major league record held by Walter Johnson. While Seaver was not expected to start the next-to-last game of the season, he asked to take the mound when his left hip condition showed some improvement. "I needed something to carry me through the winter after the kind of year I had," said Seaver.[16] Jon Matlack pitched the last game of the season and suffered another hard-luck loss as the Phillies beat the Mets in 10 innings, 3–2. The loss dropped Matlack's won-lost record to an undeserving 13-15.

When the dust cleared, the Mets found themselves in sole possession of fifth place with a 71-91 record, their worst showing in seven years.

A Team in Transition

The dust had not completely settled on a disappointing 1974 baseball season before Mets general manager Bob Scheffing handed in his resignation. Scheffing, who had taken over the position as general manager upon the death of his predecessor, Johnny Murphy, after the miraculous 1969 season, had been talking about retiring for more than a year. The dismal failings of the defending National League champions did not do anything to encourage Scheffing to change his mind.

In his stead the Mets named their 45-year-old director of minor league operations, Joe McDonald, to the post. McDonald had been with the Mets since their inception in 1962, starting out as a statistician. He rapidly moved through the system, advancing to minor league assistant in 1963, administrative secretary in 1965, director of scouting in 1966, and on to director of minor league operations in 1968. In an otherwise undistinguished career, Joe McDonald had one accomplishment he could take credit for — he kept Jerry Koosman from being released from the Mets organization. As the story goes, three players named Jerry — Jerry Koosman, Jerry Johnson and Jerry Wilde — were involved in a motor vehicle accident on their way to spring training in early 1966. The threesome, against team regulations, decided to ride together in Koosman's car instead of flying. When Koosman needed $75 to avoid being put behind bars, McDonald advanced Koosman the money he needed to extricate himself from the jam. Later in spring training, Koosman was on the verge of being released, as many in the organization believed he was not a prospect. McDonald vetoed the release because Koosman still owed the team money. The rest is history, as Koosman developed into the best left-hander in team annals.

Based on McDonald's opening remarks upon being introduced as general manager, it was clear he wasn't going to stand pat. The Mets did just that after the 1973 season when they turned down an offer to trade George Stone and Craig Swan to the Astros for power-hitting center fielder Jimmy Wynn despite being in desperate need for both skill sets. In the traditional fashion of acquiring stars long past their prime, a la Duke Snider, Gil Hodges, and Warren Spahn, less than two weeks after ascending to the position of general manager, McDonald acquired Joe Torre from the St. Louis Cardinals in exchange for left-handed swingman Ray Sadecki, who was 8-8 for the Mets with a decent ERA of 3.41, and minor league pitcher Tommie Moore. While the Mets had coveted Torre for the longest of times, they were never able to pull the trigger on a deal because the asking price was always too high, namely one of the Mets' highly touted starting pitchers. The asking price for Torre went down significantly, however, when Torre's numbers began to significantly decline. The Cardinals also decided to hand the first base job to their hot prospect, Keith Hernandez. In a bit of irony, Sadecki's return to the Cardinals was one of coming full circle. In 1966 the Cardinals dealt Sadecki to the San Francisco Giants for Orlando Cepeda. Cepeda was then traded to the Atlanta Braves for Joe Torre. Now Torre was sent to the Mets for Sadecki, who was back where he started.

Although Torre had played first base for the Cardinals the last two seasons, the Mets planned on playing Torre at third, meaning Wayne Garrett would be relegated to the bench, a role the Mets always intended for him. Ironically, it was the Mets' dissatisfaction with Garrett as a regular third baseman that created their most glaring need, a center fielder. Not comfortable with the thought of Garrett being their regular third baseman, the Mets dealt promising rookie center fielder Amos Otis to the Kansas City Royals in exchange for third baseman Joy Foy. While Foy fizzled, Otis developed into one of the elite center fielders in the game.

With the acquisition of Joe Torre and the relegation of Wayne Garrett to the bench, Ken Boswell, who became a back-up infielder when the Mets acquired Felix Millan in the spring of 1973, became expendable. The same was true of veteran catcher Duffy Dyer, given that Torre could serve as an emergency catcher as well.

McDonald wasted no time dangling his trade bait. His first catch was speedy outfielder Gene Clines from the Pittsburgh Pirates, who was acquired in exchange for Duffy Dyer. Clines, who once stole 63 bases in a minor league season, swiped 14 out of 16 bases with the Pirates in 1974. While the Mets didn't intend for Clines to solve the center field problem, he did give the team more overall speed. The addition of speed was essential, because the Mets on any given day could roll out a lineup that consisted of four slow-moving vehicles in Staub, Torre, Kranepool and Grote.

A week later Boswell was gone, sent to the Astros for Bob Gallagher. In Gallagher, the Mets received a left-handed hitting outfielder whom the Astros used strictly as a defensive replacement. While Gallagher was devoid of any power, he hit well average-wise in three minor league seasons.

The Mets' brass headed to New Orleans for the annual winter meetings with their number one need, a prominent center fielder, unfulfilled. One deal that had previously fallen through would've sent Rusty Staub to the Giants for Bobby Bonds. The Giants, however, held out for Jon Matlack, killing the deal. The Mets' opportunity to acquire Bonds ended when he was sent to the Mets' cross-town rivals and their co-tenants, the New York Yankees, for Bobby Murcer. Staub's name was also mentioned in a deal that would've sent him to Baltimore for Paul Blair as well as one that would've sent him back to Montreal for Willie Davis. The Mets rejected the latter offer.

Rusty Staub admitted he was perturbed with his name constantly mentioned in trade rumors. "I've read where I was offered in trades to both the Giants and Orioles and it upsets me," said Staub, "because I don't want to be traded. I want to play for the Mets and I want the Mets' fans to see the kind of year Rusty Staub can really have."[1] Rumor had it that Staub raised the wrath of board chairman M. Donald Grant for his refusal to make the Mets' post-season trip to Japan with his teammates as part of baseball's goodwill mission. Three others who opposed the trip — Boswell, Sadecki, and Dyer — had already been dealt. Staub defended himself by saying, "I told Mr. Grant right from the start when the trip was proposed that I did not want to go. I had two very good reasons. First of all, I detest flying. Everyone knows that. I was not anxious to make a long trip to Japan. Secondly, I have very strong business interests with Land-Baron Investments in Houston and my presence there in the off-season is a part of the deal." The Mets also had an issue with Staub regarding his weight, which at times reached as high as 215 pounds. "I agree I have had some problems with my weight," Staub admitted. "After the 1973 season, I let myself get away. But it wasn't my weight that was a problem. When I pulled a hamstring in July, it wasn't because I was out of shape. It was because of the soft infield. I stepped in a hole rounding first and I pulled up lame. Ask anybody who ran or played on that infield and they'll tell what shape the infield was in."[2]

Another Mets player who figured prominently in trade rumors was Tug McGraw. McGraw's feelings about the potential of being dealt from the Mets mirrored those of Staub. If McGraw was looking for any reassurance from McDonald regarding his status, there was none forthcoming. "He's got grounds for questioning his status," said McDonald. "He didn't have a very good year." However, McDonald was not intent on trading McGraw due to his poor year. "I still regard Tug as a quality pitcher. I still regard him as the pitcher I saw the last six weeks of the '73 season."[3] Yet the bottom line remained if the Mets received a good offer for McGraw, he would be dealt. Already the rumor mill had McGraw headed to Boston for either Rick Miller or Juan Beniquez, or to Baltimore for Paul Blair.

Ultimately, it was McGraw who was traded in a six-player blockbuster deal with the Phillies that brought the Mets their center fielder they were so desperately seeking. The Mets sent McGraw along with outfielders Dave Schneck and Don Hahn to Philadelphia in return for center fielder Del Unser, one of the promising young catchers in the game, John Stearns, and left-handed reliever Mac Scarce. In announcing the deal McDonald commented, "Tug had a bad year in 1973, except for the last six weeks, and he wasn't so good in all of 1974. We hated to lose him, but you've got to give something to get some thing."[4]

"Joe called me at 6:00 this morning," said McGraw in California, "and told me they were trying to shake things up. I'm really disappointed but I expected it, either this year or next, because I've got eight years in the big leagues and in two more years I'd have the right to veto any deal." McGraw also admitted for the first time that he wasn't pitching at 100 percent in 1974. A torn muscle in his rib cage cramped his pitching style. "I should have waited for it to heal, but like a hard headed stubborn Irishman, I rushed it," McGraw said. "I kept trying to throw and my arm kept hurting. So I kept on changing my delivery, favoring it, worrying about your arm. You do that long enough and everything goes, including your confidence."[5]

With the most heavily traded Mets team assembled in St. Petersburg for the start of spring training, McDonald pulled off his seventh and perhaps biggest deal. McDonald announced that the Mets purchased the contract of slugger Dave Kingman from the San Francisco Giants for approximately $125,000. Kingman, at 26 years old and less than four full years in the majors under his belt, already had 77 home runs to his credit. Among them was a mammoth blast of Mets left-hander Jerry Koosman that completely cleared Shea Stadium and crashed against the Giants' team bus one August afternoon in Kingman's 1971 rookie season.

Where Kingman would play was another question. Kingman, never known for his leather, had played third, first and the outfield in his brief career. However, the Mets already had Joe Torre, who could play both first and third, and John Milner and Ed Kranepool, who played the outfield as well as first base.

As a result of McDonald's wheeling and dealing, the Mets were a radically different team that graced the home dugout at Shea Stadium on April 8, as they prepared to begin the 1975 season against the Philadelphia Phillies. While the Mets, never known for their offensive prowess, had potentially the best hitting lineup in the history of the organization, for the first time in recent memory there were serious questions about the pitching staff. Despite still having the best three front-line pitchers in baseball with Seaver, Koosman and Matlack, the back of the Mets' rotation was suspect. The fourth spot in the rotation went to Randy Tate, a rookie who had yet to show he could harness his great stuff. Hank Webb, who'll always be remembered by Mets fans as the losing pitcher in the marathon 25-inning game against the Cardinals in September 1974, was slated to be the fifth starter when the schedule demanded it. George Stone, who was penciled in as the fourth starter when training camp opened, hasn't thrown a pitch in a game since August 1974. Stone had to be shut down after his first throwing session of the spring, and had shown no improvement from his season-ending injury. Stone was subsequently placed on the disabled list, with the Mets no longer counting on the pitcher.

The biggest question mark remained the bullpen. With Tug McGraw sitting in the other dugout and his designated replacement, Bob Apodaca, back in Florida on the disabled list with an inflamed elbow, Harry Parker was the only veteran to reside in the bullpen at the start of the season. Two rookie right-handers Rick Baldwin and Jerry Cram, would complement Parker. Mac Scarce, acquired in the McGraw trade, would be the only left-hander working in relief.

For the third straight year Tom Seaver faced off against the ace of the Phillies' staff, Steve Carlton. While two seasons earlier Seaver hurled a shutout with the help of the bat of Cleon Jones as the Mets downed the Phillies, 3–0, the 1974 season saw the Mets get shocked when Tug McGraw allowed a ninth-inning two-run homer to the 1974 NL Rookie of the Year, Mike Schmidt. With Mike Schmidt joining Greg Luzinski and Willie Montanez as legitimate power hitters and Larry Bowa, Bob Boone developing as stars in the National League, the Phillies were rapidly becoming a force to be reckoned with in the Eastern Division. In the meantime, the Mets' lineup contained an all-new starting out-field as Gene Clines opened in right field, subbing for Rusty Staub, who was nursing a thigh injury, and Dave Kingman resided in left field, the customary position of Cleon Jones, who was left in Florida when he failed to adequately recover from off-season knee surgery.

The game turned out to be a classic pitching duel between Seaver and Carlton. The Phillies scored the first run of the new season in the top of the third inning. Dave Kingman showed why he was considered a defensive liability when he allowed a drive hit off the bat of Dave Cash to bounce off his glove, enabling Bob Boone to score from first. An inning later Kingman demonstrated his devastating raw power by redirecting a Carlton pitch over the left field fence to draw the Mets even, 1–1.

With Seaver showing no ill effects from his injury-plagued 1974 campaign and Carlton just as dominating, the game headed to the bottom of the ninth still tied, 1–1. Felix Millan led off with a single to the opposite field; John Milner followed with a walk. With the winning run only one hundred eighty feet away, the more than 18,000 fans on their feet, and the rhythmic chanting of "Let's Go Mets!" reaching a crescendo, Joe Torre stepped in to the batter's box. After Torre worked the count to 2–0, he ripped a knee-high fastball into left field to score Millan, who outraced Luzinski's throw to the plate, sending the already frenzied crowd home euphoric.

Any leftover euphoria dissipated very quickly the next day, however, after the Mets lost the second game of the series in eleven innings, 3–2.

With the Mets sharing their home with their cross-town rivals for the second consecutive season while Yankee Stadium was being renovated, the Mets hit the road for a trip that took them to Pittsburgh, Philadelphia and St. Louis. The opener of the series saw Mets starter Jerry Koosman, who led New York in victories in 1974 with fifteen, have the unenviable task of taking on the dangerous Pirate lineup, which featured the likes of Willie Stargell, Dave Parker, Al Oliver, Richie Zisk and Richie Hebner. Koosman held the big bats at bay through the first eight innings as the Mets built a three-run lead thanks to the punch provided by the new arrivals. Kingman hit a home run in the fourth,

Four new faces graced the Mets' 1975 Opening Day lineup. Clockwise from top right: Joe Torre, Gene Clines, Dave Kingman and Del Unser (© Bettmann/Corbis).

Torre followed with an RBI double in the fifth, and Unser clubbed a home run in the eighth.

With a good portion of the over 43,000 fans starting to head for the exits, Koosman took the mound for the ninth. Three scratch singles later and Koosman's shutout was gone. Berra turned to Rick Baldwin in an attempt to put out the fire. Baldwin immediately added kerosene to the blaze by walking his first batter. After a fly out, Baldwin induced Rennie Stennett to hit a grounder up the middle. On natural grass it would have been a routine double play to end the game. Instead, the ball took an Astroturf hop over Baldwin's head into center field, scoring two runs to tie the game and deprive Koosman of his win. In an attempt to salvage the game, Berra then turned to his only lefty in the bullpen, Mac Scarce, to face left-handed power hitter Richie Hebner. The strategy backfired when Hebner smashed a single off Scarce, scoring Paul Popovich with the winning run.

Koosman, who was deprived of a twenty-win season in 1974 when the bullpen failed to hold leads on at least five occasions, was disappointed but upbeat. "It's just a shame when you go out there with a shutout to get three more outs and you don't win the game. It hurts, but it won't let us down."[6]

After a rare Saturday off-day to allow for an open date in case the Pirates' Friday night home opener was rained out, Tom Seaver took to the hill for the Mets in the second game of a short two-game series. For the third game in a row, the Mets lost in large part because of the failure of the bullpen. With the Mets trailing 3–2 at the end of six innings and Tom Seaver getting stronger as the game progressed, Berra elected to call on Ed Kranepool to pinch-hit for Seaver in the seventh inning with the tying run on base. When Ed Kranepool popped up, stranding the tying run, the responsibility fell on the shoulders of Harry Parker to hold the Pirates to a one-run lead. It took just one batter for Parker to fail in his responsibilities when he allowed a lead-off home run to Rennie Stennett. By the time the inning was over, the Mets were trailing by three runs.

After Rusty Staub hit what would've otherwise been a game-tying home run in the eighth, Berra was subject to second-guessing from both Seaver and many in the media. Yogi defended himself by saying, "If there wasn't a man in scoring position I probably would've left him in."[7] Yogi Berra was wont to say "if you ain't got a bullpen, you ain't got nuthin." After losing four consecutive games due to failures of the relief corps, it was clear the Mets had no bullpen. With this in mind, the Mets were fortunate when veteran left-hander Tom Hall of the Cincinnati Reds became available when the Reds had to clear roster space for Dan Driessen. In return for Hall, New York sent Mac Scarce, whose Mets career consisted of two pitches, back to the Reds.

"He gives us a guy who has pitched over 700 innings in the majors, who has one of the best strikeout ratios in the majors," said Joe McDonald, who made the deal after it became obvious the Mets could not continue operating with the bodies they had in the bullpen.[8]

Hall was immediately thrown into battle as the Mets opened a short two-game series in St. Louis. Hall faced six batters and retired them all, but the Mets still lost their fifth consecutive game. This time the culprits were a lack of clutch hitting and, uncharacteristically, errors by the usually sure-handed Buddy Harrelson and Felix Millan, allowing the Cardinals to score three runs in the fifth.

The Mets salvaged the final game of the series and the road trip when the new offense finally got itself going as New York pummeled the Cardinals, 14–7, while scoring six runs in the first inning. Jerry Koosman, apparently not used to such largesse, promptly surrendered four runs and was gone by the second inning. Rick Baldwin, with 5⅔ innings of relief, picked up his first major league win.

The Mets returned home with their tails between their legs after having lost five of their first seven games to start a homestand with the Cubs, Cardinals and Expos. But being back on their own friendly turf didn't help in the opener as the Cubs beat Tom Seaver, 4–2. The only good news to come out on this day was the reactivation of Bob Apodaca, who was desperately needed in the Mets' bullpen.

A Saturday rainout forced a Sunday afternoon doubleheader, and if there ever was a doubleheader the Mets could ill-afford to lose so early in the season, this was it. A doubleheader sweep by the Cubs would leave the Mets seven games behind league-leading Chicago. The Mets, who lost eleven doubleheaders in 1974, were struggling along with a 2-7 record, suffering from the same maladies they encountered the previous season, namely a lack of clutch hitting and shoddy relief pitching.

In the first game the Mets staked starter Matlack to an early 7–0 lead on the strength of doubles by Millan and Kranepool, a triple by Garrett, and a home run by utility shortstop Jack Heidemann.

The Mets, who never seemed to do things the easy way, had to hang on for dear life as the Cubs began chipping away, scoring two runs in the third and three in the fifth. With the Mets leading 8–5 in the eighth and the Cubs' potential tying run at the plate, Berra called on Apodaca, just off the disabled list, who was able to end the threat with only one run scoring. Apodaca picked up his first save of the year when he easily set the Cubs down in the ninth inning.

In the second game, home runs by Grote and Kingman, the latter a towering blast over the center field fence, staked the Mets to a 4–0 lead. Tate and Baldwin combined to shut out the Cubs for the first eight innings. With the Mets only one out away from their doubleheader sweep, New York fans had their hearts in their mouths as the Cubs loaded the bases in the ninth off Rick Baldwin. A routine single by Jose Cardenal was then misplayed into a triple by Kingman, scoring all three Cubs and leaving the tying run only ninety feet away with the dangerous Bill Madlock at the plate. Mets fans, firmly believing that another game was about to be gift-wrapped and given away on a silver platter, were able to exhale as Baldwin induced Madlock to fly out to end the game and give New York a much-needed sweep.

Fresh off their doubleheader sweep over the Cubs, the Mets kept their momentum going by crushing the Cardinals, 9–5, behind Jerry Koosman's 165-pitch complete game. While it may not have been pretty, it was good enough for Koosman to pick up his first victory of the season. Koosman allowed five runs on nine hits, but the new Met offense pounded Cardinal pitching for nine runs and thirteen hits. While the Mets were encouraged by Koosman's nine strikeouts, they still had to be somewhat concerned that the left-hander had allowed 28 hits and 12 runs in his last two starts.

The next afternoon Bob Gibson and Tom Seaver faced one another for the eleventh time in their careers. What started as a classic pitching duel ended in a Mets romp. The thirty-nine-year-old Gibson, who had announced his retirement effective at season's end, took a 1–0 lead into the bottom of the fifth. In the last half of the fifth, however, Gibson began to show his age. Singles by Heidemann and Grote and a groundout by Seaver put Mets runners on second and third with one out. Gibson proceeded to walk Garrett unintentionally, followed by a Millan double to bring home two runs and give the Mets a 2–1 lead. The Cardinals then intentionally walked the left-handed batting Unser to set up a possible double play with the slow-footed Staub at-bat. The strategy, while sensible, backfired miserably, as Staub drove Gibson's first pitch into the right field

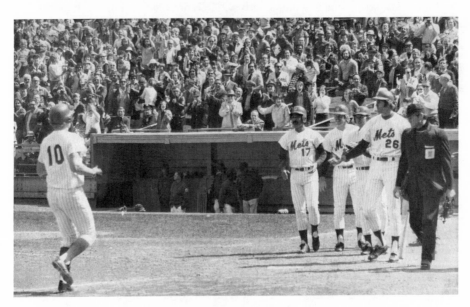

Rusty Staub is congratulated by Felix Millan, Wayne Garrett, Del Unser and Dave Kingman after hitting a grand slam home run off the Cardinals' Bob Gibson in a 7–1 Mets win (*New York Times*).

bullpen. For Staub it was the sixth grand slam of his career, and the Mets had a 6–1 lead. A seventh-inning homer by Unser off Al Hrabosky accounted for the Mets' final run in a 7–1 win. Seaver was in vintage form, allowing one run and four hits while fanning seven on his way to his second victory of the season.

The bats continued to pound and the Mets continued to win. The Mets won seven consecutive games before being stopped in Chicago by the Cubs, 7–4, on the last day of April. With the loss the Mets ended the month tied for second place with the Pittsburgh Pirates with a 9-7 record, 2½ games behind the surprising Chicago Cubs. After losing the finale of the series with the Cubs, it was back home for the Mets to start a twelve-game homestand that would see New York take on the Montreal Expos, Pittsburgh Pirates, Cincinnati Reds and San Francisco Giants.

Jerry Koosman drew the opening assignment of the homestand. Entering the game with a team-high ERA of 7.04, the left-hander knew it was time to bear down. And bear down he did, blanking the Expos on four hits and allowing a runner to get as far as third base only once. That occurred in the first, when Pepe Mangual led the game off with a single, moved to second on an infield out and stole third. Koosman stranded Mangual by fanning Bob Bailey for the third out.

With his best outing since his first start of the season, when he took a shutout into the ninth inning before watching the bullpen blow the game, Koosman was all smiles after the game. Said the pitcher, "I was really trying just to concentrate. I was out there to slow down my pace and not throw the pitches so quickly."[9]

The Mets' powerful new bats, responsible in large part for the first 10 wins, suddenly went into hibernation the next day when close to 40,000 fans showed up to watch the old man of the Expos, 35-year-old left-hander Woodie Fryman, stop the Mets on one hit. It was the third consecutive shutout for Fryman, who set an Expo record with 30⅔ consecutive scoreless innings. The rookie catcher, John Stearns, accounted for the Mets' only hit, a two-out double in the fifth. For the first time in the young season, Berra had turned to his fifth starter, Hank Webb. Webb, despite pitching exceptionally well, allowing only two runs in seven innings, was saddled with the tough loss.

The sleeping bats continued to slumber as the Mets lost their next five games, getting swept by the Pirates and then losing the first two games of their series with the Reds. With the Mets sitting on a six-game losing streak, memories of their recent seven-game winning streak were fading very quickly.

The Mets turned to their stopper, Seaver, in the hopes of ending their losing ways. One batter into the game, the prospects didn't seem to be bright, as Pete Rose led the contest off with a home run. The chances looked even less rosy at the end of the inning as the Reds managed to tack on a second run. The Mets cut the deficit in half in the bottom of the second inning, with John

Milner smashing his third home run of the year, and tied the game when Milner grounded out for an RBI in the fourth.

The Mets finally caught their long-awaited break. With Seaver cruising along after allowing two runs in the first, the Reds came to bat in the top half of the eighth inning. Seaver, who had not walked a batter in the first seven innings, issued his first base on balls to Pete Rose leading off. The next batter, Ken Griffey, drilled the ball to the wall in left-center field. With Rose racing around the bases, Del Unser picked up the ball and sent it in to relay man Mike Phillips.[10] Phillips fired a strike home to catcher Jerry Grote, who applied the tag. In a very close play, Rose was ruled out by umpire John Kibler, keeping the 2–2 tie intact. Rose, who didn't argue, did say after the game, "I'm not being derogatory of the umpire, but I think if he called me safe, I don't know if Grote would've argued."[11]

As the late Bob Murphy loved to say, "How many times after a fielder makes a great play does he get to lead off the next inning?" Mike Phillips opened the bottom of the eighth with a base hit. With Phillips at first, Millan attempted to sacrifice, laying one down in front of Reds catcher Johnny Bench. Bench's throw hit Millan, who was ruled to be out of the base line; as a result, Millan

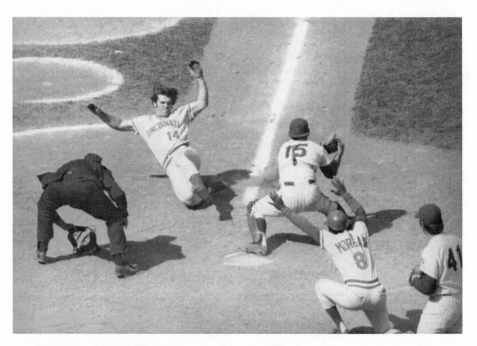

Pete Rose is about to be tagged out by Jerry Grote at the plate courtesy of great throws by Del Unser and Mike Phillips. The play was crucial in keeping a 2–2 tie intact in a game the Mets eventually won, snapping a seven-game losing streak (© Bettmann/ Corbis).

was called out and Phillips was returned to first. The Mets were only temporarily denied as Del Unser singled, putting runners on first and second. Sparky Anderson went to his pen to bring Will McEnaney in to face Staub. The moved backfired as Staub singled home Phillips with what proved to be the winning run.

Bobby Murcer and the Giants followed the Reds into Shea for a three-game series. The Mets won the first game on a double by Joe Torre with the bases loaded. Torre had been struggling with a .182 batting average and only five runs batted in. "Those are Joe Torre's first runs batted in, in 10 games," announced the press box. "With men on, that's when I'm supposed to hit it," said Torre. "The other night I got three hits. But none of them came with men on base. If I don't hit with men on base, I'm not paying my dues. They didn't get me for my glove or to hit .300. They got me to drive in runs." Torre was off to such a slow start he actually made an appointment with a doctor to have his eyes examined. He wasn't seeing the ball the way he expected to. "But in the last few games I've been more patient at the plate. I felt it coming in the middle of a game against Pittsburgh," said Torre. "I hit the ball good but right to someone." Before Torre's big hit, he hit the ball hard twice off Giants starter Jim Barr but had nothing to show for it. Torre continued talking about his big hit. "When the kid (meaning reliever Gary Lavelle) threw me two balls with the bases loaded, I knew he had to come over the plate with a fastball. There was no place to put me. And he did. It was a sinking fastball and I smoked it. It was a good feeling."[12]

Bobby Murcer, who made his first appearance back in New York since being dealt by the Yankees for Bobby Bonds, went hitless against Mets pitching. "It would be something if I hit a few homers here, but don't count on it with Matlack and Koosman pitching," said Murcer. "I'll settle for some bleeders."[13]

After rain washed out the middle game of the series, Jerry Koosman ended the homestand the same way he started it, by shutting down the Giants, 5–1, with Kingman and Staub combining for all five Mets RBIs. In this rollercoaster season, the Mets had a three-game winning streak, which followed a six-game losing string, which followed a seven-game winning streak, which followed a five-game losing streak. The Mets also found themselves with a public relations problem after Cleon Jones, who was left behind in Florida to rehabilitate his injured knee, was arrested after police found him sleeping in a compromised position with an unidentified female companion. While the charges were dropped, Jones was fined a record $2,000 and forced to publicly apologize at a press conference with his wife, Angela, at his side.

The Mets extended their winning streak to five games after taking the first two games of their road trip, which began in Houston and would continue on to Cincinnati and Atlanta. In the opener Rusty Staub and Dave Kingman hit home runs as the Mets and Seaver trounced the Astros. A five-run seventh inning in the middle game allowed the Mets to keep their streak intact. However, the streak was snapped after the Astros avenged their beatings by trouncing the Mets in the series finale.

It wasn't until the Mets reached Cincinnati on May 20 that Joe Torre produced the way the Mets anticipated that he would. Torre went 4-for-5 including his first Met home run and two doubles while driving in three runs, to back the seven-hit pitching of Jerry Koosman as the Mets defeated the Reds, 6–2, in the opener of the series. Koosman, after being hit hard early in the season, improved his record to 4–1 with the win. Rusty Staub, who was batting over .300 and leading the Mets in RBIs, knocked in two of the runs. With Rusty consistently being mentioned over the winter in trade rumors, the famous baseball saying, "Some of the best deals are the ones you don't make," certainly applied to Staub.

"The one thing I had to convince people here was that I didn't want to be traded," said Staub. "There was a bad quote in the middle of September last year claiming that I wanted to go back to Montreal. I never said that. But I was worried I would be. After the winter meetings in New Orleans last December, I personally thanked Joe McDonald and Donald Grant for not trading me. I did make Yogi one promise. That I would be truthful with him and that I would not play if I were hurt. I made that mistake last September. I jammed my hand sliding into second base against Atlanta. I played even though I was hurt. But we had so many guys out with injuries (Harrelson, Grote and Jones), I didn't think it was best for my team to have Benny Ayala playing right field. So I played and it was a mistake. I know that now. I still hope to play every day, and as long as I'm healthy I will. The way I feel, I think I can have the kind of year the Mets expect of me."[14] After losing the second game of the series to the Reds, the Mets moved on to Atlanta, where they took two out of three from the Braves before returning home to take on the Los Angeles Dodgers, San Diego Padres, Houston Astros and Atlanta Braves.

The Mets got their homestand off on the right foot as Seaver, who was coming off his worst outing of the season when the Reds manhandled him in Cincinnati, faced Andy Messersmith, who came into the game with a 7-0 record and a 1.96 ERA. With the game tied at three in the last of the ninth inning with one out, Mike Phillips lashed a triple just beyond the reach of center fielder Jimmy Wynn. After Grote was intentionally walked to set up the possible double play, Yogi Berra called on Wayne Garrett, who was suffering from tendonitis on his left ankle, to bat for Seaver. Garrett launched Messersmith's second pitch into the right field stands for a game-winning three-run homer.

In the second game of the series, the Dodgers crushed the Mets and Harry Parker, who received a rare starting assignment, 10-4. Even worse news for the Mets was the fact that Bud Harrelson was suffering from torn cartilage in his right knee, which would require surgery and in all likelihood cost him the rest of the season. The bad news was partially mitigated by the fine play of Mike

Phillips, who was picked up on waivers from the Giants after San Francisco figured he couldn't replace Chris Speier. But Phillips earned raves from his teammates in the short time he was a Met. "Anything he can get to he's going to make the play," said Jon Matlack. "He gets more velocity on the ball just letting it go than a lot of guys do if they wind up," said Ed Kranepool. "He's the future of the franchise," said Bud Harrelson before undergoing surgery. "If I didn't know he would be around, I wouldn't have agreed to the operation at this time. But from what I've seen of Mike, he could do the job."[15] The bad medical news wasn't limited to Harrelson as Wayne Garrett was diagnosed with an infection of the ankle joints, which would sideline him for at least a week. If there was any silver lining, it was the Mets activating Cleon Jones, who successfully pinch-hit in his first at-bat of the season.

Jon Matlack picked up his sixth win of the season in the series finale with the Dodgers as the Mets scored an eighth-inning run to down Los Angeles, 4–3. Next into Shea Stadium came the San Diego Padres, with whom the Mets had less success with than the Dodgers. Jerry Koosman lost to Randy Jones in the opener of a weekend series. With the game tied 2–2 in the eighth inning and the bases full of Padres, Apodaca replaced Koosman on the mound and immediately surrendered a grand slam home run to Willie McCovey. Only Tom Seaver had any luck with the Padres, as the Mets sent San Diego down to a 7–2 defeat in the middle game of the series. With the win Seaver took over the team lead in victories with seven. After the club's offense overexerted themselves with 17 hits in their 7–2 victory, the Mets' hitting attack was nonexistent in the rubber game of the series, as Alan Foster and ex–Met Danny Frisella combined to shut out New York. Despite a fine outing, rookie Randy Tate was saddled with his fourth loss of the year.

The starting pitching, considered the best in all of baseball, showed why when the next opponents, the Houston Astros, came in for a four-game series, which the Mets swept. In the opener Jon Matlack held the Astros to four hits as he shut the Astros out, 2–0. It was only in the middle game of the series, which was started by Tom Hall, that the Astros were able to score more than one run, as the Mets beat the Astros, 4–3.

Despite stranding 13 base runners in the third game of the series, the one run the Mets were able to push across the plate was enough, as Jerry Koosman, en route to his 99th major league win, shut out the Astros, 1–0. Koosman also received defensive help from Cleon Jones, recently recalled from the disabled list, when he threw out Tommy Helms at the plate from left field. "The biggest play of the game was Cleon's," said Koosman. "He charged the ball and made a perfect throw."[16] The Mets continued to roll in the finale of the series, when Tom Seaver allowed only run in a complete-game effort. Seaver flirted with trouble in the ninth inning when he surrendered base hits to Bob Watson and Jose Cruz, but struck out Doug Rader to end the game. "I felt real good at the end," said Seaver.[17]

Despite losing the first two games to their next opponent, the Braves, the Mets were able to finish a winning homestand by beating Atlanta, in fourteen innings in the final game of the long homestand. In a wild affair, the Mets had to come back from 5–2 and 6–5 deficits to send the game into extra innings, where they were finally gift-wrapped with a victory, courtesy of the Braves' defense. Joe Torre, who had hit in 15 consecutive games, contributed four hits, including a triple, and played a large role in the sequence of events that allowed the Mets to score the winning run. With Millan on first base, Torre lifted a pop fly to right-center, which was dropped by Braves center fielder Cito Gaston, sending Millan to third and Torre to second. Moments later, a wild pitch by Braves reliever Elias Sosa sent Millan home with the winning run. For Hank Webb, the winner in relief, it was his first major league win. The Mets' relief corps suffered a scare in the eighth inning when Harry Parker took a Dave May line drive off his knee and had to be removed on a stretcher. However, Parker was diagnosed with only contusions of his left knee and was listed as day-to-day.

With the long and successful homestand behind them, the Mets prepared themselves for a road trip that would take them to California to take on the Giants, Dodgers and Padres and then cross-country to Montreal before returning home.

So close, yet so far. Jerry Koosman was one good throw to second and then one strike away from winning his 100th major league game. With one out in the ninth during the opening game of the road trip at Candlestick Park, the Mets held a 4–1 lead over the Giants when Koosman surrendered a base hit to Gary Thomasson. Koosman, however, induced the next batter, Derrel Thomas, to bounce a ball back to the mound for what seemed to be a game-ending double play. In his haste, Koosman threw low to second, and all runners were safe. Bobby Murcer flied out for the second out before Koosman ran the count to 1–2 on Chris Speier. Speier proceeded to single to left to score the second Giants run. Willie Montanez, recently acquired from the Phillies, followed with another single to left. When left fielder Bob Gallagher, who entered the game for defense, let the ball get behind him, another two runs scored and the game was tied. Bob Apodaca relieved Koosman and immediately surrendered a base hit to his first batter, Bruce Miller, for the game-winning hit. So instead of celebrating his 100th win, Koosman instead was saddled with his fourth loss of the year. It was the second time during the season that Koosman took a lead into the ninth and failed to walk away with a win.

Tom Seaver was in his typical form, as he stopped the Giants on six hits while striking out nine, including the last four of the game, en route to his ninth victory and first shutout of the season, as the Mets blanked the Giants in the series finale. Despite the Mets' nine hits and four doubles, one New Yorker who went hitless was Joe Torre, who saw his 16-game hitting streak come to a halt. Torre, who was batting around .280, couldn't get his average above .200

during the first six weeks of the season. "I'm not as bad as the .150 I was hitting and I'm not as good as the .360 I once hit," said Torre. "Right now I'll settle for something around .280 and 85 or 90 RBIs. For years, there have been rumors of me coming back to play in New York. First when I was with the Braves and later with the Cardinals. I was much younger when all these rumors started. Now that I'm finally playing in New York, I'm 34. I still have the same desire to do well, but I'm not the young man I used to be. I have my days when I feel well and days when I don't. It's not easy coming out and playing a day game after a night game. The important thing now is that I'm physically as good as I can be. Confidence is so important. This streak I've been on only helps restore it. I feel I've got my stroke back."[18] Torre admitted he could not play everyday and would need occasional help from Wayne Garrett at third. In a personnel move, the Mets announced after the game that Wayne Garrett had been reactivated and Bob Gallagher, who made a key error in the previous game, was optioned to the minors.

The Mets headed on to beautiful Dodger Stadium, where better than 40,000 fans showed up as Doug Rau and Randy Tate were locked in a classic pitching duel. The Dodgers scored their first and only run in the second inning on a sacrifice fly by Joe Ferguson. Doug Rau, the Dodgers' starter, was able to keep the Mets off the scoreboard until the eighth inning. With John Stearns at first and one out, Jesus Alou, who continued to excel as a right-handed bat off the bench, pinch-hit for Tate and doubled to score Stearns and tie the game at 1–1. Dodgers manager Walter Alston replaced Rau with his ace, Mike Marshall, who got out of a two-out, bases-loaded jam by inducing Torre to ground out. Marshall was not as fortunate in the ninth inning, as he walked Staub to lead off the frame. A wild pitch moved Staub to second, who scored two outs later with what proved to be the winning run when Mike Phillips singled him home. Tate, who pitched his best game of the year, was replaced by Apodaca, the eventual winning pitcher, who retired all six batters he faced, including strikeouts of the last two batters, Steve Garvey and Willie Crawford.

For the third night in a row, the Mets received fabulous pitching as Jon Matlack pitched a complete-game, three-hit shutout in a 2–0 whitewashing of the Dodgers. The game remained scoreless until the sixth inning when the Mets struck on back-to-back doubles by Wayne Garrett and Felix Millan. The Mets scored an insurance run in the eighth on a Garrett single and another double by Millan.

With the rare sweep of the Dodgers in their home park, New York continued on to San Diego while trailing the division-leading Pirates by only one-half game. Even better was the news that the already strong pitching would be bolstered by George Stone, who was reactivated to start the opener of the series against the Padres after not appearing in a game since July 30, 1974, due to a tear in his rotator cuff.

Stone didn't disappoint by pitching seven fabulous innings. He allowed the Padres only one first-inning run as the Mets won their fourth consecutive game on their road trip. The Mets, who had been able to survive of late on great pitching while the offense was relatively quiet, exploded for seven runs on seventeen hits off a quartet of Padres pitchers.

Jerry Koosman's bid for his 100th big league victory had to be postponed for another day after a poor performance snapped the Mets' winning streak at four. The Mets actually led 1–0 after an inning and a half, and with Koosman beginning the game with a flourish by fanning four of the first five batters he faced, things were looking up. But Koosman surrendered five runs over the next three innings, and the Mets fell, 7–1.

The Mets were able to recover, however, and take the series from the Padres behind Tom Seaver's 10th win. Tom Seaver threw his second consecutive shutout while lowering his ERA to a league-leading 1.82. For six innings, Seaver was matched by his mound opponent and former teammate Brent Strom. The Mets broke the scoreless deadlock in the seventh inning when Del Unser singled, moved to third on a double by John Stearns, and scored when shortstop Enzo Hernandez booted Tom Seaver's grounder. The Mets broke the game open in the ninth when they scored five runs.

Seaver, off to a spectacular start, in large part attributed his success to finally developing a change-up, a pitch he didn't have during his first nine years in the majors. The pitch did not come easy, but with a lot of hard work he finally had what he considered a most unorthodox change. Seaver explained, "Unorthodox in that the way I hold it is different than any other pitcher. I couldn't conceive going out and showing it to a young pitcher and telling him this is the way to grip the ball. But I tried all the other ways and I just couldn't develop one. It was the way I threw my fastball that made it difficult to develop one. A couple of years ago, Ray Sadecki told me I would have difficulty coming up with one because of the way I threw. Ray was very perceptive that way."[19]

Seaver began experimenting and worked hard on his change-up in 1974. He finally got to the point where he could throw it safely and with confidence 10 to 20 times a game. "It makes a heckuva difference," Seaver said. "They have never seen me with this pitch before, so it gives me something extra they're not looking for." With Seaver throwing more change-ups and fewer fastballs, it naturally reduced his amount of strikeouts. To date, Seaver had yet to have a 10-strikeout game after entering the season with 52 in his career. "I don't think I realized how hard I threw in those days," said Seaver. "But right now I'm in a transition stage. I am 30 years old and I don't have the zip I used to have two days after a start. Now it takes three to four to feel right again. It's definitely the age factor." Seaver still believed, however, that the strikeouts would come and he would have occasional games where he fanned 10 or more batters in a game, albeit with less frequency. Already the only National League pitcher in history to strike out 200 or more batters in seven consecutive seasons, he foresaw that record being extended to eight. He had averaged six per game in 1975, and if he maintained that average over 35 anticipated starts, he would have 210 for the season.

After ending the California portion of the road trip with a highly successful 5–2 mark, the Mets headed to the final destination, Montreal, once again only one-half game out of first place. The biggest crowd of the season for the Expos, 21,710 fans, showed up to watch the Mets take on Montreal in a twilight doubleheader. The Mets began the evening quickly by scoring four runs in their first at-bat off Expos starter Don Stanhouse.

The Expos, however, immediately cut their deficit in half in their first at-bat. Each team added a run in the fourth, giving the Mets a 5–3 lead. However, the game turned in the fifth when Jose Morales and Bob Bailey singled again and a young catcher named Gary Carter crushed a Matlack pitch over the left field fence, giving the Expos the lead for good. For Matlack, it was his fifth loss against eight wins.

The second game saw Randy Tate take on the ace of the Expos' staff, Steve Rogers. While Tate pitched very nicely, allowing only two runs in six innings, his counterpart surrendered nothing during the first six innings. However, the Mets got Tate off the hook in the seventh inning when Kranepool and Phillips singled, and with two outs, Berra turned to his number one pinch-hitter, Jesus Alou, who had converted seven of his first twelve opportunities. Alou once again came through as he singled home the tying runs.

With neither team scoring any further through the tenth inning, the Mets came to bat in the eleventh against reliever Chuck Taylor. Taylor started off impressively by striking out the two tough Mets left-handed bats, Staub and Kranepool. However, he got in trouble by walking the third tough left-hander, John Milner, and Mike Phillips followed with a triple off the right field wall to score Milner. A couple more walks and a Wayne Garrett single plated another two runs, giving the Mets a 5–2 lead. Harry Parker, the winner in relief, retired the Expos in order in the eleventh inning to give the Mets a split of the long evening.

While the next day the Mets were gratified by George Stone's second consecutive good start, there could be nothing but disappointment with the end result, as the Mets' bullpen blew a three-run lead and lost to the Expos in ten innings. The game — a seesaw affair throughout — saw the Mets go on top 6–3 in the top of the eighth inning. However, reliever Tom Hall surrendered an eighth-inning home run to Bob Bailey and a two-run single to Gary Carter in the ninth, sending the contest into extra innings for the second consecutive game.

After the Mets failed to score in the tenth, Apodaca took the mound for the bottom of the inning but was not effective. Newly acquired Nate Colbert led off the inning with a booming double and scored the winning run on a single to right by Pete Mackanin.

The finale of the road trip, another nail-biter, took thirteen innings before Gary Carter once again inflicted his punishment by sending the Mets once again down to defeat. In a pitching matchup that pitted two crafty veteran left-handers, Jerry Koosman and Woodie Fryman, the game remained scoreless through the first four innings. The Mets broke through off Fryman in the fifth when Kingman slammed his ninth home run of the year. The Mets extended their lead to 2–0 in the sixth when Koosman doubled and scored on a single by Felix Millan. In the last of the sixth, the Expos cut the lead to 2–1 when Barry Foote hit his second home run of the year. The Expos tied the game in the eighth when Koosman walked Mackanin, who advanced to second on a wild pitch and scored on a bloop double by Larry Parrish. Koosman continued pitching through the tenth, but the Mets were not able to push across another run for him. Two innings later, a Gary Carter single off Rick Baldwin finished the Mets. For Koosman, it was his third consecutive attempt at the elusive 100th career win. Commenting after the game about his failure to secure his 100th win, Koosman said, "I don't think about 100 wins as any kind of milestone. To me, a milestone is 20 wins a season, or 100 strikeouts, something that helps a team."[20]

The Mets returned home on June 20 after a disappointing 6–5 road trip. It was disappointing because the team went 5–2 on the difficult part of the trip, but only 1–3 in Montreal, traditionally a venue where the Mets did fairly well. Even more disappointing was the fact that each loss was by only one run, and with a break here and there, the Mets could have easily swept the series.

The homecoming was anything but pleasant as the Mets took on the league-leading and defending National League East champion Pittsburgh Pirates. Over 47,000 fans entered Shea Stadium to welcome the Mets home and watch Tom Seaver take on the Pirates' promising rookie left-hander John Candelaria. For the first eight innings, the patrons were treated to a good old-fashioned pitching duel. The rookie matched the veteran goose egg for goose egg for the first six innings, as the game remained scoreless. In the seventh, the deadlock was broken when Willie Stargell deposited a Seaver pitch into the Mets' bullpen. The home run was significant, not only because it gave the Pirates a 1–0 lead, but it was also number 358 of Stargell's career, tying him with Mets manager Yogi Berra for 26th on the all-time home run list. It was also Stargell's 49th home run against the Mets, the most any one player had hit against the team.

The Mets got the run back in the last of the eighth when John Stearns lined a one-out single and moved to third on another successful pinch-hitting appearance by Jesus Alou. Jack Heidemann, batting for Seaver, brought Stearns home with a sacrifice fly to left field. However, the evening was ruined for the 47,000 New York fans when the Mets' bullpen took over in the ninth. Tom Hall was the first of the culprits, allowing consecutive singles to Stargell, Dave Parker and Zisk, for the go-ahead run. With no outs and runners on first and second, Apodaca relieved Hall and immediately loaded the bases by allowing a base hit to catcher Manny Sanguillen. Apodaca made things interesting for a while as he struck out Ed Kirkpatrick and pitcher John Candelaria. With the bases loaded and two outs, Rennie Stennett stepped to the plate. If Apodaca retired Stennett, the Mets would bat in the ninth trailing by only one run. Stennett, however, got Apodaca for a bases-clearing triple, putting the game out of reach.

The Mets appeared to have the second game of the series well in hand, scoring three runs before anyone was out in the bottom of the first. Pirates starter Bruce Kison pitched to five batters, walked the first two, gave up three singles to the next three batters—good for three runs—and was given the rest of the day off. A quartet of Pirates relievers—Sam McDowell, Larry Demery, Ramon Hernandez, the eventual winner, and Dave Guisti—held the Mets scoreless the rest of the way. Contrary to his counterpart Bruce Kison, Mets starter Jon Matlack kept the Pirates off the scoreboard for the first six innings. But the tide of the game changed in the seventh inning when Richie Zisk and Richie Hebner singled. Manager Danny Murtaugh then went to his bench and called on Dave Parker to pinch hit. Murtaugh was made to look like a genius when Parker drilled a Matlack pitch over the fence in right-center for a game-tying home run.

With the game tied at three, Harry Parker took over the pitching in the ninth and retired the first two batters he faced. But Rennie Stennett beat out an infield hit and immediately stole second, his first stolen base of the year. Another Mets killer, Manny Sanguillen, then singled Stennett home for the tiebreaking run. After Al Oliver followed with a single and Bob Robertson walked to load the bases, Berra replaced Parker with Baldwin. Unfortunately for Berra and the Mets, Baldwin could do no better, walking the next batter, Zisk, to force in the second run of the inning. Bill Robinson, who killed the Mets the previous time the Pirates were in town, continued his assault on New York pitching by singling in two more runs, putting the Mets in a 7–3 hole. The Mets, who had not scored since the first inning, failed to score in the ninth inning as well, as they lost their fourth consecutive game.

The losing continued the next afternoon when the Pirates again dominated the Mets, beating them for the eighth consecutive game without a defeat during the season. With their win, the Pirates extended their division lead over the third-place Mets to 6½ games. Despite a stellar performance by rookie starter Randy Tate, who allowed only one run in seven innings, the Mets were unable to do anything against Pirates starter Dock Ellis. The only run allowed by Tate came in the second inning, and again it was the wildness of Tate that produced the Pirates' run. Tate walked four and hit a batter in the inning. The Pirates scored an insurance run off Bob Apodaca in the ninth. With the shutout, the Pirates' earned run average against the Mets stood at a collective 1.67.

Mets backup outfielder and former Pirate Gene Clines commented on his former team's domination of his new employer, saying, "They've got momentum now and they're going to get rougher. Unless they run into a tailspin, they're going to be tough to catch."[21] Clines sounded as if he would've rather been on the other side.

The St. Louis Cardinals followed the Pirates to town for a four-game series, starting with a Monday evening twilight doubleheader. For the Mets, the evening was an exercise in futility as the New York bats remained ice cold, failing to score in either game of the twinbill. With the double loss, the Mets extended their losing streak to seven games and their scoreless streak to 35 innings. The pitiful effort spoiled two solid pitching performances by starters Hank Webb and George Stone.

In the opener the Cards scored the only run of the game in the first inning. Lou Brock led the game off with a walk against starter and loser Hank Webb and then promptly stole second. Two outs later, a single by Ron Fairly scored Brock. On the other hand, the Mets could do absolutely nothing against Cardinals starter Ron Reed, recently acquired from the Braves.

In the second game, the contest remained scoreless for the first seven innings as George Stone tossed his third solid outing since returning from the disabled list, and Cardinals' starter John Denny similarly shackled the Mets. However, in the eighth inning, John Denny led off for the Cardinals with a base hit, his first in the majors. Bake McBride, the Cardinals' leadoff batter, sacrificed Denny to second, and the next batter, Mike Tyson, drew a walk. Louis Melendez followed with an infield hit off the glove of shortstop Mike Phillips, and for the first time the Cardinals had a threatened with the bases loaded. In a surprise move, Berra, who had received no help from his relief corps of late, decided to call on Jon Matlack, who had been doing some tune-up work in the bullpen. The bullpen's arsonist tendencies immediately rubbed off on Matlack when the first batter he faced, pinch-hitter Ted Simmons, slammed Matlack's third pitch over the fence for a grand slam and a 4–0 Cardinals lead. Even though Matlack could not be considered a full-fledged member of the bullpen, the blast marked the fifth time in the seven-game losing streak that the bullpen failed.

The bullpen wasn't given an opportunity in the middle game of the series as Koosman snapped the Mets' losing streak with a spectacular outing and picked up his 100th career win after failing in his three previous outings. Another dubious distinction the Mets entered the game with, namely their 35-inning scoreless streak, came to an abrupt halt in the team's first at-bat. Gene Clines led off with a single to center and immediately stole second. After Felix Millan grounded out, Jesus Alou, manning right field and batting third in Berra's revised lineup, drilled the ball to left-center, which Lou Brock after a long run touched with his glove but couldn't hold. Clines, meanwhile, scored the first Mets' run in 35 innings. The occasion was marked with the crowd of just under 20,000 rising in unison to give the team the Bronx cheer. Dave Kingman added to the New York lead in the fourth when he blasted a 425-foot home run with a runner on to give the Mets a 3–0 advantage. The Mets finalized their scoring in the seventh when Unser singled, was sacrificed to second by Jerry Koosman, and came around to score on Gene Clines' second hit of the game. A base hit by Millan sent Clines to third before he scored when Jesus Alou bounced to first. The Cardinals finally broke through against Koosman in the eighth when they scored their lone run as the Mets prevailed, 5–1.

Before the game it was learned that Harry Parker was suffering from tendonitis, thus partially explaining his poor performances in his last few outings, and was placed on the 21-day disabled list. To take Parker's place on the roster, the Mets recalled right-handed relief pitcher Ken Sanders.

After Tom Seaver and Rick Baldwin combined on a five-hitter to beat the Cardinals, 2–1, and split the series, the Mets welcomed in the Phillies for a big four-game weekend series. A crowd of 27,935 showed up to watch as the Mets began the series, which included the annual and popular Old-Timers Day game and a Sunday afternoon doubleheader, on the right foot as they beat the Phillies, 4–2. Jon Matlack, back in his familiar role as a starter, was lights out as he held the Phillies to five hits, struck out eight, and picked up his ninth win of the season. Dave Kingman provided the power as he homered with one on in the first inning to cap a four-run outburst.

The Phillies couldn't touch Matlack until Greg Luzinski blasted his 18th home run in the top of the fifth. In the sixth, Larry Bowa singled, and "Downtown" Ollie Brown blooped a base hit to right field. When Staub's throw to the shortstop got away from Phillips, who was charged with an error, Bowa headed home to score the Phillies' second and final run. The Mets' precarious two-run lead was a hairbreadth away from disintegrating when in the eighth inning and Ollie Brown at first, Greg Luzinski, who had already taken Matlack deep once, blasted another drive to deep left that seemed certain to be heading out of the park for a game-tying two-run home run. Though not known as a defensive whiz, left fielder Dave Kingman, with his back against the fence and using all of his 6 foot 6 inch height, was able to reel in Luzinski's drive.

Matlack, on his confrontation with Luzinski said, "I dread hitters like Luzinski. The idea is not to get behind him in the count. I threw that first pitch right in the strike zone as hard as I could and once I get that first strike, I can throw my kind of pitches and he'll have to go for them."[22] In the stands was Casey Stengel, on hand for the 14th annual Old-Timers Day at Shea Stadium. When asked about the current year's edition of the team he once managed, he answered in usual Stengelese. "I saw them in Los Angeles and they were wonderful, they won two games and I saw them last night and they win again, and look at some of the college men they've got coming up. You've got super and amazing men to go out on the field for you, who can run and field and those young arms are like a whip you can crack, not like an old arm like mine, which is like a board."[23]

More than 37,200 fans showed up for the Saturday afternoon Old-Timers Day game, followed by the regularly scheduled Mets-Phillies contest. In a season of streaks, the Mets extended their latest winning streak to four. While on the field the game was marred by heavy rain, including a 90-minute delay, Randy Tate ended a month-long winning drought, stopping the Phillies and their ace, Steve Carlton, 5–2. Tate, who'd been plagued with streaks of wildness, opened the game by walking Phillies leadoff batter Dave Cash. Cash stole second and was sacrificed to third by Larry Bowa. Tate then continued his wild ways by walking Jay Johnstone, putting runners at the corners. Joe Torre and pitching coach Rube Walker headed to the mound in an attempt to calm the wild right-hander. Whatever was said must've worked as cleanup hitter Greg Luzinski hit the ball on a line to right, only to have Staub make one of his trademark sliding catches. Cash tagged up on the play and scored the first run of the game. Tate then struck out Dick Allen to end the inning. The Mets got that run back in the bottom of the first, and went ahead in the third inning, 2–1, after the game was delayed by rain for 90 minutes in the second inning. The Phillies retied the game off Tate in the fourth, but the Mets took the lead right back in the fifth when Kingman singled home two runs with the bases loaded. The Mets added their fifth run courtesy of the Phillies slipping and sliding on the mud-filled field. Tate, after allowing the Phillies' second run, was virtually untouchable the rest of the way, fanning nine batters in the process. For Tate it was his third victory against six defeats.

Over 45,000 fans attended the series finale, a Sunday afternoon double-header. A day that started bright and sunny for the Mets ended dark and dreary seven hours later. With the Mets having taken the first two games in the series and sending their aces, Koosman and Seaver, against Phillies rookies Larry Christenson and Tom Underwood, there was every reason to believe that New York would emerge from the weekend winning at least three out of four or possibly even sweeping the series.

Unfortunately, Jerry Koosman, the starter in the opener, showed up without his stuff. Shortstop Mike Phillips showed up with butterfingers, making two errors in the first two innings. The combination led to the Phillies scoring seven runs in the first two innings to chase Koosman with the Mets trailing, 7–0. Ken Sanders, making his first appearance in relief, replaced Koosman in what appeared to be a mop-up assignment.

The Mets, however, made it a game by scoring five runs in the fifth and cutting their deficit to 8–6. The Mets threatened again in the sixth while loading the bases, but Jesus Alou, who had been so reliable coming off the bench, bounced into a force play to end the threat. Tug McGraw entered the game in the seventh, facing his ex-teammates for the first time since being dealt, and allowed the Mets nothing as the Phillies held on to beat New York, 9–6.

The second game began on a much better note for the Mets as they scored three runs in the fourth inning. Seaver kept the Phillies off the board until Jay Johnstone took him deep in the sixth. Seaver, with 11 strikeouts under his belt, took the mound for the ninth carrying a tedious 3–2 lead, and was three outs away from walking off with his twelfth win. The inning started innocently enough as Luzinski grounded out. But the next batter, Seaver's perpetual nemesis, Tommy Hutton, worked a walk and Mike Schmidt singled. Out came Seaver, and in came Apodaca. Apodaca's first batter, Johnny Oates, greeted him with a smash off his nose, loading the bases. Apodaca, who lay on the ground bleeding profusely, was removed from the field on a stretcher. His replacement, Rick Baldwin, struck out his first batter, but walked Ollie Brown to force in the tying run. Baldwin got out of the inning without further damage by striking out his next batter. However, the Mets couldn't escape Greg Luzinski's powerful stroke as he blasted his 19th home run in the top of the twelfth, giving the Phillies a 4–3 lead. Tug McGraw, the beneficiary of Luzinski's power, retired the Mets in the 12th to pick up the win. If McGraw had any motivation for revenge against the team that dealt him, he couldn't do it in more impressive fashion as he hurled seven shutout innings. McGraw, commenting on his return to Shea, said, "What an emotional thing it is to come back here and do a good job. Shea has a magnitude, an intangible air that other stadiums don't have."[24]

Up next for the Mets were the Chicago Cubs, who came into Shea Stadium for a four-game series. The opener pitted a couple of Stones facing one another — George for the Mets and Steve for the Cubs. In the end it was George that came out on top as he continued his remarkable comeback from a serious shoulder injury with his fourth consecutive outstanding performance. Stone was brilliant throughout, allowing the Cubs only an unearned run in the third inning. The Mets tied the game in the sixth inning and scored four runs in the last of the eighth as they beat the Cubs, 5–1.

For Stone, it was his second win against one loss in four starts, and he lowered his ERA to a sparkling 1.84. Stone, commenting on his pitching performance, said, "When you don't have the velocity, you have to compensate for it. I compensate by pitching to spots and changing speeds. I concentrate extra hard on where I'm throwing the ball. The comeback has been better than I anticipated. If I can be as effective the rest of the season, I'll be satisfied. I want to be able to give the club six, seven or eight strong innings every time out. If I can do that consistently, I feel I will have done my job."[25]

Considering the fact that the Mets were on the verge of releasing Stone during spring training, the team had to be thrilled with his performance. Stone, the first pitcher ever to return successfully from a torn rotator cuff injury, the same injury that ended the career of Mel Stottlemyre, was initially placed on the disabled by the Mets on August 9, 1974, and was ordered not to touch a baseball until he arrived at spring training. When Stone reported to camp, he threw three pitches and had to quit because the pain was so severe. The Mets, realistic about Stone's situation, were not counting on him for the season. "Yes, we did even consider giving him his unconditional release," said general manager Joe McDonald. "I mentioned it to him at contract time. I told him it might happen that we have to give him his unconditional release. He understood."

After Stone showed up at training camp and couldn't throw after a long winter of rest, Mets team physician Dr. James Parkes decided it was time to change tactics. Parkes ordered Stone to start some isometric exercises as well to begin soft tossing from 30 to 40 feet. While many of the Mets believed they had seen the last of Stone as a teammate, they failed to take into account his determination. Joe McDonald praised Stone for his work ethic. "He deserves everything good that's happened to him. He really worked hard to get back, most of the time by himself. And he didn't mind pitching against minor leaguers and kids who had never played before."[26]

Bob Apodaca was diagnosed with a broken nose and placed on the 21-day disabled list. Nino Espinosa, a right-handed pitcher, was recalled from Tidewater to take Apodaca's roster spot. With both Parker and Apodaca on the disabled list, the Mets' bullpen was once again in disarray.

The Mets lost the second game of the series by a score of 5–4. What was particularly tough about the loss was the fact that the Mets climbed back from a 4–0 deficit only to lose the game in the tenth inning on an extremely close play at first. After starter Hank Webb spotted the Cubs a quick 4–0 lead after three innings, the Mets began to make their move in the bottom of the fifth as they scored two runs. The newest Mets relievers, Sanders and Espinosa, kept the Cubs off the scoreboard, combining for four innings of scoreless relief to give the Mets' offense a chance to tie the game in the eighth inning. Singles by Millan and Garrett and a sacrifice fly by Kranepool brought home one run while Kingman singled home the tying tally.

Rick Baldwin, who relieved in the tenth, started the inning and the trouble by walking Don Kessinger, who promptly stole second base, as shortstop Mike Phillips was slow to cover the bag. Phillips, to his credit, was the first to admit his gaffe. Kessinger advanced to third on an infield out and then stood his ground as Monday bounced back to the mound. Jerry Morales followed with another dribbler, this one down the third-base line, which Garret picked bare-handed and made a nice throw to first. While Baldwin and the Mets were sure the throw beat Morales, first base umpire Chris Pelekoudas thought otherwise and called Morales safe as the go-ahead run scored. "I thought we might have had him," Baldwin said diplomatically after the game. "Anybody but Morales, and we would've had him," was Berra's comment.[27]

Jon Matlack, whose wife had a baby boy early Wednesday morning, was the winner in the third game of the series as the Mets topped the Cubs, 7–2. Matlack celebrated the birth of his child by pitching a complete game and picking up his 10th win of the season. Joe Torre hit his second home run of the year, his first as a Met at Shea, in the first inning to give the hosts the early 1–0 lead. The Cubs temporarily took a 2–1 lead in the third, but the Mets tied the game in the fourth, regained the lead by scoring two runs in the fifth, and broke the contest open by scoring three runs in the sixth.

Jerry Koosman, who was shelled in his last start against the Phillies while allowing eight runs in less than two innings, was spectacular in the Thursday afternoon matinee as he shut out the Cubs, 4–0, on four hits. Koosman, who went through four sweatshirts, four uniform tops and two caps during his afternoon of work at a muggy Shea Stadium, admitted he'd rather pitch in cool weather. "I know I've had some good games in the heat, but I'd rather it was cool," said Koosman. "It gets real bad out there when there is sweat running in your eyes, ears and down your arm and off your fingers."[28]

John Milner, making his first start since May 12, was the hitting star of the game as he slammed his fifth home run of the year in the last of the sixth inning. Milner, who had lost his starting job due to the solid hitting of Kranepool and the power of Kingman, was happy to get the opportunity to start. The Mets scored their final two runs of the afternoon on a two-run double by none other than pitcher Jerry Koosman. For Koosman, it was his seventh win of the season.

The Mets ended the homestand winning seven of the fifteen games, which was remarkable considering they lost the first five games. Now it was on to Philadelphia to celebrate the Fourth of July weekend in the "City of Brotherly Love" with a big four-game series against the powerful Phillies. Following the first leg of a road trip, the Mets would make stops in Atlanta and Cincinnati before breaking for the All-Star Game, which was scheduled to be played in Milwaukee.

The large crowd of over 55,000 Philadelphia fans showed up to the opening game of the series, but left disappointed as the Mets scored three runs in the top of the ninth to beat the Phillies, 4–3. Tug McGraw, the hero of Sunday's doubleheader, was the goat as he surrendered ninth-inning home runs to Dave Kingman and Jerry Grote. "Some nights you got it, some nights they've got it," said McGraw.[29]

The Phillies took an early 1–0 lead in the bottom of the second inning off Mets starter Tom Seaver. The Mets tied the game in their half of the fourth inning when Dave Kingman smashed a drive off the kneecap of Phillies starter Larry Christenson, scoring Joe Torre. Christenson had to be removed from the game and was diagnosed with a severe bruise. For the second game in a row between these two teams, a pitcher had to depart the contest due to being hit by a batted ball. Seaver, despite surrendering the lead, was the beneficiary of the Mets' ninth-inning power outburst and was credited with his 12th victory of the year.

For the third time in a two-week span, the Mets were swept in a doubleheader as they lost both ends to the Phillies, 8–2 and 10–7. The Mets, who had been bugged all season by inconsistencies from their fourth and fifth starters, received no help as neither starter, Tate in the first game and Stone in the second, made it past the fourth inning. The Mets were never in the first game as the Phillies scored five runs off Tate in the first three innings and built a 5–0 lead. The Phillies' long reliever, Ron Schueler, got a rare start in the first game and stopped the Mets on four hits. The biggest blow for New York was John Stearns' second career home run. George Stone, the second game starter, had his first poor outing of the season, surrendering four runs on ten hits, despite the fact that only one of the runs were earned. Stone didn't figure in the decision as he left with the game tied at four. The Mets took a 4–3 lead in the third, with three runs scoring on a John Milner home run, his sixth of the year. Milner had to leave the game in the seventh inning after he injured his knee while crashing into the left field wall while catching a ball. Nino Espinosa, who followed Stone to the mound, was tattooed for six runs on seven hits and was tagged with his first major league loss.

A combination of poor pitching, a lack of clutch hitting and shoddy defense sent the Mets to their third straight loss in the finale of the series with the Phillies. Uncharacteristic of a front-line pitcher, Jon Matlack was racked for eleven hits and eight runs, six of them earned, in 7⅔ innings. In all fairness to Matlack, however, the defense behind him was almost comical at times. With the game tied at three in the last of the fifth inning with a runner at first and two outs, Ollie Brown smashed a hard grounder that Mike Phillips allowed to get by him for an error. When Kingman fumbled the ball in the outfield, Brown took second. With runners on second and third, Greg Luzinski, who was having a monster year, followed with a double, scoring two runs and putting the Phillies ahead, 5–3. After the Mets cut the lead to one run by scoring once in the sixth, New York handed the Phillies the game on a silver platter in the eighth. A misjudged fly ball, three walks and Dave Kingman tripping over a rolling ball gave the Phillies three runs and the victory. Mike Phillips' two-run homer in the ninth was too little too late, and the Mets went down to defeat, 8–6. The game was best summed up by Matlack, who said, "They were lousy, we were lousier, and I was the lousiest."[30]

After Philadelphia, the Mets returned to the "Launching Pad" and the home of Chief Noc-A-Homa. In the first of a three-game series, all the power belonged to Rusty Staub and Dave Kingman as the Mets downed the Braves, 3–1, behind a complete-game six-hitter by Hank Webb. Kingman, whose two-run blast in the seventh put the Mets in front 3–0, had the dubious distinction of striking out his other three at-bats. With his three strikeouts, Kingman had whiffed 58 times in 60 games, while at the same time slamming 14 home runs and driving in 36 runs.

A scant crowd of only 4,942 showed up for the second game of the series. In a contest that saw home runs hit by Garrett and Kingman for the Mets and Earl Williams and Clarence Gaston for the Braves, New York had the advantage in that Kingman's blast came with two runners on board, as the visitors edged the Braves, 4–3.

Mets starter Jerry Koosman felt fortunate to get through the game with so little damage, as the short foul poles encouraged home runs. "It's got to be a pop fly before you feel it's going to stay in the ball park," said Koosman. "I didn't have good control, I didn't have a good curveball and my fastball wasn't much tonight."[31] For Koosman it was his eighth win of the year. Ken Sanders relieved Koosman in the ninth and picked up his first save as a Met.

The Mets completed their three-game sweep of the Braves and recouped the three games they lost against the Phillies. Rusty Staub hit the deciding home run off Maximino Leon in the tenth inning of a 1–1 game. Tom Seaver pitched a 10-inning complete game as he picked up his 13th win against only four losses.

Any momentum the Mets carried into their weekend four-game series with the Reds in Cincinnati was immediately deflated as they opened with a twilight doubleheader loss. Once again, doubleheaders were the Mets' Achilles' heel. While the first game was a tightly contested affair in which the Reds wrung out a 4–3 win over Matlack, the second game was over in the first inning after Johnny Bench blasted a three-run homer off Randy Tate as the Reds cruised to a 4–1 victory. Tate, the loser, was saddled with a record of 3-8. For the Reds, the hottest team in baseball, it was their eighth straight win.

The Reds made it nine in a row the next day when they pulled out another one-run victory courtesy of a couple of Astroturf base hits. Jerry Koosman, the starter and hard-luck loser, bemoaned his bad luck after the game. "If Abner Doubleday had experimented with Astroturf, he would've never invented the game of baseball," said Koosman.[32] Koosman was referring to the grounders that skidded and accelerated off the rain-slick artificial turf, allowing the Reds to score three unearned runs in the first inning, as they held on to beat the Mets, 3–2.

Pete Rose led off the game for the Reds with a base hit. Concepcion followed with a skidding grounder near second, which Millan snared with a nice diving stop, but made a high throw from his stomach and all hands were safe. Millan was charged with an error on the play. Joe Morgan then lined a base hit just over the outstretched glove of Millan to load the bases. Koosman was in an unenviable situation — bases loaded, nobody out, and the next three batters due up were Johnny Bench, Tony Perez and George Foster. Koosman got Bench to pop out to the infield, but Perez lined another base hit just beyond the reach of Millan, scoring one run. Koosman induced Foster to pop out as well and was just about out of the inning while incurring only minimal damage. But the next batter, Merv Rettenmund, lashed a grounder that exploded off the Astro-turf and into center field to score two runs, which turned out to be the difference in the game. The Mets fought back, scoring two runs in the second off Reds starter Pat Darcy, but couldn't add any further tallies as they went down to defeat, 3–2. The Mets, who arrived in Cincinnati on Friday on a high note after sweeping the Braves, left town depressed and demoralized, a whopping 10½ games out of first place after the Reds completed a four-game sweep of the New Yorkers.

For a while it seemed the Mets would be able to ride the arm of Tom Seaver into the All-Star break with a win. Alas, it was not to be. Seaver, who chose to start on three days rest instead of starting the All Star Game in Milwaukee, took a 3–0 lead into the seventh inning. Seaver, who through the first six innings allowed the Reds no runs and two hits while fanning seven, began the last of the seventh by walking Joe Morgan. After Morgan stole second and Bench grounded to third, Dan Driessen doubled Morgan home for the Reds' first run. Seaver then struck out Perez, and just like Koosman the day before, was a hair-breadth away from escaping with minimal damage. But an infield single by Geronimo and a base hit by Concepcion cut the Mets' lead to one. Seaver, admittedly out of gas, walked pinch-hitter Terry Crowley to load the bases. Berra removed Seaver in favor of Rick Baldwin. A base hit by Rose scored two more runs, and the Reds had the lead and the game.

While Tom Seaver and Jon Matlack, who were named to the All-Star team by National League manager Walter Alston, headed to Milwaukee, the rest of the Mets scattered for their three-day break and to contemplate the upcoming second half of the season. "We're just not playing good defensive ball," said Joe Torre. "We've got to cut down on our mistakes in the field if we're going to do better in the second half. We're making mistakes that don't go into the box scores as errors, but they are errors ... missing the cutoff man, throwing to the wrong base ... those kinds of things." Tom Seaver agreed. "We cannot make the mistakes we have been making if we hope to cut down the lead the Pirates have on us," said Seaver. Aside from improving the defense, the Mets needed more consistency from their offense. After a fantastic start that had him heading for a 100-RBI season, Staub's RBI pace dropped off dramatically during the first half off July. Torre was a major disappointment in the RBI department as well, having driven in only nineteen runs. The only one who was taking up the slack was Kingman, who led the team in home runs with 15 and owned 40 RBIs, 19 less than team leader Staub. Yet, despite Kingman's proficiency as a legitimate power hitter, he had not won the status of a regular player, starting less than a quarter of the club's games. In light of Kingman's power numbers, why he had not earned permanent employment was a question only Yogi could answer. Yogi was increasingly losing the respect of his players due to a lack of discipline as well as constant questioning of his managerial decisions.

Berra, for his part, was airing his eternal optimism. "We've been further down than this and we came back," said Berra. "If we have a good homestand (referring to the long homestand following the All-Star break), we can get back into it. And don't forget we have 10 games left with the Pirates."[33] What Berra seemed to forget was that his Mets had lost all eight games they had played thus far with the Pirates.

Turmoil

M. Donald Grant, the Mets' chairman of the board, gave an impromptu inspirational speech shortly before the team began play for the second half of the season. His words seemed to have some effect as Staub, Kingman and Torre blasted home runs to lead the Mets to a 4–3 come-from-behind victory over the Atlanta Braves. "After we left Cincinnati like we did (being swept in a four-game series), the guys were down," said Joe Torre. "I guess Mr. Grant wanted to start the second half off right and pep us up, as the only clubs that are successful are the ones that fight back from adversity."[1] It was the first time Grant had addressed the team all season. An inspirational speech by Grant that will long be remembered by New York fans was the one he held in 1973, when the Mets also found themselves 10½ games behind at the All-Star break. They went on to win the National League East as well as the pennant and fell one game short of becoming world champions. It was that meeting that precipitated Tug McGraw's famous "Ya Gotta Believe" cry.

Koosman, who started for the Mets and was not around when the team mounted its comeback, surrendered a solo blast to Cito Gaston in the fourth inning and left in the sixth inning, trailing 3–0. The Mets immediately tied the game in their half of the sixth inning when Ed Kranepool led off with a base hit. Rusty Staub followed with a blast into the right field bullpen for his 11th home run of the year. Kingman followed Staub's blast with one of his own, and the game was tied. The Mets took the lead for good when Braves reliever Tom House, who came into the game having pitched 28 scoreless innings in relief, hung a screwball around Torre's eyes. Torre, despite struggling along with only 20 RBIs, wasted no time depositing the ball over the left-center field fence.

With a solid outing, Rick Baldwin picked up the win relief. The bullpen received more good news, when right-handed reliever Harry Parker, on the disabled list suffering from tendonitis, was reactivated before the game. To make room for Parker, Nino Espinosa was sent down to Tidewater. Bob Apodaca, suffering from a broken nose and a deviated septum, still had a ways to go before he would be ready to rejoin the big club.

The team was thrust into turmoil two games into the second half after

Cleon Jones openly defied manager Yogi Berra in the seventh inning of the second game of the series against the Braves. Jones, who pinch-hit in the last of the seventh, was asked to take over left field in the eighth, but refused. A shouting match between the two ensued on the bench and ended with Jones flinging his glove down, pulling towels off the rack and storming up the runway to the clubhouse. "I told him to go out and play left field, but he wouldn't go," said Berra. "I couldn't wait for him all day to go, so I sent someone else out. It made me change my whole lineup because I had to use another player. It was the most embarrassing thing that happened to me since I became manager."[2] Berra, who was always criticized for his lack of discipline, took a surprisingly tough stance, and demanded that Jones be suspended. Jones, for his part, was teed off by his lack of playing time, having lost his regular left field job to Dave Kingman.

In the game itself, the Mets committed four errors and wasted 15 hits as they went down to defeat, 4–3. Jon Matlack, the winning pitcher in the All-Star Game who shared the game MVP award with Bill Madlock, held the Braves scoreless through the first four innings and left after the fifth when he surrendered three unearned runs. Joe Torre celebrated his 35th birthday with mixed results as he collected three hits, but dropped a throw from Mike Phillips that opened the floodgates that led to three runs for the Braves in the fifth inning. A Mets rally in the last of the ninth fell just short as Jerry Grote, who bounced a high chopper to second with both the tying and winning runs on base, just missed beating the throw from second baseman Marty Perez.

The Mets took the rubber game of the three-game series, 5–4, with another complete-game effort by Tom Seaver, who picked up his 14th win of the season. Seaver also picked up six strikeouts, giving him a career total of 1,999. His next strikeout meant a new milestone for the star right-hander. Ed Kranepool and Rusty Staub were the hitting stars of the game for the Mets, combining for five hits and driving in four of the five runs.

While off the field the Mets unsuccessfully kept trying to trade their mutinous left fielder, Cleon Jones, on the field they played their most exciting game of the season upon welcoming the Houston Astros for a rare Sunday afternoon Monday evening two-game series. The Astros scored five runs in the top of the fifth to take a commanding 7–1 lead. However, Kingman, who had already driven in the only run scored by New York, blasted a three-run homer in the last of the fifth, cutting the deficit to 7–4. The Mets scored two more runs in the inning when with two outs and two runners on base, Jack Heidemann hit a short fly to center field, which Cesar Cedeno lost in the glare. The ball struck his thumb as two more runs scored, and the Astros now carried a precarious 7–6 lead. Cedeno had to leave the game since he cut his thumb and required stitches. The Mets called on Hank Webb to hold the Astros, but immediately surrendered two runs to give Houston a 9–6 edge. The Mets, however, refused to die, and in the eighth inning Jesus Alou and Felix Millan doubled for one run. Joe Torre followed with a base hit scoring Millan, and once again the Mets trailed by only one run. Dave Kingman then followed with a blast off the auxiliary scoreboard on the left field balcony for his second home run of the game, his 18th overall, and his fifth and sixth RBIs of the game, giving the Mets an exhilarating 10–9 victory.

A dejected Joe Torre walks back to the dugout after grounding into a double play. Torre put himself in the record books with the dubious distinction of hitting into four double plays in one game. All four at-bats by Torre followed base hits by Felix Millan (*New York Times*).

Rusty Staub and Dave Kingman again went deep for the Mets in the series finale with the Astros. But the story of the game was the National League record set by Joe Torre. Torre had the dubious distinction of grounding into four double plays after four singles by Felix Millan. "It would've been fun if we won," said Torre. "I'll just tell the kids I hit four bullets."[3] Twenty previous National Leaguers, including Ted Martinez, who hit into three double plays in 1974 as a Met, held the record broken by Torre.

The Cincinnati Reds followed the Astros into town for a three-game series. The Mets were looking for revenge after the Reds swept New York four straight in the weekend preceding the All-Star break. One of the more humorous events in the short history of the franchise occurred in the opener of the series. After striking out Johnny Bench on a classic changeup with the bases loaded to end the top of the third inning, Jerry Koosman led off with a base hit to start the bottom of the frame. What happened next caught everyone by surprise, for Koosman took off on a delayed steal. When no one covered catcher Bill Plummer's throw to the bag at second, the ball went sailing into center field and Koosman slid safely into third. With the Mets already leading 1–0, Koosman scored the team's second run of the game on a sacrifice fly by Wayne Garrett. Koosman explained his motive behind his sudden mad dash. "Nobody in the ballpark expected me to steal. Their shortstop and second baseman were laying back, and I figured it would be easy for me to do."[4] One person not amused by Koosman's mad dash was manager Yogi Berra. "If he wouldn't have made it, I would've shot him."[5] More impressive for Koosman than his running was his pitching, as he carried a 3–0, three-hit shutout into the ninth. While Koosman faltered slightly by allowing a run and three hits, he had enough left to close out an impressive 3–1 victory.

After Tom Seaver presented Jerry Koosman with the base he stole the night before, jokingly calling it the Lou Brock Award, the Mets went out and completed part two of the payback behind a five-hitter by Jon Matlack in a 5–2 win over the Reds. Ed Kranepool continued to star at the plate as he had three hits and drove in three runs. Team RBI leaders Kingman and Staub drove in the other Mets runs. "The Mets have the best three pitchers in baseball as a group," said Reds manager Sparky Anderson. "Seaver, Koosman and Matlack may not be the best individually, but when they come at you in a one-two-three order, they're the best bunch."[6]

The 51,882 fans that showed up at a hot and muggy Shea Stadium hoping the Mets would take the broom to the Big Red Machine went home disappointed as New York dropped a 2–1 decision. Mets pitchers Tom Seaver and Rick Baldwin kept their part of the bargain by holding the Reds to only two runs on seven hits. Seaver, however, had to settle for the honor of being the 27th major league pitcher to reach 2,000 strikeouts after fanning Dan Driessen in the second inning. A lack of clutch hitting did the Mets in as they stranded 12 runners on base off a trio of Reds pitchers. The biggest culprit was Dave Kingman, who struck out four times and stranded four runners on base, including the potential tying and winning runs in the last of the ninth inning. Ed Kranepool, the hottest bat in the lineup, began the game on the bench as the Reds started left-hander Fred Norman, but it was Kranepool that scored the Mets' lone run as he singled as a pinch-hitter in the last of the ninth and came around to score on a sacrifice fly by Felix Millan.

That ended a week of exciting baseball on the field as well as a tumultuous one off it as the Mets headed to Chicago, the first stop on a three-city, 12-game road trip. The Mets had gained one game on the division-leading Pirates, trailing now by 9½ games. Conspicuously missing on the trip was Cleon Jones, who was suspended indefinitely four days after his mutinous act. While Yogi Berra wanted Jones suspended immediately, board chairman Grant, fearful of reprisals from the Players Association, insisted on not making any rash decisions. There was a lot of dissension in the front office as the Mets tried to convince Berra to forgive and forget. Berra, never known for his discipline, surprisingly stood his ground and insisted that it was either he or Jones. As a result, the Mets waited four days before suspending the outfielder, trying to deal Jones in the interim. In fact, the Mets had agreed in principle to send Jones to the California Angels in return for outfielder Terry Harper. Jones, being a "five-and-ten player" (ten years in the majors, five with the same team) rejected the deal.

The Mets were back to the friendly confines of Wrigley Field along with the camaraderie that comes with it, including the ivy-covered walls and the Bleacher Bums. Dave Kingman atoned for his four-strikeout game the day before by going 4-for-5, including his 20th home run of the year, as the Mets downed the Cubs in the opener of the series, 6–3. Ed Kranepool picked up two more hits in the game to raise his batting average to .353, which would have led the league if he had enough at-bats to qualify. Felix Millan, who singled in his first at-bat, extended his hitting streak to 18 consecutive games. Randy Tate, allowing three runs and five hits over seven innings, picked up his fourth win of the year, with Ken Sanders earning his second save.

The second game of the series was a classic Wrigley Field affair with the Mets edging out the Cubs in 10 innings, 9–8, after exchanging leads several times.

The Cleon Jones saga finally came to an anticlimactic end with the Mets handing Jones his unconditional release. The Mets had reached an impasse with the disgruntled outfielder. Jones vetoed a trade that would've sent him elsewhere; at the same time, Berra was sticking to his guns, insisting he wouldn't manage if Jones were reinstated. Joe McDonald released a statement: "Having exhausted all avenues in attempting to reconcile this problem, we are offering Cleon Jones his unconditional release. We see nothing to be gained in going through the arbitration procedure. Regardless of the result, the problem would not be resolved. We have no desire to hurt anyone. The suspension is being lifted and Cleon will be paid in full. We feel another club will sign him and we wish

Top: Jerry Koosman slides into third base after stealing second; the ball sailed into center field when no one covered second. The Reds' Pete Rose awaits the late throw at third (*New York Times*). *Bottom*: The next day Tom Seaver presented Koosman with the base he stole. The base was facetiously called "the Lou Brock Award" (MAB Celebrity Services).

Tom Seaver strikes out Dan Driessien of the Reds. The strikeout was Seaver's 2,000th of his distinguished career (© Bettmann/Corbis).

him well." Yogi was relieved as well. "I wish Cleon all the luck in the world," said Berra. "I know he has talent. I think he wasted a lot of his talent and I believe I bent over backwards to help him, but I wasn't going to take anymore from him. That's all. If I were dealing with a white man, I'd do the same thing. It's not a matter of black and white. It's a matter of I wouldn't be able to face any of my players if I took him back. I'm easy to forgive. Like I said, I covered for Jones a lot. His refusing to play was the icing on the cake."[7] If the Mets were hoping to avoid angering the Players Association, however, they were disappointed, as Marvin Miller, leader of the union, scheduled a Monday grievance hearing. Miller's office said that the suspension smacked of coercion because the Mets suspended Jones after he had refused to be traded.

Cleon Jones' roster spot was taken by Bob Apodaca, who was reactivated off the disabled list after recovering from a deviated septum, courtesy of Johnny Oates of the Phillies.

The Mets completed their series in Chicago by barely escaping with a Sunday afternoon doubleheader split. The Cubs won the first game, 4–2, on the strength of two home runs by Bill Madlock, whose bat had been torrid in the series, off Mets starter and loser Jerry Koosman. A tenth-inning, bases-loaded single by Wayne Garrett keyed a three-run rally as the Mets beat the Cubs, 4–1, in the second game of the twinbill, thus escaping the humiliation of being swept in four consecutive doubleheaders. Hank Webb, scattering eight hits over nine innings in the second game, allowed only one run as he picked up his third win of the year. Cubs pitchers Tom Dettore and Darold Knowles were just as dominating through the first nine innings while holding the Mets to one run as well, sending the game into extra innings. But in the tenth the Mets loaded the bases off Cubs reliever Paul Reuschel, the younger brother of Cubs starter Rick, setting the stage for Garrett's big hit.

The arrival of Paul Reuschel, just recently called up from the minors, increased the number of sets of brothers pitching in the majors to four. The others were Phil and Joe Niekro, Bob and Ken Forsch, and Gaylord and Jim Perry.

Having gotten their road trip off to a good start, winning three out of four, the Mets headed to St. Louis to take on the Cardinals in a four-game series, including another doubleheader.

The Mets banged out 17 hits in a slugfest and downed the Cardinals, 11–7, to take the opening game of the series. The final score made the game seem closer than it actually was, as the Mets carried a 10–1 lead before the Cardinals came to bat in the last of the sixth. The Cardinals refused to quit, however, scoring four runs in the inning and sending Matlack to the showers before he could get out of the frame. Apodaca, who was making his first appearance since returning from the disabled listed with a broken nose and a deviated septum, replaced Matlack. The Mets' attack was a complete team effort as every position player contributed at least one base hit. Wayne Garrett, who had hit in seven of his last eight games, had a base hit and scored a run. The red-hot Millan added four hits, including two doubles, while driving in three runs. Ed Kranepool extended his hitting to streak to 13 games, which was the longest on the club. Rusty Staub pitched in with three hits and drove in his 69th run of the year, which led the team. Jerry Grote, having by far his best offensive season while batting .299, chipped in with two more hits, while Del Unser broke a 1-for-10 dry spell with a base hit that drove in two runs. Mike Phillips and Bob Apodaca had two hits apiece as well. While the Mets outscored St. Louis by a healthy 11–7 margin, the Cardinals nearly matched the Mets in base hits as they had 16 safeties of their own. Bake McBride was the only position player on either side who failed to get at least one hit. Jon Matlack picked up his 12th win of the year, while Apodaca notched his eighth save.

The Mets and Cardinals continued their series the next night with a twilight doubleheader, their second in three days. The two clubs combined for 54 hits while splitting the doubleheader, with the Cardinals taking the opener, and the Mets salvaging the nightcap with a decisive 11–6 victory.

While the Mets out-hit St. Louis, 15–10, in the opener, the Cardinals were able to make the most of their hits as they outscored the Mets by a 5–3 margin. The key play in the first game was one that was not made. With two outs in the last of the fifth and the game tied at one, Willie Davis bounced a grounder to first baseman Ed Kranepool. Kranepool, however, could not get the ball out of his glove, and Davis was safe. The Cardinals went on to score three runs off starter and loser Tom Seaver. Kranepool, to his credit, shouldered all the blame. "I've made that play a thousand times," said Kranepool. "The ball stuck in the pocket of the glove as it should have, but I had to grab twice for it, and with Willie's speed it was too long."[8] While the Mets tried to claw back, they couldn't come up with the big hit, stranding twelve runners in the process. Good defensive work by the Cardinals didn't help the Mets' cause, either.

The Mets took an early 5–0 lead in the second game, but the Cardinals with three in the fifth made it a close game as they chased Mets starter and winner Tom Hall. The Mets added two runs in the sixth and four in the eighth and were never headed.

The Cardinals salvaged a split of the series when they tattooed Randy Tate for five runs in the second inning on the way to an easy 5–2 win.

With the Mets winning five of their first eight games on the road trip, they arrived at the moment of truth. Trailing the division-leading Pirates by nine games, the Mets headed for the lion's den — Pittsburgh — for a huge five-game weekend series, including another doubleheader. In the previous eight contests against the Pirates, the Mets had yet to beat Pittsburgh. Yogi Berra said of the upcoming series, "I wish we were in their position. We got to take three out of five; I'd like to get four out of five to get back in there with Philadelphia and Pittsburgh."[9]

Jerry Koosman picked up his 10th win of the season by stopping the Pirates, 6–2. Koosman allowed two first-inning runs and shut the Pirates down the rest of the way. Dave Kingman blasted his 23rd and 24th home runs of the year, while Joe Torre added his fourth.

The Mets took the second game of the series as well, 4–2, behind George Stone. Stone, whose previous few outings were poor, pitched well while allowing the Pirates two runs on only four hits. He lasted into the seventh inning and picked up his third win of the year.

Dave Kingman, who had been driving in runs in droves, usually by hitting balls over walls, drove in a run in an unexpected manner from the big man — a perfectly laid bunt down the third base line. With the score tied at two in the fifth inning, and the Mets with runners on second and third, left fielder Jesus Alou drove in what proved to be the winning run with a sharp single. The Mets were aided defensively as well when Rusty Staub, not known for his glove work, made two outstanding plays, robbing the Pirates of a couple of extra-base hits. The first came against long-time Mets nemesis Bill Robinson, who lined a ball to deep right-center, which Staub practically out-ran to make the catch. The second was a tumbling grab off the bat of Richie Hebner. "I made it to the right place at the right time," said Staub. "You got to go for them and if you make the catch, you're a hero; if you miss...."[10] There was no need for Staub to complete his sentence.

The third game of the series saw Jon Matlack fire a five-hitter, and the

Mets scored five runs in the seventh inning to shut out the Pirates, 6–0. For Matlack it was his 13th win of the year. Wayne Garrett struck the big blow for the Mets with a bases-loaded double in the seventh inning. The Mets now trailed Pittsburgh by only six games as they went into the big Sunday double-header. All they had to do was gain a split, and they would return home only six games out. A sweep, which was unthinkable, would bring the Mets home only four games behind.

While the Mets fought valiantly, they fell short by one run in each game. The first game, a 15-inning affair, was decided when ex–Met Duffy Dyer, traded for Gene Clines, hit a walk-off home run. Tom Seaver pitched the first 10 innings, allowing four runs, and didn't figure in the decision. While the Pirates broke out to an early 3–0 lead, the Mets tied it in the sixth when John Milner crashed his seventh homer of the year. The teams exchanged runs in the seventh, and the game headed into extra innings tied at four. Seaver, usually known for his strikeouts, only fanned five, but induced three double-play grounders in the last three innings to keep the tie intact. Bob Apodaca, who replaced Seaver, stranded seven runners, as he consistently pitched himself out of trouble in his first four innings of work. In the 15th inning, he needn't have to worry about stranding runners, as the first batter he faced, Duffy Dyer, greeted him by blasting his third home run of the year to send the Mets to their first defeat of the series. Duffy Dyer, after the home run, commented on his game-winning blast. "In that sort of situation, you look for a certain pitch in a certain place. I got just what I wanted, a ball a little up in the strike zone."[11]

The Mets took a gigantic step backwards when they lost the second game as well. The second game belonged to Richie Hebner, who drove in all four of the Pirates' runs with a double and his 12th home run of the year. All of the Pirates' runs were scored against the Mets' starter and loser, Hank Webb, as Pittsburgh scored two in the first and added two more in the third. With the Mets trailing 4–1 after three, New York pushed a run across in the fourth on a triple by John Stearns and a groundout by Hank Webb. The Mets cut the Pirates lead down to 4–3 in the fifth on an RBI single by Jesus Alou, but could come no closer. For the fifth time in a little over a month, the Mets lost both ends of a doubleheader.

If there was any solace for the Mets as they headed home for a long home-stand trailing the Pirates by eight games, it was Ed Kranepool's hitting streak, still alive at 17 games, after he collected two base hits in the opener of the doubleheader.

The Mets returned home on August 4 against the Expos. Randy Tate flirted first with a no-hitter and then a shutout, but at day's end all he had to show for his efforts was another loss, his 10th of the year, as the Expos downed the Mets, 4–3. The Mets jumped out to an early lead by scoring three runs in the fifth inning. Two runs came on a Gene Clines triple, and Clines scored when

Mike Jorgensen booted a grounder. In the meantime, Randy Tate was mowing down the Expos in rapid order by not allowing a hit and fanning 11 through his first seven innings of work. In the eighth, Tate began where he left off by striking out pinch-hitter Jose Morales. And then the roof caved in. Manager Gene Mauch sent up Jim Lyttle to bat for the pitcher. Lyttle lined a clean single to left, ending Tate's no-hitter bid. Pepe Mangual followed with a walk, but Jim Dwyer struck out for Tate's 13th strikeout. Tate needed just one more out to keep his shutout intact, but that out came too late. Gary Carter, who tormented the Mets in a series in Montreal in late June, continued to inflict his pain as he singled to left-center, scoring Lyttle and ending the shutout bid. The next batter, Mike Jorgensen, who could not express his regret any better for his fifth-inning miscue, proceeded to blast a Tate fastball into the right field bullpen, giving the Expos a 4–3 lead that they would maintain.

Once again Berra was second-guessed, this time for his decision not to pull Tate before Jorgensen came to the plate. "Nobody but Jorgensen hit a ball hard off him. If Jorgensen had hit only a single or got a walk, I'd have taken him out, but what are the odds that he'd hit a home run?"[12]

Things didn't get any better the next night. For the sixth time that season, the Mets lost a doubleheader. And for the second time that season, they lost a doubleheader without scoring a run in either game, losing both by identical 7–0 scores. The games were a mirror image of each other as the Mets managed only five hits in both contests while only one batter reached third.

In the first game, Jerry Koosman was rocked for six runs in less than three innings. The newest Met, Skip Lockwood, recalled from Tidewater after Monday night's debacle, replaced Koosman and gave the Mets 2⅔ innings of relief, allowing only a Barry Foote home run. While second-game starter Tom Hall fared slightly better than Koosman did in the first game by allowing three runs in five innings, the damage was enough to send the Mets down to defeat for the fifth consecutive game.

After the game Berra bemoaned his team's misfortune with doubleheaders. "Sure it hurts, because that's twelve games we lost in doubleheaders alone," complained the manager. When asked by reporters, what the team would do next, Berra responded, "Regroup, that's what we do—regroup for tomorrow night and hope we start hitting again."[13]

Unfortunately for Yogi, he would not get the opportunity to manage the next night for the Mets. The Mets' front office made a decision in between games of the doubleheader to relieve Berra of his managerial duties. Berra was not informed of the decision, however, until the next morning.

Donald Grant, the Mets' chairman of the board, commented on the decision. "It's a decision that has been going through our heads for some time. We have considered it many times in the past. We were on the verge of telling Yogi he was out, but always the team would bounce back. It was a yo-yo season. Like grapes the wins and losses would come in clusters. One day we were in the thick of the pennant race and five days later disaster had struck. It had nothing to do with failing attendance, dissension on the team, the increasingly turbulent problem we had over Cleon Jones or the Yankees' change of managers.[14] Nothing had anything to do with it but the performance of the team, and what happened Monday and Tuesday on the field climaxed our decision."

The criticism of Berra was not that he did not know his baseball, but that he was unable to control his players. Players laughed at him behind his back, ridiculed his actions and complained about his indecisiveness.

Donald Grant was aware of all this. He had learned the pulse of the clubhouse with frequent visits and by talking to the veteran players. He had also learned it from at least one player who went upstairs to bare the facts. Tom Seaver, the alleged culprit, advised Grant of the complete disregard the players had for Berra's managerial ability.

In Berra's place the Mets named their first-base coach, Roy McMillan, as interim manager. In McMillan, the Mets saw another Gil Hodges, a strong but quiet personality. McMillan's first order of business was to call a clubhouse meeting in which he made clear that he did not believe the Mets were out of the pennant race, despite the fact that they were 9½ games out of first.

The players' reactions to the firing of Berra and the hiring of McMillan was decidedly mixed. Jerry Koosman said "Yogi was making moves that didn't sit well with the team. They didn't seem to be the proper moves, though the players probably didn't have all the information."[15] Felix Millan commented, "It's really sad to see him go. He always treated me good. He's one of the best managers I ever had."[16] "I've played with a lot of managers, but he's the nicest man I ever played for. To me he's not the worst manager right now. Look around. You see guys who have never won anything and they still have their jobs,"[17] said Jesus Alou. According to Tom Seaver, "I felt it was coming for a long time. There's a different man managing. I'm sure things will be different in a very positive way."[18]

Some 9,000 fans showed up to a rainy and dreary Shea Stadium to watch Roy McMillan make his managerial debut. For the first three and one-half innings of the McMillan era, it didn't appear that the Mets' response would be any different to their new manager as the Expos opened up an early 4–0 lead off New York starter George Stone. Stone had to leave the game after pitching three innings due to a strained back, which was not considered to be serious. However, the Mets' offense began to show some life in the last of the fourth when Wayne Garrett connected for his fourth home run of the year with a man on to cut the Expos' lead in half. The Mets then exploded in the sixth inning for seven runs after two were out, with the big hit being a bases-clearing double by Del Unser. The Mets had what seemed to be a commanding 9–4 lead, but the Expos would not go down easily in defeat. Montreal scored two runs off Bob Apodaca in the ninth inning and had the bases loaded with no one out when Mother Nature intervened. The skies opened up, deluging the field and forcing a rain delay. After waiting for an hour and a quarter, the game was called and McMillan had his first managerial win.

Tom Seaver was pressed into service on three days rest after Jon Matlack couldn't start due to injuries sustained in an automobile accident. The end result was McMillan's second victory in as many games as Seaver fired a three-hitter and the Mets downed the Expos, 7–0, in the finale of the five-game series. For Seaver, it was his 15th victory of the year. Tom Seaver was surprised that he got through the game with so little trouble. "Warming up, it seemed like I was very stiff," said Seaver. "It was nice to be in the cool weather, but I certainly wasn't overpowering."[19] That was an assessment Montreal may have argued with. The Mets put the game away early, scoring five runs in the top of the first. Mike Phillips swung the big bat with three hits and three RBIs, including a double.

McMillan's winning streak as the manager lasted only two games as the Dodgers followed the Expos into town and took the opener of a three-game series, 4–3. Randy Tate, coming off his failed no-hitter bid, had another strong outing but didn't figure in the decision. Tate allowed solo home runs to Steve Garvey in the second and Jimmy Wynn in the fifth. Tate was also helped by a great back-to-the-plate catch by Gene Clines, which was turned into a double play. The Mets, trailing 1–0, took the lead in the fourth on doubles by Torre and Staub and a base hit by Jack Heidemann. After Wynn's home run in the sixth tied the game, the Mets regained the lead on Heidemann's sacrifice fly.

The Mets, however, couldn't hold the Dodgers. Ken Sanders, who replaced Tate in the seventh, took the mound again in the eighth. Jimmy Wynn and Garvey struck again, this time with base hits. After a sacrifice, Ron Cey singled home both runners for what turned out to be the game-winning hit. For Ken Sanders, it was his first loss as a Met.

A night later, there was good news and bad news for Mets starter Jerry Koosman. The good news was that Koosman, coming off his horrendous start against Montreal earlier in the week, pitched a solid eight innings and allowed only two runs. The bad news was that the Mets scored no runs for Koosman. As a result, he suffered his 10th loss of the season against 10 wins.

The Mets' offense continued their sabbatical as the Dodgers took the broom to New York, 2–1, despite another solid pitching performance by a quartet of Mets pitchers. Hank Webb, who pitched the first five innings, surrendered two runs on five hits and was the losing pitcher. The game was marred by a bench-clearing brawl in the fifth inning, when Dodgers starter Don Sutton hit Felix Millan with a pitch. After Millan was hit and started to first base, he shouted something at Sutton, then headed for him. Joe Pignatano, who replaced McMillan as the Mets' first base coach, and Dodgers catcher Steve Yeager rushed to intervene. Then Joe Torre led a charge of about twenty Mets out of the dugout, and the Dodgers bench followed suit. After a few moments of milling around, the teams parted with no punches thrown to resume play. After the game Sutton denied that he had intentionally hit Millan. "Anybody who knows anything about pitching knows you don't put the tying run on base. Millan's the kind of guy who stands right on the plate."[20] In the eighth inning, a bizarre incident felled reliever Ken Sanders when a return throw from catcher John Stearns during warm-ups glanced off his glove and hit the pitcher in the eye. Sanders, who received a cut above his eye, had to leave the game and was taken to the Eye Institute of Columbia Presbyterian Hospital for examination. "I don't know what happened," said catcher John Stearns. "He was standing there waiting for the throw. Maybe it sailed a little bit. I don't know. It barely hit the side of his glove but that didn't stop the momentum at all. As far as I could tell it hit him right in the eye."

The Mets breathed a sigh of a relief when the Dodgers left town and the San Diego Padres came calling for a three-game series. In fact, the Mets had less trouble with the Padres as they took two out of three. George Stone, who strained his back a week earlier, became an emergency starter in the opener, when scheduled starter Jon Matlack had to be scratched due to an upper respiratory infection. Matlack missed his second straight start, the first due to an automobile accident on a rain-slicked highway, in which Matlack luckily escaped with only stitches. Stone lasted just two innings, allowing four runs in the second inning after the Mets had staked him to a 3–0 lead in the bottom of the first off Padres staff ace Randy Jones. Jones entered the game with a 15-6 won-lost record and a league-leading 1.85 ERA. Skip Lockwood, who replaced Stone, entered the game in the third inning with the score tied at four and pitched five scoreless innings as he picked up his first win as a Met. The big hit for the Mets was Ed Kranepool's three-run homer, which increased a slim Mets lead from 5–4 to 8–4. For Kranepool it was his third home run of the year and his first since May 27. The Mets continued to pound away against the Padres in the second game of the series as they beat San Diego, 9–4, behind Seaver's 16th win of the season.

The Padres avoided being swept by scoring five runs in the eighth inning on the way to an 8–5 victory. The loss was doubly painful, as not only did the Mets carry a 4–2 lead into the eighth inning, but had they won, the Mets would've trailed the front-running Pirates by only 5½ games. With the Mets leading 4–2 in the eighth and Randy Tate sailing along, the Padres ambushed Tate and his successor, Rick Baldwin, scoring five runs in the inning, with the big blow a three-run homer by Bobby Tolan off Baldwin. For Tate, it was the third game in a row he had late-inning difficulties. In the three games he struck out 28 in 24 innings, but had only two losses to show for his efforts, as his record dropped to a disappointing 4–11. The Mets scored four runs in the first inning, batted around and chased Padres starter Dan Spillner, but could do nothing against his successor, Dave Freisleben.

On August 15, it was the Giants who came into Shea for a big four-game weekend series, including a Friday night twilight doubleheader. The Mets split the doubleheader and cut a half-game off the Pirates' lead to trail by only 5½ games. And if not for one disastrous inning in the first game, the Mets would have trailed by only 4½ games. With Ed Halicki and Jerry Koosman locked in a scoreless duel for the first five innings, Koosman suddenly became very hittable as the first six batters in the top of the sixth inning reached base and scored. Marc Hill had the last and longest hit, a three-run homer, which gave the Giants a 6–0 lead and an eventual 6–2 win. Hank Webb pitched a complete game and Rusty Staub, John Stearns and Wayne Garrett homered as the Mets took the nightcap with a resounding 9–4 victory.

Craig Swan was called up from the minors after winning 13 of 20 decisions at Tidewater to take the start in the middle game of the series. Swan went 8⅓ innings, allowing only five hits as he picked up his second major league win in the Mets' 4–2 victory over the Giants. After the Giants took an early 1–0 lead in the second inning, the Mets quickly gained the advantage for good in their half of the second when Joe Torre hit a two-run homer off Pete Falcone, a fellow Brooklyn native. After the game the Mets announced that George Stone was placed on the 21-day disabled list and Mike Vail, who was leading the International League in hitting with a .346 batting average, was recalled from Tidewater.

Tom Seaver and Jerry Koosman combined on a four-hitter to shut the Giants out, 3–0, in the finale of the series. The Mets climbed to within 3½ games of the Pirates, who were mired in a six-game losing streak. While Seaver picked up his 17th win of the season, Koosman earned his first save of the year. "They called me into the manager's office before the game," said Koosman after his first relief appearance in three years. "I had a feeling they were going to ask me to go to the bullpen. I read about where the Pirates asked Dock Ellis to go to the bullpen and then it dawned upon me that maybe it would happen to me. I just had a feeling. So when I went into Roy's office, I spoke up even before they had a chance to ask me. 'Sure, I'll go to the bullpen,' I told Roy, that whatever he wanted me to do, I'll do." The idea to use Koosman in the bullpen didn't originate with either Roy McMillan or with pitching coach Rube Walker. Rather, it came from former manager Yogi Berra. "Yogi Berra always used to tell me he thought I'd make a good reliever," Koosman said. "He said I could get loose in a hurry and throw often. It only takes me about 12 or 15 pitches to get ready."[21] Despite Koosman's 10-11 record, McMillan went to some lengths to establish that Koosman was not being demoted. In fact, if not for about five disastrous innings, Koosman's record actually could have been 15-5.

The Mets scored one run in the third and two more in the fifth to build a 3–0 lead. Seaver cruised into the eighth inning, having held the Giants scoreless while allowing only three hits when he ran out of gas. In came Koosman, who ended the inning with a couple of force plays. In the ninth, Koosman allowed a lead-off single but induced the next batter to hit into a double play and then struck out Chris Speier to end the game.

The Mets headed to Houston on the first leg of a two-week, 14-game road trip that would see them also travel to San Francisco, San Diego and Los Angeles before returning home to face the Pirates in a key series beginning on Labor Day. The Mets dropped the opener to the Astros, 4–0, despite of the fact that their pitchers allowed Houston only two hits. Randy Tate, the snake-bitten rookie right-hander, who walked the first three batters he faced, was fortunate enough to escape the inning with only one run scored. The Astros scored two more runs in the fourth with the only two hits they would garner all evening. In the meantime, Astros starter J.R. Richard scattered six hits, including doubles by Ed Kranepool and Wayne Garrett, while fanning nine on his way to his ninth victory of the year.

Despite the setback, two Mets reached milestones. Del Unser opened the game with his 1,000th big league hit, while Mike Vail, in a pinch-hitting role, picked up his first major league hit in his first at-bat. Both players were given the ball to commemorate their accomplishments. With the Pirates having the day off, the Mets dropped a half-game in the standings to trail Pittsburgh by four games.

The merry-go-round of managers continued as the Astros fired their skipper, Preston Gomez, before the start of the second game of the series. In his stead the Astros hired Bill Virdon, who was relieved of his duties as Yankees manager a week before the Mets let Berra go. Virdon was rumored to be Berra's replacement before the Mets elected to go with McMillan.

Jon Matlack, in his first game back after missing seventeen days due to an automobile accident and an upper respiratory infection, held the Astros scoreless through eight innings while the Mets built a 6–0 lead. Matlack tired in the ninth, however, yielding a leadoff double to Enos Cabell. After Matlack retired the next two batters, he surrendered back-to-back home runs to Cesar Cedeno and Cliff Johnson, cutting the Mets' lead in half. After Johnson's blast, Lockwood replaced Matlack, but only succeeded in bringing the tying run to the plate after walking his first batter and giving up a base hit to the next batter. McMillan then turned to his new-found closer, Jerry Koosman, who induced the next batter to bounce out to end the game as he picked up his second save in three days. After the game, McMillan announced that Koosman was returning to the starting rotation to take the place of Randy Tate, who had lost his last four decisions and was struggling along with a 4-12 record. McMillan, however, did not rule out Koosman returning to the bullpen at a later date. "It's great having a guy like that around," said McMillan. "He can go either way." Koosman's response to his return to the rotation was, "It's a relief."[22] Del Unser and Wayne Garrett powered the Mets' attack with home runs. The Mets, despite the victory, could not move up in the standings as the Pirates won as well.

The Mets lost the rubber game of the series in heart-breaking fashion as the Astros squeezed out a ten-inning 5–4 victory. The loss dropped the Mets to five games back after the Pirates won their game.

The Astros took an early 3–0 lead off Mets starter Hank Webb, but a monstrous home run by Dave Kingman with two aboard tied the game. For Kingman it was his 25th home run of the year. The Astros went ahead again in the last of the eighth inning on an RBI single by pinch-hitter Jose Cruz, but the Mets tied it in the ninth on Gene Clines' third hit of the game. After reliever Rick Baldwin retired the Astros in the ninth and Jim Crawford retired the Mets in the tenth, Baldwin remained on the mound for the Mets in the last of the tenth. Cesar Cedeno led the inning off with a single, and on a hit-and-run play, Cliff Johnson drilled a ball between Clines and Staub for the victory.

On to windy Candlestick Park where the Mets took the opener of the series with a 6–4 decision over the Giants, scoring five runs in the first inning. Tom Seaver, with relief help from Apodaca, picked up his 18th win of the season.

Jerry Koosman returned to the starting rotation of the second game of the series after his short stint in the bullpen. Koosman pitched like he had never left the rotation, hooking up in a dynamic pitching duel with Giants starter John Montefusco. The only run scored through the first eight innings came on a Del Unser home run in the fourth. Each pitcher allowed only two hits and struck out 11 through the first eight frames.

In the ninth, Koosman took the mound clinging to a 1–0 lead but was removed in favor of Skip Lockwood after allowing a leadoff double to Gary Thomasson. After Lockwood got the first out of the inning, Willie Montanez followed with another double, tying the game and depriving Koosman of a well-earned victory. After Chris Speier was intentionally walked, McMillan went back to the mound and replaced Lockwood with the left-handed Hall. Hall proceeded to walk the next two batters, forcing in the winning run.

Over 24,000 fans filed into Candlestick Park for a Sunday afternoon Jacket Day doubleheader. While in the opener the Mets' offense was alive and well, pounding Giants pitching for nine runs and twelve hits, the Mets bats were silenced in the nightcap, as they were no-hit for only their fifth time in history. The four other no-hitters were hurled by known and established pitchers, none less than Sandy Koufax, Jim Bunning, Bill Stoneman and Bob Moose. This time the honors belonged to rookie right-hander Ed Halicki, who had just been recalled from the minors in May.

The Mets climbed out to an early 7–0 lead in the opener, with Dave Kingman supplying the power by blasting a grand slam home run in the top of the fifth inning, his 26th home run of the year. With Matlack on the mound, the Mets carried a 9–2 lead into the last of the seventh inning. Matlack, however, tired in the seventh as he allowed three Giants runs to score before he could retire the side. Apodaca was summoned to end the Giants' uprising and continued to hold San Francisco at bay. Apodaca was credited with his 12th save, while Matlack picked up his 15th win, equaling his career high.

The nightcap was basically over before it began as the Giants scored two

Dave Kingman is congratulated by third base coach Eddie Yost after home run number 28 (AP Images).

quick runs off Mets starter Craig Swan. Ed Halicki, who entered the game with a 7-10 record, struck out 10, walked two and didn't come close to giving up a hit.

The ninth inning began with Jesus Alou, the Mets' prolific pinch-hitter, leading off. After fouling approximately four pitches out of play, Alou fouled one that was caught, leaving Halicki with two more outs. The next batter, Del Unser, walked, which brought Felix Millan to the plate. "I consider him their best hitter," said Halicki. "And I was actually amazed that I could strike him out because he swung over a slider that wasn't a good pitch."[23] And, in fact, he did, then Wayne Garrett bounced out to first baseman Montanez to seal the no-hitter. With the split of the doubleheader, the Mets dropped in the standings by another half-game and now trailed the Pirates by six games as they headed on to San Diego.

With the Mets being tamed by a rookie the day before, it was the New York rookies that took center stage as the Mets opened their three-game series with the Padres. Mike Vail, a recent call-up, went 4-for-4 and Hank Webb scattered five hits on his way to his first big league shutout. The Mets took a 1–0 lead in the second inning when Dave Kingman doubled and Grote tripled. The triple was controversial, because the Mets argued that the ball hit by Grote was actually a home run; on replay, it seemed the Mets had a case. The Mets added a run in the fourth when Gene Clines singled, moved to second on a hit-and-run grounder, and scored on Vail's third hit of the game. A double by Staub in the ninth scored two more runs to give Webb a 4–0 cushion as he took the mound for the final frame.

The rookies continued to shine as Randy Tate returned to the starting rotation for the second game of the series and picked up his first win in more than a month in the Mets' 7–2 victory over the Padres. Mike Vail continued his torrid hitting by picking up another three hits. While the Mets trailed 1–0 as they came to bat in the top of the fourth, they scored two in that frame and added three in the fifth and two more in the seventh.

The Mets completed a sweep of the Padres as they routed San Diego, 7–0, behind Tom Seaver, who picked up his 19th win and fanned 10. Dave Kingman connected for his 27th home run while Staub hit his 15th. Mike Vail added another two base hits.

With the Pirates losing, their lead on the Mets was once again reduced to five games. With their series in San Diego over, the Mets packed their bags and headed on to Dodger Stadium for a big four-game weekend series with Los Angeles. The Mets had won their two previous games against the Dodgers at Dodger Stadium.

Jerry Koosman opened the series and in a masterful performance scattered eight hits while only allowing one run as the Mets won their fourth game in a row, 4–1. For Koosman, who fanned 10, it was his 11th win and second consecutive excellent start since returning from the bullpen.

With Pittsburgh not playing, the Mets gained a half-game on the Pirates, reducing their lead to only 4½ games.

Break up those Mets! The Mets had won five in a row after Jon Matlack stopped the Dodgers on just six hits in a 6–1 victory. For Matlack, it was a career-high in victories after he picked up his 16th. For the Mets' pitching staff, it was the fifth consecutive complete game thrown by New York's starters. Matlack had a 6–0 lead before he even threw his first pitch as the Mets scored six runs in the top of the first, three of them coming on Dave Kingman's 28th home run. With the Pirates being rained out, the Mets gained another half-game and now trailed Pittsburgh by only four games.

The Mets' streak came to an abrupt halt after the Dodgers and Andy Messersmith stopped New York, 7–0. Ron Cey blasted two home runs—his first a three-run blast in the first inning—and the Dodgers were never headed. Hank Webb was the starter and loser for the Mets. The Mets didn't lose any ground as the Pirates lost as well; however, it was a lost opportunity, as New York could've crawled to within three games of first.

The finale of the series saw Ron Cey once again hit two more homers, and once again the Mets lost, yet lost no ground as the Pirates lost again. Thus ended the month of August, and as baseball entered the stretch drive, the Mets found themselves only four games behind the division-leading Pirates, who were coming into Shea Stadium for a big three-game series, beginning with a Labor Day afternoon contest.

The Pennant Race That Wasn't

The first game of the series belonged to Tom Seaver and the crowd of more than 54,000 that gathered for the Labor Day afternoon matinee as the home stretch of the season officially began. Not only did Seaver pick up his 20th win of the season and record his second shutout in a row, but he also fanned his 200th batter of the year, marking the ninth consecutive season that he had done so. That broke the record he had previously held with Rube Waddell and Walter Johnson.

"I'm very happy to have it," said Tom Seaver, sipping champagne after the game. "The two guys you pass aren't too shabby."[1] With the win the Mets jumped back to only four games out with two games left in the series, during which the Mets were going to throw Koosman and Matlack at the Pirates.

There were more highlights and more good news for the Mets on this afternoon. Mike Vail, in his first Shea Stadium at-bat in the first inning, hit his first major league home run, giving the Mets a 1–0 lead. The Mets scored two more runs in the sixth inning on RBI singles by Staub and Torre. Additionally, Bud Harrelson was reinstated and started his first game in more than three months after undergoing knee surgery.

The Mets' dream of another pennant began to slip away after the Pirates banged Jerry Koosman around for seven runs and eight hits in less than four innings. The Pirates bounced back from their loss in the opener of the series and beat the Mets in a slugfest. Bill Robinson got the scoring going in the second inning by blasting a home run just over the leap of Rusty Staub's outstretched glove. The Mets bounced right back with two runs when Dave Kingman led off the second inning with a walk and Torre homered to center. Unfazed, the Pirates came back with three base hits and a Manny Sanguillen two-run blast that was just inside the left field foul pole to give Pittsburgh a 4–2 lead. The Mets, however, struck again in their half of the third when rookie sensation Mike Vail tripled and scored on a Staub groundout before Kingman launched his 29th home run of the year. However, that didn't last past the next Pirates' turn at bat. Richie Hebner led the inning off with a base hit, and Frank Taveras lined a ball down the left field line and made it all the way around the bases as Vail couldn't dig the ball out of the corner. Taveras was credited with a triple and an error charged to Mike Vail. Rennie Stennett followed with another home run and Koosman was done for the day, joining his mound opponent, Ken Brett, who was removed in the third inning. Pirates relievers Kent Tekulve and Dave Guisti were able to keep the Mets off the scoreboard the rest of the way, while the Pirates scored one more run off reliever Skip Lockwood for a final 8–4 Pittsburgh win.

Jerry Koosman was asked after the game to comment on his pitching performance. "It was only the second time in my career that I went out with good stuff and I got ripped. Two of their three home runs were hit off good pitches, and I thought the third was going to go foul."[2]

The Mets moved one more step backwards in their quest for the division title after losing the rubber game of the series to the Pirates, 3–1. The Mets were now six games behind the Pirates with 24 games left to play. While the Mets took an early 1–0 lead in the first inning on a single by Felix Millan and a double by Mike Vail, they could not do any other scoring against Pirates starter Jerry Reuss. Reuss threw a complete game, scattering eight hits, while picking up his 15th win. Mets starter Jon Matlack kept the Pirates off the scoreboard for the first three innings, and when the Pirates finally scored in the fourth, it

The Mets' chances of winning another pennant rested on the arms of the big three. From left to right: Jon Matlack, Tom Seaver and Jerry Koosman (© Bettmann/Corbis).

Mike Vail hits a home run in his first Shea Stadium at-bat (*New York Times*).

was with the assistance of the Mets' infield, which committed two errors in the inning. Manny Sanguillen led off the inning with a bouncer to third, which wasn't handled by Garrett. Al Oliver followed with a single to right, and Willie Stargell bounced a hard grounder to Dave Kingman, who was playing first. Kingman, trying for a double play, fired to Harrelson, who was covering second. Harrelson, however, couldn't handle the throw, which skipped into the outfield, scoring Sanguillen with the tying run. The game became untied in the seventh, when Bill Robinson, who had killed the Mets all year long, killed them again by launching a screaming line drive over the left field fence, just under the auxiliary scoreboard. Robinson continued his obsession with the Mets when he led off the ninth inning with a double and scored when Dave Parker followed with another double.

A very upset Matlack minced no words in his comments after the game. "They wanted it more than we did, that's why they won. If there ever was a critical series, this was it."[3]

For the first time since McMillan was named manager, there was some second-guessing on the part of the players behind the manager's back. At issue was McMillan's decision to start Wayne Garrett, a left-handed batter, against left-hander Jerry Reuss. Garrett made two errors, struck out twice, and otherwise went hitless. A guy like Garrett typically came to the ballpark thinking he's not going to play. When he found out he's in the lineup against a left-handed pitcher, it's a whole other matter to him. At the same time, Joe Torre was surprised that he was not in the starting lineup. When questioned about his decision, McMillan said he thought Garrett hit left-handers pretty good and was the best man for the job on this day.

While the Mets were down, they were not out. The St. Louis Cardinals came in for a three-game weekend series and the Mets behind Seaver and Apodaca prevailed, 5–2. For Seaver, it was his 21st win of the year and seventh straight, while Apodaca picked up his 13th save of the season. Mike Vail hit a two-run homer in the third to give the Mets a 2–0 lead. After the Cardinals tied the game in the top of the fifth, Dave Kingman's 30th home run in the last of the sixth put the Mets ahead to stay. Kingman's home run made him the first Met to hit 30 home runs in a season since Frank Thomas did it during the franchise's inaugural season of 1962.

The Mets continued to play themselves out of contention by falling to the Cardinals in the middle game of the series. Poor defensive play in the first inning did the Mets in as two errors contributed to four runs in the 6–3 loss. With one out in the top of the first, Bake McBride singled. When Mets starter Jerry Koosman attempted to pick McBride off first, Dave Kingman allowed the throw to get by him and McBride waltzed to third. Willie Davis followed with a walk, and both runners moved up on a wild pitch, giving the Cards a 1–0 lead. Ted Simmons popped a fly ball to left, an easy out except for the fact that Mike Vail made a rookie mental mistake by forgetting to take the field with sunglasses. Vail lost the ball in the sun, and the Cardinals now had runners at first and second. Reggie Smith followed with a walk to load the bases. Hector Cruz then flied out to Mike Vail, scoring the second run of the inning. However, Vail then made his second mental error of the inning by throwing to the plate to try to nab Davis, even though he had no chance. The other runners, meanwhile, advanced to second and third.

A Ted Sizemore double scored two more runs and the Mets were in a 4–0 hole before they even came to bat. While Koosman pitched superbly through the sixth inning, the Mets had too much of a hill to climb. An obviously frustrated Koosman said after the game, "You can't spot anybody anything, especially the guys you're contending with for the pennant. We should've been out of that inning with no runs scored, but instead things went wrong, and it took us out of the game."[4]

The Mets continued their descent downward as the Cardinals in the finale of the weekend series drubbed New York, 12–4. With the loss the Mets dropped to a seemingly insurmountable 7½ game deficit. An obviously dejected team met reporters in the clubhouse after the game. "It was not a pennant week," said Tom Seaver. "We screwed up," said Matlack, who had seen his teammates commit six errors behind him in the last two crucial games he pitched.[5] "I pitched one very good and one decent game, and didn't win either." "We had a bad week on defense," said Rusty Staub. "We made mistakes in more places than defense," said manager Roy McMillan. "You would hope to win two out of three in each series this week instead of lose two out of three. In the history of the Mets they've always been able to come back. But I don't know if there's time now."

The Mets' dispirited play continued as they took to the road. Their first stop was Montreal, where they lost all three to the Expos, including a twilight doubleheader, sending the Mets into a five-game losing streak and putting their pennant hopes on life support. Hank Webb and George Stone, making his first start since pulling a muscle in his back on August 11, were the starters for the Mets. Both pitchers were hit hard, with Webb not getting out of the first inning and Stone not making it through the fourth. The only bright spot for the Mets was Mike Vail, who extended his hitting streak to 16 games.

An ex–Met did New York in during the series finale, when Mike Jorgensen lashed a Bob Apodaca pitch into right-center field for a double in the 10th inning. That hit led the Expos to a 2–1 victory and a sweep over the Mets.

The Mets moved into Pittsburgh for a two-game series that at this point no longer had any bearing on the pennant race. The Mets' poor play of late seemingly rubbed off on Tom Seaver as he uncharacteristically allowed six runs on seven hits in less than six innings of work, as the Mets went down to defeat for their sixth loss in a row. "I felt uncomfortable out there," said Seaver after the game. "And I'll say this. Every bad pitch I made, they hit."[6]

Again the bright spots in the loss were the hitting of Dave Kingman, who smacked two more home runs, and Mike Vail, who extended his hitting streak to 18 games. After the game the Mets announced they were recalling third base prospect Roy Staiger and catcher Ron Hodges from Tidewater, which had just won the International League championship. Jerry Koosman put an end to the Mets' losing streak by throwing his third shutout of the season as the Mets stopped the Pirates, 7–0, in the final game of the season between the two teams. "I just hope a strong pitching performance will help the club out of its rut," said Koosman after the game. "The chances of catching the Pirates are very, very slim, but we've got to keep plugging away and maybe get second or third."[7]

Like a broken record, it went without saying that the offensive stars of the game were Dave Kingman, who tied the club record for home runs in a season with 34 and tied Mike Schmidt for the National League lead, and Mike Vail, who hit safely for the 19th straight game.

After losing two out of three in St. Louis, a deflated Mets team headed home for the final homestand of the season. The only thing the Mets had to play for was the consolation prize of third place on the team level, and on the personal level, to see how long Mike Vail could extend his hitting streak, which was one short of tying the National League record for rookies at 23, attained by Joe Rapp and Richie Ashburn, both while members of the Phillies. Another

Mets record being threatened was for the most home runs hit in a season, previously set by Frank Thomas in 1962 and currently tied by Dave Kingman. Kingman was also in a battle with the Phillies' Mike Schmidt for the National League home run title.

It was a skimpy crowd of just over 7,000 that showed up to watch the Mets take on the Expos in the opener of the series. The Expos scored two early runs off Mets starter Jerry Koosman in the second inning, but the left-hander recovered to hold Montreal in check through the eighth inning. With the Mets trailing 2–0, they came to bat in the bottom of the sixth. Del Unser walked and stole second, bringing Vail to the plate. A chant of "Let's go Mike" replaced the standard restrain of "Let's go Mets" as Vail settled into the batter's box. Vail, who grounded to short his first time up and lined out hard to third in his second at-bat, drilled a clean single into center, scoring Unser. The game was stopped as Vail was given the ball as a memento to his record-tying feat. The Mets tied the game in the seventh on what ranked as the weirdest sequence of the season. Kingman bounced a ball to Expos third baseman Larry Parrish, who bounced a throw past first baseman Jose Morales. When Kingman headed for second, Morales threw wildly into left field, sending Kingman to third. Kingman completed his trip around the bases to tie the game when Expos starter Steve Rogers threw a wild pitch. Vail drove in the game-winning run in the last of the eighth after Garrett, batting for Koosman, singled to open the inning. Gene Clines, who ran for Garrett, was sacrificed to second by Del Unser and scored on Vail's second hit of the game. Koosman, who picked up his 13th win of the season, got relief help from Lockwood, who earned his first save as a Met. After the game Mike Vail spoke to reporters, commenting on his feat. "I just try to hit the ball, hope they fall in. I just look for the good pitch, a pitch I can handle and then I try to drive it."[8]

Mike Vail had eight at-bats as he tried to have the National League consecutive game hitting streak record all for himself, but couldn't manage more than a walk as the Mets and Expos battled for 18 innings. Don Demola walked Del Unser with the bases loaded to force in the winning run as the Mets prevailed, 4–3, in a game they were trailing, 3–0. Two games after Mike Vail tied the record for hitting in consecutive games by a rookie, Dave Kingman broke the club record for home runs, when he belted his 35th, a two-run blast in the last of the ninth inning that snapped a 5–5 tie to give the Mets a 7–5 win. "I don't know why, but I haven't been swinging the bat real well since tying the club record," Kingman confessed after the game. "Now I can forget all about records and go back to the frame of mind I was in before thinking about home runs."[9] Rusty Staub also set a Mets record when he drove in his 100th run with his home run.

While the Mets were unofficially out of the pennant race after losing four of six to the Pirates and Cardinals in the first week of September, it wasn't until September 18th that New York was officially eliminated after losing to the

Phillies, 4–3, in the opener of the final series at Shea Stadium. The Mets were able to roll out one final home victory after

Ron Hodges' first home run in more than two and one-half years with two outs in the eleventh inning lifted the Mets to a 9–7 win over the Phillies in the middle game of the series. In a roller-coaster affair, the Mets carried a 7–5 lead into the ninth inning, but reliever Rick Baldwin couldn't close it out after Mike Schmidt, competing with Dave Kingman for the National League home run championship, blasted his 38th of the year. Rusty Staub hit his 19th home run for the victors.

The Mets closed down their home season in front of over 50,000 fans while losing to the Phillies, 4–2. The Mets were completely lifeless until Ron Hodges hit his second two-run homer in two days in the last of the ninth, this one off Tug McGraw. McGraw, however, was able to strike out his next two batters as he picked up his 14th save of the year. McGraw was thrilled with his performance over the weekend against his former teammates. "It was fun, getting them out three days in a row," said McGraw.[10] Jon Matlack, who surrendered all four Phillies runs, was charged with his 12th loss. Matlack had been a major disappointment in the month of September, failing to win a single game.

With the home schedule completed and third place still a very distinct possibility, the Mets headed on the road for a trip that included visits to Chicago

Joe Wallis is about to break up Tom Seaver's attempt at a no-hitter with a two-out single in the ninth inning (© Bettmann/Corbis).

for two games and Philadelphia for four games to finish out the regular season. In the opener of the series at Wrigley Field, the Mets erased a 6–0 deficit and rallied to beat the Cubs, 8–6. While Mets starter Craig Swan was raked early for six runs and didn't get out of the second inning, his replacements—Skip Lockwood, Rick Baldwin, Bob Apodaca and Ken Sanders—held the Cubs scoreless the rest of the way. The Mets cut their deficit in half by scoring three runs in the fourth and sliced it down to one run when Kingman drove in two runs in the fifth with a double. New York finally took the lead for good in the eighth.

What do Jimmy Qualls, Leron Lee and Joe Wallis have in common? They are the three players of little renown who have broken up Tom Seaver's attempt at no-hitters with singles in the ninth. Jimmy Qualls was the first to do it when he broke up Seaver's quest for a perfect game with one out in the ninth in a game at Shea Stadium against the Cubs in July of 1969. Leron Lee was the culprit in the first game of a July 4, 1972, doubleheader against the San Diego Padres when he singled with one out in the ninth, the only hit Seaver would surrender. On September 24, 1975, Seaver came within one out of a no-hitter, only to have Joe Wallis single to right with two outs in the ninth. Even if Seaver had accomplished his dream of pitching a no-hitter, he wouldn't have come up with his 22nd victory, as the Mets had been unable to put a run on the scoreboard. The Mets came within inches of scoring when Rusty Staub was cut down at the plate trying to score from first base on a double by Dave Kingman in the fourth. The Cubs eventually won the game in the 11th inning when Skip Lockwood walked Bill Madlock with the bases loaded to force in the only run of the afternoon.

The final weekend of the regular season began with a Friday evening doubleheader at Veterans Stadium. The Mets showed no inclination towards wanting the season to end as they took the Phillies to 12 innings of each game before settling for a split. In the opener, with the game tied at three in the last of the 12th, Larry Bowa hit his second triple of the game off losing pitcher Bob Apodaca and scored on a Garry Maddox single. Mets starter Jon Matlack continued his September win drought despite pitching well into the seventh inning, allowing three runs on seven hits. For the Mets offensively, Dave Kingman hit his 36th home run of the year.

In the nightcap Jerry Koosman assured himself of a winning season when he pitched a solid 11 innings and allowed only one unearned run while fanning 10. The Mets scored two unearned runs in the 12th, but New York fans had to hold their breath in the bottom of the inning when Johnny Oates singled off reliever Ken Sanders and Tim McCarver walked. With two outs Mike Rogodzinski doubled, scoring Oates, but McCarver, trying to score right behind him, was thrown out to end the game. For Koosman it was his 14th win against 13 losses.

After Randy Tate and the Mets were crushed in the middle game of the series by Steve Carlton and the Phillies, Tom Seaver picked up his 22nd victory of the season in the finale. With the win it appeared that Seaver would be the early favorite to be the 1975 Cy Young Award winner. Seaver finished the season with a 22-9 record and 242 strikeouts along with the third-best ERA in the league behind Randy Jones and Andy Messersmith.

The Mets also clinched a tie for third place with their win and finished the season with an 82-80 record, 11 games better than their disappointing 71-91 record of a year ago, but not as good as the Mets' brass and all their tinkering had hoped for. In fact, the Mets' 11-game turnaround could be attributed solely to the return to form of Tom Seaver, who won 11 games more than the previous season when he was bothered with chronic sciatic hip problems.

10

The New Manager

Two rookie managers promoted from the minors were sitting in the opposing dugouts as the Mets opened their 15th season. For the Expos, beginning their seventh season, sitting in the third base dugout was 38-year-old Karl Kuehl, promoted from Memphis. In the Mets' dugout, getting ready to manage his first major league game, sat Joe Frazier, promoted from Tidewater.

Three days after the 1975 regular season ended, in a move that surprised nobody, the Mets announced that Roy McMillan would not return as manager for the 1976 campaign. In his stead, the Mets promoted Joe Frazier from Triple-A Tidewater, where he had won the pennant three years in a row.

The New York team assembled in the dugout resembled very much the team that ended the 1975 season with one notable exception: Rusty Staub was no longer with the team. Staub had earned a reprieve the previous winter when the Mets failed to trade him despite entertaining offers, but he was not so lucky this off-season, and New York sent him to the Tigers in return for 35-year-old left-hander Mickey Lolich. While the trading of Staub was not a surprise in itself since he was one year away from being a 10-5 man and would have had veto power over any potential trade after the next season, what was surprising was that the Mets would trade their leading run producer for an aging and overweight pitcher. Lolich, the hero of the 1968 World Series and owner of spectacular career numbers, having won 207 games for the Tigers over his 13-year career with 2,679 strikeouts as well 39 shutouts, slipped to a 12-18 record in 1975 as his career began to take a downward spiral. Even more surprising was the fact that the Mets went into the winter meetings with obtaining a right-handed hitting third baseman and a left-handed reliever as their priority. "I know, I know,"[1] McDonald responded, when asked about the Mets' apparent change of direction. "I said we needed a right-handed third baseman and a left-handed relief pitcher. I still do. But this was the best deal offered to us. We could have gone in another direction, but we felt this was the best deal we could make or we would not have made it." In fact, the Mets turned down an offer to acquire Doug DeCinces, the heir apparent to Brooks Robinson, in exchange for Staub. However, the Mets felt that pitching was the name of the game; that's what

The Mets and their fans sorely missed the bat and the legendary sliding catches of Rusty Staub after the Mets dealt the popular player to the Tigers over the off season. Board Chairman Donald Grant ordered GM Joe McDonald to dispose of the outfielder (AP Images).

brought them the world championship in 1969 and brought them within one out of winning another world championship in 1973. "When we go into a city now for a three-game series, the other team knows that they are going to see somebody like Seaver, Koosman, Matlack or Lolich in every game," McDonald said, commenting on the trade. "One of the reasons we didn't win last year was because we didn't have a dependable No. 4 starter. If Randy Tate were ready to be the pitcher we think he will be someday, we might not have made this trade."[2]

The Mets' grandiose plan of having their 1975 rookie sensation Mike Vail replace Staub in right field didn't even make it to spring training after Vail dislocated his ankle in a pickup basketball game shortly before training camp was slated to open. John Milner, who spent most of 1975 in Yogi Berra's and then Roy McMillan's doghouse, was slated to replace Vail in right field. The salivating thought of having a rotation of Seaver, Koosman, Matlack and Lolich was not assured either. Frazier began contemplating using Koosman as the left-handed short man out of the bullpen because the Mets weren't comfortable

Top: It was an aggressive Mets lineup that opened the season under new manager Joe Frazier. Dave Kingman steals second as ex–Met Tim Foli awaits the late throw (AP Images). *Bottom*: Jerry Grote was not as fortunate as he was tagged out at the plate by Expos catcher Barry Foote while trying to score in the second inning (AP Images).

with Tom Hall handling that pivotal role. Other changes instituted by Frazier were switching Torre to first, where he would platoon with Ed Kranepool, and platoon Wayne Garrett at third with right-handed hitting rookie Roy Staiger. While Staiger was highly touted defensively, he was not known for his prowess with the bat.

Less then 16,000 fans showed up to a chilly Shea Stadium as Tom Seaver took the mound for the ninth consecutive Opening Day. He was opposed by the ace of the Expos' staff, Steve Rogers. Seaver picked up where he left off in 1975 as he pitched a solid seven innings, holding the Expos to one run over seven innings while fanning eight. With the Mets leading 3–1 after seven innings, the new ace of the Mets' bullpen, Skip Lockwood, took over the pitching and immediately had fans of all ages reaching for their Rolaids as he surrendered three consecutive hits to cut the Mets' lead down to one, with the tying and go-ahead runs on base. Lockwood, however, was able to reach back and get out of further trouble, preserving Joe Frazier's first major league win and Seaver's first of the new season.

"I was cold all over and there was no feeling in my fingers much of the time," said Seaver after the game. "But it's usually chilly the first three weeks of the season, and both of the pitchers have to live with it."[3]

On offense the little guy, Bud Harrelson, struck the big blow. Harrelson, who missed most of the 1975 season due to knee surgery, was healthy once again, and with the score tied 1–1 in the last of the fourth, stepped up to the plate with runners at first and second. Harrelson drilled a ball over the head of left fielder Larry Biittner, who was playing shallow, scoring both runners and giving the Mets a 3–1 lead.

Jon Matlack fired a complete-game four-hitter as the Mets won their second straight game for their new manager. Again the big inning for the Mets was the fourth, and again it was Harrelson who displayed the power, this time driving the ball over right fielder Ellis Valentine's head for a triple. Felix Millan followed with a double, and that was it for the scoring on another chilly early spring afternoon.

The Mets had only one scary moment all afternoon and that was in the ninth inning. With Matlack clinging to his 1–0 lead, Mike Jorgensen sent Dave Kingman to the wall in right field to reel in his long drive. Manager Frazier hurried out to the mound and told Matlack, "You just gave the whole bench a heart attack." Matlack responded, "If you think you were worried, I was already looking for a hole to crawl into."[4]

Poor defensive play and 14 runners stranded on base ended Joe Frazier's unbeaten streak as a big league manager despite a Mets' ninth-inning rally, which fell just short, as New York lost the final game of the series with the Expos, 7–6. On a bitter cold afternoon, Mickey Lolich's first Mets and National League start lasted just two innings as he surrendered three runs in the top of the second. Poor defense played a big role in the Expos' big inning, with Lolich misplaying a bunt and Benny Ayala misplaying a ball, which ended as a double and two runs scoring. With the Mets loading the bases in the last of the second, Frazier had Stearns pinch-hit for Lolich. Stearns flied out, ending the Mets' threat. Frazier commented after the game on his decision to lift Lolich after only two innings, "It was so miserable out there, that I took him out for his own good. Besides a base hit there and we'd have a shot at the game."[5] With the Expos leading 7–4 in the eighth, Dave Kingman hit the first home run of the season for the Mets, cutting the Expos' lead to 7–5. The Mets were able to add a single run in the ninth inning, but a double play short-circuited the rally.

The Mets headed for Chicago to play against the Cubs in their home opener. Again the combination of too many stranded base runners and poor defensive play did the Mets in. Fifteen runners were left on base as the Mets fell, 5–4, when the Cubs scored a run in the last of the ninth inning. With the game tied 4–4 in the last of the ninth and one out, Cubs second baseman Manny Trillo tripled off Skip Lockwood. After the Mets intentionally loaded the bases by walking the next two batters, pinch-hitter Tim Hosey popped out to Millan, giving Lockwood an even chance to send the game into extra innings. Lockwood almost did escape when Rick Monday popped a fly into short center field. However, center fielder Bruce Boisclair hesitated before running in and the ball eluded his desperate lunge, hitting the ground and scoring Trillo from third with the winning run.

"I blew the play," a dejected Boisclair said after the game. "It was my mistake and it cost us the game."[6] Frazier, however, was not that quick to blame Boisclair. Frazier actually blamed the loss more on Dave Kingman, who stranded five base runners in his first three at-bats, and also over-slid second base after getting aboard on a base hit in the seventh. The Mets followed their second one-run loss with their third consecutive one-run setback.

Tom Seaver was staked initially to a 3–0 lead and then to a 5–2 advantage before he had to come out of the game with an injury to his right calf muscle after pitching five innings. Seaver was injured in the top of the fifth while running the bases and scoring the Mets' third run of the game. John Milner drove in the Mets' first three runs with a base hit in the top of the first inning and a sacrifice fly in the fifth. Rick Monday's two-run homer in the last of the fifth off Tom Seaver cut the Mets' lead to 3–2. The Mets regained their three-run advantage in the top of the sixth when Garrett singled and Dave Kingman followed by smacking the ball completely out of Wrigley Field and into a home on Kenmore Street. The blast traveled an estimated 630 feet, one of the longest home runs in Wrigley Field history.

Apodaca replaced Seaver in the sixth inning and allowed a run when the Mets botched a run-down play. Things went from bad to worse in the last of the seventh when Randy Hundley, who was claimed off waivers from the Padres, led off with a double versus Apodaca. A single by Jose Cardenal scored Hundley, and Apodaca was sent to the showers. Webb replaced Apodaca but fared no better as Bill Madlock greeted him by tripling in the tying run. A base hit by Jerry Morales gave the Cubs a 6–5 lead, a lead they wouldn't relinquish. After the game Frazier bemoaned his team's poor play. "The second line pitching's just not doing the job. You don't throw a guy who's been out of baseball for so long [referring to Hundley] a fastball right in there."[7]

Dave Kingman salvaged the final game of the series for the Mets by slamming two more tape-measure blasts, the latter a three-run homer in the top of the ninth to give the Mets a 10–8 come-from-behind victory. The Cubs raked Mets starter Jon Matlack for seven runs in the three innings he lasted and carried a 7–2 lead as the Mets came to bat in the fourth. The Mets, however, refused to quit and began pecking away at the Cubs' lead, scoring one in the fourth, three in the sixth and eventually tying the game with a run in the eighth. The Cubs took the lead right back in their half of the eighth inning, courtesy of wildness by Mets relievers Lockwood and Webb, which included two walks and a hit batsman.

So it was when the Mets came to bat in the ninth inning on the verge of losing their fourth straight one-run game. John Milner, continuing with his hot bat, stroked his third hit of the game, which was followed by another base hit by Del Unser, bringing Kingman to the plate with runners on first and second. After several conferences on the mound that included the entire infield and Cubs manager Jim Marshall, presumably on how to pitch to Kingman, Cubs pitcher Tom Detorre was ready. One moment later the ball was on Waveland Street for Kingman's third mammoth blast in the series. The Mets had a 10–8 lead, which winning pitcher Skip Lockwood made stand as he held the Cubs at bay in the ninth. For once Frazier had something to smile about. "Now that's what I call a major league home run."[8]

The Mets traveled next to Pittsburgh for a weekend series with the National League Eastern Division champions. The opener of the series pitted two transplanted American League veterans against one another. Doc Medich, formerly of the Yankees, took the hill for the Pirates, while Lolich, formerly of the Tigers, toed the rubber for the visiting Mets. While Lolich allowed the Pirates only three runs in the six-plus innings he worked, Medich was better, allowing only a John Milner home run in pitching the Pirates to a complete-game 3–1 victory. Jerry Koosman, who started the season in the bullpen, was given the start in the middle game of the series. The move paid handsome dividends, as Koosman held the Pirates to only one run while pitching a complete game.

The Mets put the game away before they got out of the first inning by scoring five runs off Pirates starter Bruce Kison. Kison didn't make it out of the first inning, getting credit for pitching only two-thirds of an inning, and was replaced by Kent Tekulve. But it was off the Pirates' fourth and final pitcher, Dave Giusti, that the Mets did most of the damage, smacking him around for ten runs on eleven hits, including Dave Kingman's fifth home run and

Kranepool's first. By the time the fun was over, the Mets amassed 17 runs as they demolished the Pirates, 17–1.

Koosman was thrilled with Frazier's decision to put him back in the starting rotation. "I have always wanted to be a starter," said Koosman. "If you have the potential and show it, then that's what they should make you." A bigger accomplishment for Koosman on this afternoon was the fact that his win marked the 20th time in his career he had beaten the Pirates. "Beating one of the best teams in baseball 20 times makes me feel most proud."[9]

The Pirates took the rubber game of the series, 7–5, as they scored six runs in the last of the fourth inning off Mets starter Craig Swan and reliever Tom Hall, thereby breaking a 1–1 tie after Kingman and Stargell exchanged home runs in the early innings. The Pirates had to hold on for dear life, however, as Dave Kingman put on another power display, adding a three-run homer in the top of the eighth to cut the Mets' deficit to 7–4. The Mets were able to bring the tying run to the plate in the ninth inning, but groundouts by Torre and Milner ended both the threat and the game.

Having lost two out of three to Chicago and Pittsburgh, the Mets headed on to St. Louis for a three-game series with the Cardinals. The opener of the series, which started late due to a rain delay, ended very late after it took the Mets 17 innings to outlast the Cardinals, 4–3, on Del Unser's homer in the 17th inning. In a game of redeeming features, Unser atoned for misjudging a fly ball to center field that allowed the Cardinals to score two first-inning runs off Tom Seaver. Seaver, who showed no ill effects from his calf injury, pitched eight innings and allowed three runs. The next day saw the Mets continue where they left off the evening before as two-run homers by Felix Millan, Del Unser and John Milner off Cardinals starter Lynn McGlothen in the first two innings gave the Mets an early 6–0 lead. An obviously frustrated McGlothen wasted no time in plunking Del Unser on his right elbow when he came to bat in the third inning. In response, Mets starter Jon Matlack brushed back McGlothen when he came to bat in the bottom of the inning. Following Matlack's brush-back pitch, Matlack and both managers received a warning from home plate umpire Bruce Froemming. Nevertheless, it didn't stop McGlothen from brushing back Matlack when he came to bat in the fourth inning, which earned the Cardinal pitcher a warning of his own from Froemming. After Harrelson was ejected from the game and Frazier nearly followed for razzing Froemming for not ejecting McGlothen, the St. Louis hurler on his next pitch nailed Matlack, earning an ejection from the game. Both benches cleared shortly thereafter, and after plenty of pushing and shoving, order was finally restored.

After the game, which the Mets won handily, McGlothen readily admitted that he purposely threw at Unser and Matlack. McGlothen maintained that not only did he have a right to retaliate as a pitcher, but it was his duty as a major leaguer to do so. Jon Matlack reacted angrily to McGlothen's rationale. "I used to have a lot of respect for McGlothen," said Matlack. "I thought he was a good pitcher, but now I think he stinks."[10] Subsequently, McGlothen was suspended for five days and fined $300.

A comedy of errors prevented the Mets from sweeping the series against the Cardinals. The comedy started in the second inning after Ted Simmons doubled off Mets starter Mickey Lolich. Lolich's wild pitch advanced Simmons to third, and when Grote had trouble locating the ball, Simmons headed home. After Grote recovered the ball, a good throw would have nabbed Simmons. However, Grote's high throw glanced off Lolich's glove, and the Cardinals had a 1–0 lead. The comedy continued after Lolich struck out the next batter, Mike Anderson, but again the ball got by Grote, who threw wildly to first, allowing Anderson to reach. The Cardinals scored their second run in the fourth courtesy of an error by left fielder Benny Ayala. Still, the Mets carried a 4–2 lead into the last of the sixth inning when the comedy show began again. Vic Harris, leading off, hit a high pop behind first base, where Kranepool and Millan converged on the ball before letting the ball drop between them for a two-base hit. Lolich proceeded to get the next two batters on grounders, but instead of being in the dugout with his two-run lead still intact, he now had the task of getting Reggie Smith out. Smith proceeded to hit the ball out of the park, and the game was now a brand-new affair, all tied 4–4. But the fun wasn't over yet. Mike Anderson, the next batter, popped a ball over shortstop, where Mike Phillips, Bruce Boisclair and Benny Ayala converged again with no one touching the ball, as it fell in for another two-base hit. Snake-bitten, Lolich exited, replaced by Lockwood, who surrendered a clean single to Ron Fairly, giving the Cardinals the lead once again. Don Kessinger followed with a double, scoring Ron Fairly for the fourth Cardinal run in the inning. St. Louis went on to beat the Mets, 7–4.

The last leg of the unusually long April road trip took the Mets to Houston for a weekend series. In the opener Jerry Koosman, wishing the Mets would've saved some of the 17 runs they scored in Pittsburgh for him, lost a two-hitter and a ballgame when Cesar Cedeno belted a two-run homer off him in the last of the seventh inning. The Mets, meanwhile, managed only one run off Astros starter Mike Cosgrove and reliever Ken Forsch.

Tom Seaver fired a three-hitter and the Mets exploded for seven runs on 12 hits as New York downed the Astros, 7–1, in the middle game of the series. Every Met in the lineup with the exception of Jerry Grote had a base hit, including Tom Seaver, whose base hit in the eighth inning drove in two runs.

The Mets took the rubber game of the series, 4–2. For the third straight game Cesar Cedeno drove in the only runs the Astros would score when he slammed a two-run homer in the last off the fourth inning off Mets starter Jon Matlack. Jerry Koosman noted after the game, "If it hadn't been for Cedeno, we'd have shut them out all three times."[11]

That was little solace for both Koosman, who took the loss on Friday night despite pitching exceptional ball prior to Cedeno's blast, as well as Matlack, who allowed nothing before Cedeno's home run and nothing after it but didn't figure in the decision.

Cedeno's blast eclipsed a 1–0 Mets lead, which held up until the Mets came to bat in the seventh inning and scored a lone run, knotting the game, 2–2. With Matlack being pinch-hit for in the seventh inning, Ken Sanders came on to pitch in the last of the seventh and was the beneficiary of the two runs the Mets scored in the top of the eighth to pick up his first win of the year.

In another first, manager Joe Frazier was tossed for the first time from a major league game when he came out of the dugout to question home plate umpire Jim Quick on a balk call on Matlack in the fourth inning. Frazier was unaware of a rule that prohibits anyone leaving the dugout to question a balk call.

All of 3,342 fans showed up to Shea Stadium to watch the Mets return home after their 12-game road trip to take on the Atlanta Braves. Mickey Lolich earned his first win in the National League and as a member of the New York Mets, as New York downed the Braves, 3–1. In addition, Lolich chalked up the 2,700th strikeout of his career. "It feels super," said Lolich. "That was the Lolich I traded for," said a thrilled Joe Frazier.[12] The hitting star for the Mets was catcher Ron Hodges, whose two-run single in the second inning put the Mets ahead to stay.

The Mets won their fourth game in a row the next day in dramatic fashion, scoring three runs in the ninth while coming back to beat the Braves, 6–5. Singles by Dave Kingman and pinch-hitters Jerry Grote and John Milner produced the Mets' fourth run and brought rookie Bruce Boisclair to the plate against Braves rookie reliever Pablo Torrealba. Boisclair drilled Torrealba's fifth pitch to the right-center field fence, scoring Grote and Milner with the tying and winning runs. "I was delighted when they left him in," said Boisclair after the game, commenting on Braves manager Dave Bristol's decision to leave Torrealba in to face Boisclair. "I faced him about twelve times in the International League the past three years and I got something like ten hits."[13]

The Braves scored all their runs off Jerry Koosman, building a 5–1 lead after six innings, with the big blow being a two-run homer by Vic Correll in the fifth inning. The Mets started to cut into the Braves' lead in the seventh inning when Dave Kingman hit another tape-measure blast, completely clearing Shea Stadium, for his eighth homer of the year. They added another run in the eighth to bring the Mets' deficit down to two heading into the last of the ninth. Tom Hall, the third Mets pitcher, picked up his first win of the season.

The winning streak was extended to five games as Dave Kingman blasted a three-run homer in the first inning and Craig Swan pitched a complete-game shutout, stopping the Braves on five hits while fanning 11, as the Mets won the third game of the four-game series with Atlanta.

Tom Seaver allowed just five hits as the Mets, for the second consecutive game, received shutout pitching. They swept the Braves in the four-game series

Mickey Lolich en route to his first Mets win (AP Images).

and won their sixth consecutive game. Seaver retired the first seven batters he faced and later set down 12 in a row while fanning nine. "He pitches like a winner," a proud Frazier said after the game. "You get him a couple of runs in the latter stages of the game and you don't beat him."[14] On this day the latter stages meant the sixth inning when the Mets scored their two runs, one coming on a Dave Kingman single and the other on an error by Wayne Garrett.

Sad to see the Braves leave town, the Mets welcomed the Astros into Shea for a three-game weekend series. In the opener, only a wild pitch prevented the Mets' pitching staff from hurling three consecutive shutouts, as New York won its seventh consecutive game. Jon Matlack pitched a complete game, upping his record to 3-0.

One controversial note in the game occurred in the seventh inning, when an errant pickoff attempt by Jon Matlack got by Dave Kingman at first base and bounced directly to the ball girl, Christina Anderson, down the right field line. Anderson picked the ball clean while it was still in play and flipped it back to Kingman. While the base runner, Roger Metzger, stopped at second, the Astros argued that he should be allowed third due to interference by the ball girl. The first base umpire, Dick Stello, maintained, however, that Metzger advanced as far as he possibly could, and made him stay at second. While Metzger was the tying run at the time, it was all academic as the next batter flied out to end the inning. The Mets ended April with 13 victories, the most in team history. They also owned the most wins in the majors and the longest winning streak thus far in the 1976 season.

After rain washed out Saturday's regularly scheduled game, the contest was rescheduled for a Sunday afternoon doubleheader. Close to 30,000 fans showed up to Shea Stadium hoping the Mets could extend their winning streak to nine games. Those hopes were dashed when the Astros scored a ninth-inning run in the first game, sending the Mets to defeat for the first time in eight games. While the Mets built a 3–0 lead in the first game, shoddy defense in the fifth inning behind the snake-bitten Lolich allowed four runs to score, giving the Astros a 4–3 lead.

The Mets were able to tie the game in the last of the sixth inning when Kranepool launched his second home run of the young season. Bob Apodaca, pitching in relief of Lolich, was able to hold the Astros off the scoreboard until the ninth inning, when he allowed two hits and a sacrifice before Larry Milbourne's single to left field scored the tie-breaking run. The Mets, however, were able to capture the nightcap behind the pitching of Jerry Koosman and the power of Wayne Garrett and Del Unser, as the Mets stopped the Astros, 7–4.

The world champion Cincinnati Reds arrived at Shea on an uncharacteristic chilly May evening, with the thermometer dipping to 48 degrees. Both starting pitchers, Tom Seaver for the Mets and Fred Norman for the Reds, suffered with their control. Fred Norman left the game after two innings, walking five without allowing a base hit, as the Mets scored two runs in the second inning. The Reds got one run back in the third inning when Seaver suffered with his control as well. Dave Kingman's two-run homer in the bottom of the third, his 10th of the year, gave the Mets a 4–1 advantage. The Mets were able to eventually extend their lead to 5–2 and hold off a ninth-inning Reds rally to win their ninth game in ten outings. Tom Seaver remained undefeated as he picked up his fourth win, while Skip Lockwood earned his third save of the year.

The middle game of the series was a classic nine-inning scoreless contest between Gary Nolan of the Reds and Jon Matlack. The game turned against the Mets after Matlack had to leave with two outs in the tenth inning due to cramps in his pitching hand. While his replacement, Ken Sanders, was able to get out of the inning without any further damage, Tom Hall, who replaced Sanders in the eleventh inning, was not as fortunate. A walk to Morgan and RBI singles by Foster and Griffey supplied the Reds with all the offense they would need, as Cincinnati would go on to beat the Mets, 2–0.

The closest the Mets came to scoring was in the seventh inning when they loaded the bases on a walk and singles by Joe Torre and Jerry Grote. However, Nolan was able to get out of the jam when Harrelson lined out to right field. For Harrelson, who went hitless, it was the first game of the season he had been kept off base.

The Mets continued their fine play as they completed their series with the Reds by winning two out of three from the defending world champs while earning their 10th victory out of their last 12 outings. Again, the Mets received excellent pitching as Craig Swan, fresh off his shutout of the Braves, held the Reds to two runs over 7⅓ innings, while Skip Lockwood picked up a five-out save, his fourth save of the year.

With the Reds leaving New York, the San Diego Padres came in for a weekend series to wrap up the homestand. Dave Kingman slammed another two home runs while Jerry Koosman allowed only six hits as the Mets beat the Padres, 6–2. Kingman drove in four runs with his home runs and now led the National League in RBIs as well as tying Mike Schmidt for the home run lead.

Despite Koosman's outstanding performance, the trade of Tom Hall earlier in the day to the Kansas City Royals for a minor league infielder led to talk once again of Koosman returning to the bullpen as the lone left-handed reliever. "I've told the Mets that I prefer starting, but naturally I'll do anything to help the club," said Koosman. "I thought about the fact that we don't have any left-handed relief in the bullpen when I heard the news."[15] With the win the Mets moved back into first place over the Philadelphia Phillies.

The Mets kept right on rolling as they won their third straight game, pounding out 12 singles as they handily beat the Padres behind Mickey Lolich for their 12th win in 14 games. While the Padres scored a first-inning run off Lolich, the Mets came right back by scoring four runs in their half of the first and were never threatened thereafter. "It doesn't frighten me that they're off to such a great start," said Frazier. "Ever since our first road trip, they've been playing like hell."[16]

The Padres avoided a sweep by beating the Mets and Tom Seaver, 2–0. The Mets who smacked the Padres' pitching around for 12 hits on Saturday, could only muster two hits and no runs off Padres starter and former Met Brent Strom. "I wasn't very good today," said Seaver. In addition to losing his first game of the year, Seaver also received a $50 fine after hitting Winfield with a pitch in the eighth inning. This followed after Seaver just barely missed hitting Winfield with the pitch before. "The first ball I threw him was a fastball and I was trying to get it inside to him," said Seaver. "But the pitch I hit him with was a changeup."[17]

With the conclusion of the successful homestand, the Mets set off to Atlanta to take on the Braves, a team in the midst of a 13-game losing streak. In an attempt to break the losing streak, the Braves held a prayer service and fired off a cannon. Braves maverick owner Ted Turner culminated the ceremony, making a complete fool of himself by running around the bases with a broom and turning a somersault.

The game itself was a seesaw affair, alternating with the Braves taking the lead and the Mets catching up, until the Braves won the game when they scored a ninth-inning run off Bob Apodaca. With the losing streak over, Ted Turner continued his antics by doing somersaults and jumping around as if the Braves had won the World Series.

In the next game the Kingman-Koosman combination struck again, with Kingman belting another pair of home runs and Koosman keeping the Braves off the scoreboard until there were two outs in the ninth, when Jimmy Wynn connected for a pinch-hit three-run homer. While Kingman's blasts were of the solo variety, coming in the second and the fifth off Braves starter Andy Messersmith, the Mets also put together a three-run fourth inning. During that inning, Joe Torre, wielding a red-hot bat, led off with a single and surprised all 8,500 fans in attendance by stealing his first base as a Met. A walk, a couple base hits and a sacrifice fly and the Mets had three more runs across the plate.

After splitting the two-game series with the Braves, the Mets took off for Cincinnati on their next leg of their second road trip of the season. Mickey Lolich continued to suffer from poor defensive play behind him as a three-hit, eight-strikeout performance went to waste. The Mets' defense committed three errors, leading to the Reds scoring four unearned runs. "You can't win games playing like that," commented Joe Frazier on the poor effort turned in by the defense.[18] On the other hand, the Reds had nothing but praise for Lolich after the game. Johnny Bench, who homered off Lolich, called him a "flirter of the corners who makes you hit his pitch."[19] The Mets could muster only four hits off Reds starter and winner Jack Billingham, one of them being a pinch-hit home run by Benny Ayala in the ninth inning for the Mets' only run.

The Mets failed to score a run for Tom Seaver for his second straight outing as New York fell to the Reds for the second consecutive game. While it was a controversial call that allowed the Reds to score their two runs, at best it would've resulted in a scoreless game after nine innings, as the Mets were able to muster only four hits off Reds rookie pitcher Santo Alcala. John Milner, who started a game for the first time since April 25, had two of the Mets' hits; doubles by Joe Torre and Dave Kingman accounted for the other two Mets hits.

The Reds managed seven hits off Seaver but were only able to tally twice. In the second inning with two outs and Tony Perez on second and Dan Driessen at third, the runners took off. While a replay showed that Tony Perez was out, second base umpire Dick Stello ruled otherwise, despite a lengthy and vigorous argument by Felix Millan. "My glove was between the bag and his foot," said Millan. "The ump blew the call," said a disgusted Frazier.[20]

With Perez ruled safe at second, Driessen's run counted and the Reds had an early 1–0 lead. The next batter, Dave Concepcion, hit a long fly ball to right field that Dave Kingman never saw and fell for a triple, giving the Reds their final run of the game.

The Mets completed the series in Cincinnati by splitting a Sunday afternoon doubleheader. The opening-game win marked the first time the Mets won a game at Riverfront Stadium since May 20, 1975, when Jerry Koosman stopped the Reds, 6–2.

The Mets returned home for a short two-game series with the Phillies before heading off to Montréal. In a battle for first place as well as a showdown between the league leaders in home runs, Mike Schmidt and Dave Kingman with 14 each, the Phillies took the opener, 2–1. While Mets starter Mickey Lolich again came up with another strong performance, he was let down by the Mets' inability to come up with key hits in key situations, resulting in 12 stranded base runners and Lolich's fifth loss of the year. While the Phillies were able to bunch together hits in both the fourth and fifth inning, accounting for the Philadelphia runs, the Mets, though constantly threatening, were not able to put any runs on the board until the last of the eighth when they scored their lone run on a pinch-single by Jerry Grote. The Mets nearly took the lead in the eighth inning when a drive by Joe Torre, which had home run distance, was foul by inches.

The Phillies were assisted by a well-rested bullpen, which had not seen action in a week. As a result, the Phillies were able to call on a trio of relievers, including McGraw, Gene Garber and Tom Underwood. McGraw was the first of the relievers, coming in during the seventh with two Mets base runners aboard. McGraw ended the threat when Unser popped up and Felix Millan grounded into a double play.

McGraw, obviously still hurt by the trade, had this response when asked about the health of his shoulder. "My shoulder is okay, but I've still got a scar where the Mets stuck the knife in my back."[21] The Mets recalled outfielder Leon Brown from the minors before the game. Brown responded with a pinch-hit double in his first major league at-bat.

In his next start, Tom Seaver finally got some runs to work with. Seaver, however, gave up more runs than he received as he lost his third game of the year. The Mets were swept in their mini-homestand and had lost their last five out of six games. The Phillies got to work early off Seaver as they sent nine men to the plate in the first inning, scoring four runs on five hits. Seaver settled down after his shaky first and allowed the Phillies nothing until the eighth inning, when Mike Schmidt crashed his 15th home run of the year. In the meantime, the Mets could do nothing off Phillies starter Jim Lonborg until the sixth inning, when Dave Kingman launched his 15th home run of the year with John Milner on base, cutting the Phillies' lead to 4–2. The Mets drew within one in the seventh inning when Felix Millan doubled and Mike Phillips singled. With left-handed batters Garrett and Milner due up next, Phillies manager Danny Ozark went to his bullpen to call on Tug McGraw. McGraw, who had made a living tormenting his old team since his exile to Philadelphia, did the job once more by retiring both Garrett and Milner on pop flies.

McGraw's resentment over the deal ratcheted up a notch as McGraw and McDonald exchanged nasty words before the game. McGraw was bitter about being dealt because the Mets considered him to be damaged goods. "I resent the things Tug said about my honesty," said McDonald. "We traded him because he had a bad year, not a bad arm. And it wasn't just me; Yogi Berra approved the deal too. We needed a center fielder and we got one."[22]

The Mets traveled on to Montreal and old Jarry Park, where the Expos were spending their last season before moving into Olympic Stadium for the 1977 slate. Wayne Garrett drove in all four Mets runs as New York came from behind to beat the Expos, 4–3. Andre Thornton, recently acquired by the Expos from the Cubs, drove in all three Expos runs, with the first two coming on a two-run homer in the bottom of the first inning off Mets starter Jon Matlack.

The Mets, held off the scoreboard for the first six innings by Montreal starter Steve Rogers, tied the game in the top of the seventh inning when Bruce Boisclair, pinch-hitting for Matlack, bunted his way on. Wayne Garrett then followed with his second home run of the year, tying the game. "It was a high changeup," said Garrett. "I was just saying to myself, 'Throw the ball up and I'm going to lean on it.'"[23]

The Expos, however, were able to regain the lead in the last of the seventh, when Dave Kingman had trouble playing a ball in the outfield. After reliever Bob Apodaca walked Pepe Mangual, Jerry White hit a drive to deep right-center field. Dave Kingman, going back for the ball, slipped on the wet ground and couldn't recover until Mangual was rounding third and heading home. Kingman got the ball into the relay man, Millan, who fired a perfect strike to Grote to nab Mangual. However, on the play, White was able to coast into third and scored on Thornton's base hit.

With the Mets now trailing by one in the last of the ninth, Grote walked to lead off the inning. Ron Hodges, batting for Harrelson, followed with another base hit. Joe Torre, batting for Lockwood, bounced back to the mound, forcing Grote at third, but Garrett then drilled a ball into the gap, scoring both Hodges and Leon Brown, who was running for Torre. The Mets now had a 4–3 lead, which Ken Sanders was able to preserve while picking up his first save of the year. Skip Lockwood, who pitched an inning and a third, earned his second win of the year.

The thrilling win was followed by the 1,000th victory in franchise history as the Mets downed the Expos with another come-from-behind effort. The Expos scored first in the third inning on a sacrifice fly by Gary Carter. However, the Expos were unable to do anything more against Mets starter Jerry Koosman, who allowed Montreal only four hits over the seven innings he worked. With Expos starter Don Stanhouse shutting out the Mets over the first seven innings, Frazier pulled Koosman in favor of pinch-hitter Bruce Boisclair to start the eighth. Frazier's strategy paid off as Boisclair singled. Expos manager Karl Kuehl then pulled Stanhouse in favor of the left-handed Fred Scherman to face the left-handed batting Garrett. Scherman walked Garrett, and Kuehl took another stroll to the mound and brought in Wayne Granger to face Millan. Granger induced Millan to pop up, but surrendered an infield hit to John Milner, loading the bases for Dave Kingman. The Expos nearly escaped trouble when Kingman popped up, but Granger could not retire Kranepool, who ended up drawing a walk to force home the tying run. The fourth pitcher of the inning, Dale Murray, was then brought in by Kuehl in an attempt to stem the tide, but Del Unser singled to center, scoring two runs, and the Mets were up 3–1. An infield single by Jerry Grote scored the fourth run in the inning.

For Koosman, who started the season as the left-hander out of the bullpen, it was his fourth win in a row, and upped his record to 5–1. Skip Lockwood, who pitched the last two innings, picked up his sixth save of the year.

A two-run seventh inning off Mets starter Craig Swan prevented New York from sweeping the weekend series in Montreal. As in the previous two games, the Mets fell behind early when the Expos scored two runs in the first inning. In a back-and-forth game, the Expos scored two unanswered runs in the last of the eighth inning to salvage the final game of the series.

The next stop on the Mets' venue was Philadelphia to take on the Phillies for a big four-game series. In the opener the Phillies ripped Lolich apart for six runs in less than two innings as the left-hander suffered his sixth defeat since joining the Mets. With the loss, the Mets dropped into third place, 5½ games behind the division-leading Phillies.

The Phillies' bats continued to dominate the Mets' pitching staff after tearing into Tom Seaver and beating New York by an 8–4 decision. Seaver was knocked around for seven runs and 14 hits in the six innings he worked. "When you're bad, you're bad," said Seaver, lamenting the low number of pitches he threw that he was satisfied with.[24] What made the loss particularly painful for Seaver, his fourth consecutive defeat, was that he was given an early 3–0 lead when Kingman hit his 16th homer in the first with two aboard. The Mets culminated their scoring in the seventh inning when Jerry Grote hit his first homer of the year. The winning pitcher for the Phillies, Jim Lonborg, improved his record to a perfect 7–0.

While Lonborg kept his perfect winning record alive with his win, Jon Matlack's perfect record went by the wayside in the third game of the series after Steve Carlton and the Phillies clipped the Mets, 5–0. While the Phillies' offense continued to pound Mets pitching, with both Luzinski and Ollie Brown taking Matlack deep with a base runner aboard, the Mets couldn't muster more than three hits off Carlton, the ace of the Phillies' staff.

For the Mets it was their fourth loss in a row, and they fell to 7½ games behind the Phillies, who were beginning to run away with the division. After the game the Mets optioned Hank Webb to Tidewater and recalled left-hander Bob Myrick and right-hander Rick Baldwin in order to bolster the relief corps.

The Mets avoided a sweep at the hands of the Phillies behind the clutch pitching of Jerry Koosman and the clutch hitting of Wayne Garrett as they came from behind in the ninth inning to beat the Phillies, 5–2. The Mets, who were trailing 1–0 as they came to bat in the seventh inning, tied the game when Kingman hit his 17th homer of the year. The tie, however, lasted only as long as it took the Phillies to come to bat in the last of the seventh, as Ollie Brown continued to terrorize Koosman when he led off with a home run against the left-hander.

In the ninth, John Milner, batting for Koosman, led off with a base hit. An attempted sacrifice by Bud Harrelson was booted by Jim Kaat, and the Mets now had runners on first and second. Leon Brown attempted to bunt the runners over, but failed to do so as Milner was forced at third. Danny Ozark pulled Kaat and brought in right-hander Gene Garber to face the right-handed batting Joe Torre. Frazier countered by sending Kranepool to bat for Torre, and Kranepool responded by sending a base hit into short center field. Seemingly, the Mets had the game tied. But the Mets didn't count on Garry Maddox, who aggressively charged the ball to throw a strike to Bob Boone, who had the plate blocked and easily tagged Harrelson out. "I couldn't move that son of a gun," said the minuscule Harrelson. "He's too big."[25] After the Mets loaded the bases, Phillies manager Ozark made a trip to the mound to call on McGraw, who had tormented his former mates ever since the trade, to face the left-handed batting Garrett. After getting two quick strikes on nasty sliders, McGraw threw a couple of balls and Garrett fouled off a couple of pitches. McGraw then threw a meatball down the middle of the plate. Garrett wasted no time depositing the ball deep into the gap in right-center field, clearing the bases.

With the disappointing 3–4 road trip behind them, the Mets returned home for a weekend series against the Cardinals. For the second time in three games, the Mets couldn't manage more than three hits against an opposing left-hander, and for the second time in three games, the Mets were shut out. Willie Crawford hit a grand slam off Mets starter Craig Swan, who went down to defeat for the fourth time of the season. If there were any good news for Mets fans on the evening, it was the work of the two relief pitchers the Mets had called up. Bob Myrick pitched a perfect third of an inning, while Rick Baldwin pitched three innings, allowing only two harmless singles and two harmless walks.

The Mets lost the second game of the series as well despite a well-pitched effort by Mickey Lolich. The left-hander failed in his attempt to pick up his third win as a Met, as the Mets' offense failed to provide more than two runs for the luckless Lolich. While Lolich allowed only two runs himself, the Mets lost the game in the 10th inning when Reggie Smith led off the frame with a home run off Ken Sanders.

Tom Seaver was one out away from breaking his four-game losing streak, and the Mets were one out away from salvaging the final game of the series with the Cardinals. Seaver never got that last out, and instead the Mets lost for the seventh time in eight tries and their 12th out of their last 16 games. The Mets were rapidly falling out of the National League East race as they fell 9½ games behind the Phillies.

With the Mets taking a 5–2 lead into the ninth, the big blow being John Milner's sixth home run of the year, Tom Seaver took the mound needing three outs to register his fifth win of the season. Seaver walked the bases full and then surrendered a two-run single to Lou Brock. Lockwood replaced Seaver to face Don Kessinger, who smacked a line drive to left field, where Leon Brown attempted to make a diving catch. The ball hit off Brown's glove and the game was tied.

The Mets then gave the game away in the 11th inning. Willie Crawford led off with a single, and Lockwood had two runners on with nobody out when he booted Vic Harris' sacrifice bunt. After Al Hrabosky struck out, Lockwood dug an even greater hole for himself when he threw a wild pitch, advancing the runners to second and third. The Mets then lost the game on a rookie mistake, when Don Kessinger hit a foul fly across the left field line. Instead of allowing the ball to drop, Leon Brown caught the ball as Crawford tagged and scored what proved to be the winning run. However, the big story of the game was the manager's criticism of the home plate umpire's judgment on calling balls and strikes in the ninth inning, which Frazier believed cost the Mets the game. "Did you ever see such awful stuff?"[26] complained Frazier. Frazier was referring to Artie Williams, the lone black umpire in the league.

The Pirates followed the Cardinals into Shea for a three-game series, beginning with a twilight doubleheader. After combining to score 12 runs in the last five games, and averaging only 2½ runs in the last 16 games, the Mets exploded for 13 runs in the first game of the twinbill as they trounced the Pirates, 13–2. It was the second time of the season the Mets manhandled the Pirates in a game, the first coming early in the campaign in Pittsburgh when the Mets pasted the Pirates, 17–1.

With the Mets carrying a 2–1 lead into the fourth inning, they exploded for six runs in the frame and added five more in the sixth. While Pirates starter Jerry Reuss was knocked around for seven runs on six hits before being removed from the game, his replacement, Kent Tekulve, bore the brunt of the Mets' assault, as he was charged with five runs on five hits in less than two innings. The Mets' offense was a joint effort, with six Mets coming up with two hits apiece. Surprisingly, the only spot in the lineup that failed to get a hit was the leadoff spot, where Leon Brown and Del Unser combined to go 0-for-5. Jon Matlack scattered five hits and fanned seven in picking up his fifth win of the season in the first game of the doubleheader.

The Mets' bats went back into hibernation for the second game, managing only a home run by Ron Hodges after two were out in the last off the ninth inning off Pirates starter and former Yankee Doc Medich. Bob Apodaca got a rare starting assignment and pitched well despite picking up his third loss of the year. Apodaca allowed only an unearned run in the first inning after Mike Phillips dropped a flip on a force play in his haste to complete a double play, and a Duffy Dyer solo homer in the second inning.

After the doubleheader, Joe Frazier apologized for what many considered to be racist remarks in his criticism of umpire Art Williams. "I want you to print my apology to the umpire, Mr. Williams," said Frazier. "In regards to my good black friends in the country, I meant nothing about race in what I said about his umpiring."[27]

In a roster move, the Mets sent Benny Ayala down to the minors and recalled utility shortstop Jack Heidemann to give the team more infield depth with both Harrelson and Millan nursing minor injuries.

The month of June began the same way the Mets ended the month of May by struggling for runs. A solid pitching performance by the Mets' stopper, Jerry Koosman, and two home runs by Joe Torre were not enough to stop the Mets' recent losing ways as the Pirates beat them, 3–2. With the loss, the Mets had lost 14 of their last 19 games.

The Mets took a rare 1–0 lead in the first inning when Torre connected off Pirates starter John Candelaria for his third homer of the year. The Pirates took the lead, however, in the top of the fourth inning, when Bill Robinson, who had made a living killing the Mets, singled to lead off the frame. Two outs later, Bob Robertson and his minuscule .128 batting average took Koosman deep. The Pirates extended their lead in the sixth when Robinson struck again, this time doubling down the left field line and scoring on a Richie Zisk base hit. The Mets cut into the Pirates' lead when Torre hit his second home run of the year in the last of the ninth inning. However, Torre's blast was too little, too late.

After New York lost two out of three to the Pirates, the Cubs came into Shea and swept the Mets in a two-game series. A four-run fifth inning in the opener sent the Mets limping to their 10th loss in 12 games and their 17th in their last 23 games. A season, which after one month seemed so promising as the Mets posted an 18-9 record and resided in first place, seemed to be heading for disaster after two months. The Mets' record dropped to 24-26 and a whopping 11½ games behind the first-place Phillies. A combination of injuries, lack of clutch hitting and atrocious defense were the main ingredients in the Mets' sudden but rapid descent. Bud Harrelson was nursing a bruised right leg, which was only getting worse, while Felix Millan was nursing a sore right shoulder. A strained groin muscle slowed John Milner, who offensively got off to a sizzling start. Mike Vail, Rusty Staub's designated replacement, was still hobbling along on his damaged right ankle and was nowhere close to returning to the active roster. "You can't fight injuries," said Frazier. "That's what we've got. Half the team's out."[28]

The game itself was symptomatic of the Mets' troubles. In the first inning, the Mets loaded the bases with no outs and their leading run producer, Dave Kingman, at the plate. Kingman, however, grounded into a double play, and the Mets settled for just one run. The Mets scratched out another run in the second inning, but gave it back in the fifth inning. A leadoff single by Rick Monday was the equivalent of a triple after Mets starter Craig Swan threw the ball away while trying to pick Monday off first. Swan compounded his problems by hitting the next batter, Jose Cardenal. Three straight base hits and a throwing error by Kingman along the way netted the Cubs four runs and the ball game.

A disastrous homestand, which saw the Mets win only one of eight games, came to an end after the Mets lost the finale of the series to the Cubs, 2–1. Again the Mets were done in by a lack of clutch hitting and poor defense. Dave Kingman was the biggest culprit, stranding seven base runners, including the tying and winning runs in the last of the ninth inning. Mickey Lolich didn't help himself, either. With the score tied at one in the seventh inning and a runner on first, Lolich bounced a pitch, advancing the go-ahead run to second base. Lolich compounded his problems when Frazier asked him if he wanted to walk the No. 8 hitter, Mick Kelleher, intentionally and face the pitcher, only to have Lolich elect to pitch to Kelleher. Lolich got burned when Kelleher singled home what proved to be the winning run.

Now it was time for the Mets to make their first cross-country flight of the season, starting a long road trip against the California clubs. Mets fans could only hope that a change of scenery would bring a change in luck.

During the first two months of the season, the trend was, as Dave Kingman went, so did the Mets. When Kingman was driving in runs by the droves early on, the Mets were winning games in droves and were within one game of first place at the end of April. When Kingman's bat cooled off during May, the Mets lost 18 out of 24 games. The real Dave Kingman returned to open the trip as he slammed three home runs on three consecutives pitches and drove in eight runs as the Mets romped all over the Dodgers, 11–0.

With the game scoreless after three innings, John Milner singled and Kingman crushed the first pitch he saw from Dodgers starter Burt Hooton. In the fifth inning, Roy Staiger led off with a single and advanced to second on a sacrifice by Tom Seaver. Mike Phillips singled home Staiger and Garrett followed with a walk. After Milner flied out, Hooton, who went by the nickname "Happy," was none too pleased after Kingman again deposited the first pitch he saw from Hooton over the wall, good for a three-run homer and a 6–0 Mets lead. Ed Kranepool, the next batter, followed Kingman by blasting another home run, thus ending Hooton's unhappy night. Kingman struck again in the seventh inning. With the Mets leading 7–0 and Mike Phillips and John Milner on base, Dave Kingman took the first pitch he saw from Dodgers reliever Al Downing and launched it over the left field wall, extending the Mets' lead to 10–0. Tom Seaver snapped out of his personal four-game losing streak in grand fashion as he allowed the Dodgers only three hits and fanned eight, while picking up his fifth win of the season.

The Mets won the second game of the series as well before the Dodgers avenged their Friday evening rout by roughing up Jerry Koosman for six runs and 10 hits in just two innings of work on their way to a 10–3 rout.

The next stop on the Mets' itinerary brought them to San Diego, where a key fielding error by Mike Phillips with two outs in the sixth inning opened the door for the Padres. The hosts scored two unearned runs on their way to a 5–1 decision over the Mets in the opener. With the Mets leading 1–0 in the sixth inning, and Mets starter Craig Swan pitching a masterpiece, Swan was on the verge of getting out of the inning on a grounder to short. Phillips threw the ball away, extending the inning and setting up Willie McCovey's double, which scored two runs. "If you can't make routine plays, you can't win," said an angry Frazier after the game.[29]

The Mets' offensive sabbatical continued the next day as they failed to muster more than three hits off Padres starter Dave Freisleben and did not score a run as they went down to defeat for the third game in a row. Even worse was another wasted pitching performance as Mickey Lolich allowed only two runs on three hits in the five innings he worked. "I've never seen anything like it," said a frustrated and angry Frazier. "We can't get no runs, or we get them all at one time."[30] With the trading deadline just a week away, Frazier hoped that GM Joe McDonald would be able to come up with another hitter.

Despite Frazier's attempt to light a fire under his beleaguered offense, nothing changed as the Mets were shut out and lost by the same 3–0 score in the third game against the Padres. Tom Seaver was the victim of the Mets' impotence at the plate as his record dropped to an even 5-5. Randy Jones, rapidly climbing the ranks toward being one of the top pitchers in the National League, was Seaver's opposition and picked up his 11th win of the season against only two losses. After the game, Jones' mound opponent was full of praise for the Padres' young left-hander. "He pitched a hell of a game," said Tom Seaver. "He kept the ball down and when we hit it, we hit at somebody."[31]

The Mets salvaged the last game of the series behind a five-hit shutout by Jon Matlack. Despite only managing six hits, the Mets combined clutch hitting and poor Padres defense as the Mets won for only the fifth time in the last twenty games. Dave Kingman blasted his 22nd home run of the year, a solo shot in the sixth inning. The Mets also received a boost when Bud Harrelson returned to the lineup for the first time in 15 games. Harrelson contributed two hits along with solid defense. Matlack, in an overpowering performance, fanned eight as he boosted his record to 7-1, his best start since joining the Mets in 1971. "It feels good," said Frazier after the game. "I'd like to win a few more now."[32]

The weekend brought the Mets to Candlestick Park in San Francisco where the Mets' offense returned to the form they've been in for most of the last month, as in non-existent. John Montefusco and the Giants shut the Mets out on three hits, 5–0. It marked the third time in four games that the Mets were held scoreless. It also marked the second time in four games they failed to manage more than three hits. Jerry Koosman surrendered a three-run homer to Bobby Murcer in the first inning and a two-run homer to Marc Hill in the second inning, which accounted for all the scoring.

In the middle game of the series, the Mets managed one hit less than the day before but still beat the Giants, 3–1. Nine walks by Giants pitcher John D'Acquisto as well as poor defensive play by San Francisco assisted the Mets in their victory.

The Mets ended their California trip with a winning record after sweeping the Giants in a doubleheader. "Winning two changed this road trip, didn't it?" Frazier asked after the sweep.[33] Mickey Lolich, who had given up only 10 earned runs in his last six games, was the rare recipient of good fortune as the Giants committed three errors, resulting in the Mets scoring two unearned runs in the first game of the doubleheader. Despite the Giants scoring twice in the first inning, Mickey Lolich and Bob Apodaca kept the Giants off the board the rest of the way, as the Mets were able to come back from their 2–0 deficit. Tom Seaver won his second game of the road trip, keeping the Giants off the board until the ninth inning, when they scored on three consecutive singles after the Mets had amassed a four-run lead. With the road trip behind them, the Mets returned home basically in the same position as when they left — in third place and 11½ games out of first place.

Back home to play the California teams on their home turf, Jon Matlack, with another strong performance, raised his record to 8-1, as the Mets took the Dodgers in the opener, 2–1, to win their fourth consecutive game. The game was scoreless for the first six innings, as the Mets wasted several opportunities off Dodgers starter Burt Hooton. The Dodgers tallied first, scoring a run off Matlack in the seventh inning. But the Mets were able to tie the game in the seventh inning when a pop fly by Wayne Garrett fell in due to a miscommunication between shortstop Bill Russell and left fielder Dusty Baker. Russell was under the impression that Baker had called him off, while Baker said he had never called for the ball. The Mets scored the go-ahead run in the eighth inning when Bud Harrelson reached on a drag bunt, despite the Dodgers arguing that Harrelson ran out of the base line. Dave Kingman drove Harrelson home when he reached for an outside pitch by Burt Hooton and stroked it into the outfield for a base hit. In addition, the Mets were aided by a terrific catch by John Milner in left field.

After the game the Mets' brass felt they had to defend their inability to trade for a legitimate hitter by the National League trading deadline, despite the team struggling mightily offensively. "Joe (McDonald) has worked tirelessly to acquire players beneficial to our team, but no deal was offered to us that we thought would be worthy of what we have to give up," said board chairman M. Donald Grant. "No one was willing to sell, and we've made some really good cash offers."[34] Grant further bemoaned the fact that the only players other teams were interested in were Seaver, Koosman and Matlack, for less than equal value.

The Mets did make some personnel moves, activating Mike Vail and demoting Rick Baldwin. They also placed Ron Hodges on the 15-day disabled list and recalled backup catcher Jay Kleven from Tidewater.

Two lefties, Doug Rau and Jerry Koosman, squared off in the middle game of the series. The Mets scored their daily one run in the last of the fifth inning, and for the first six innings, it appeared that would be enough as Mets starter Jerry Koosman kept the Dodgers off the scoreboard. With one out in the Dodgers' seventh inning, Steve Garvey bunted for a base hit. The next three batters hit balls that just barely eluded Bud Harrelson, and very quickly the Dodgers had a 2–1 lead. A moment later, after Lockwood replaced Koosman on the mound, Ted Sizemore stroked a double, driving in two more runs, and the Mets' offense was no longer in position to challenge the Dodgers, going down to a 4–1 defeat. Koosman, the hard-luck starter and loser, saw his record drop to 6–5 after getting off to a 6–1 start.

The Mets again scored their one run in the series finale with the Dodgers, though it took the Mets 14 innings to score their run of the day. Met pitchers Craig Swan and Skip Lockwood had the foresight to keep the Dodgers off the scoreboard as well. Craig Swan pitched an overpowering 10 innings, allowing just three hits while fanning eight. Skip Lockwood, who was overpowering in his own right by virtue of pitching four hitless innings while fanning six, was the winning pitcher.

A day earlier, Dave Kingman fanned against Dodgers relief ace Charlie Hough with the tying run at the plate in the last of the ninth inning. Kingman got his revenge off Hough in the 14th inning, when he drilled a Hough pitch deep into the left field bullpen for a walk-off home run. "The home run didn't make me feel any better," said Kingman. "Winning did a little bit, but I'm still swinging bad and I'm still in a slump."[35] Incidentally, for Kingman it was his 23rd home run of the season.

The Giants were the next California team to come calling, and despite the struggling offense, home runs by John Milner and Ed Kranepool powered the Mets past San Francisco, 3–2. With the win the Mets had won six out of their last seven games, while the loss for the Giants was their seventh in a row. Tom Seaver, who pitched a complete game two-hitter and had won three out of his last four starts after suffering a personal four-game losing streak, believed his change in fortunes stemmed from adjustments he made in his delivery.

The Giants snapped their seven-game losing streak and split the series by beating the Mets, 5–0. Mickey Lolich, who was charged with his ninth loss, lasted only four innings before leaving with a headache, most likely caused by Giants shortstop Marty Perez, a .234 hitter, who drove in three runs with a single and a two-run homer.

With the Mets' offense struggling as mightily as it was to score runs and Mickey Lolich suffering his ninth loss in twelve starts, the Rusty Staub trade was beginning to emerge as another disastrous deal in a litany of bad Mets trades consummated over the years. Who was to blame? While board chairman M. Donald Grant made it clear to Joe McDonald that Staub was not to be a Met after the winter meetings due to his contract demands as well as his becoming a 10-and-5 man if he would've played with the Mets for another season, ultimately it was McDonald who pulled the trigger on the deal. He came back with an old, overweight pitcher who wasn't interested in coming to New York and had to be persuaded by Grant to accept the trade.

The Mets traveled on to St. Louis where Jerry Koosman suffered another poor outing, allowing five runs and nine hits in four innings as he lost his fifth consecutive game to even his record at 6-6.

The Mets' offense continued to operate on life support, more dead than alive, and managed only three hits off Cardinals starter John Denny in the second game of the series. New York lost its fourth game in a row, shut out once again. "Maybe it wasn't meant to be," said Frazier. "Maybe we weren't meant to hit the damn ball."[36] After the game the Mets dealt utility infielder Jack Heidemann to the Milwaukee Brewers for a minor league pitcher.

The final game of the series saw the Mets match their run production of their last four games when they scored four runs in the fourth inning. Still, it was Jerry Grote's ninth-inning home run that propelled the Mets to victory, ending their four-game losing streak and salvaging the final game of the series with the Cardinals. The other big story of the game was Mike Vail, who started his first game of the season. Vail, still not at 100 percent, put in six innings before being replaced.

The Mets headed east to Chicago, where slowly the anemic Mets' offense began to show signs of emerging from their month-long melancholy as they downed the Cubs, 7–4. A Dave Kingman three-run homer and a two-run homer by Mike Phillips fueled the Mets' offense. In addition to his home run, Phillips added a single, double and triple to become the third player in Mets history to hit for the cycle. Like Grote the day before, who was mired in an 0-for-23 slump before hitting his game-winning home run, Phillips was in the midst of an 0-for-22 slump before breaking out in grand fashion.

Reminiscent of Gil Hodges during the 1969 season when he pulled Cleon Jones out of a game due to a lack of hustle, Joe Frazier did the same to John Milner. While Hodges' move was more dramatic, as he walked out to left field to bring Jones in with him, Milner was benched after failing to run out a pop-up that eventually fell in. The play occurred in the fifth inning, with the game tied, 3–3. Mike Phillips opened the inning with a triple, and after Millan grounded out, Milner popped the ball up down the right field line. While second baseman Manny Trillo angled under the ball, Milner just watched. After Trillo dropped the ball and Phillips scored, Milner coasted into first base. A moment later, Bruce Boisclair was standing at first base, pinch-running for Milner. Joe Frazier denied Milner was removed for disciplinary reasons, rather he "figured" Milner was hurt as players on his team are expected to hustle at all times. The fact that Milner didn't hustle could mean only one thing—that the groin injury Milner was troubled by on and off during the season was bothering him. While Frazier admitted he didn't ask Milner if he was hurt or not, he maintained that he didn't have to. "Hell, I don't have to ask, I can see. If he has got a bad leg, I don't want him playing."[37] John Milner had even less to say after the game. In fact, he refused to make any comments at all. Jon Matlack picked up his ninth win of the year, scattering nine hits in a complete-game effort, as he fanned six and didn't walk a batter.

If there was any bitterness between Milner and Frazier over the incident, by the end of the next game, it was all smoothed over. The grand slam Milner hit in the third inning, of course, didn't hurt. "We never had any words," said Frazier. Milner, for his part, played down the incident as well. "Yesterday is behind me."[38] After the Cubs took a 1–0 lead in the first inning when leadoff batter Rick Monday homered off Mets starter Jerry Koosman, the Mets roared back with six runs of their own, four coming on Milner's grand slam and another when Kingman went back-to-back with Milner for his 25th home run of the year. With his home run, Kingman was well on his way to overtaking Hack Wilson's National League record for home runs in a season with 56. Mike Phillips hit his second home run in as many days, in the eighth inning, as the Mets coasted to its first victory in a long time. A fine pitching performance by Jerry Koosman, who ended a personal five-game losing streak, further bolstered the Mets.

After the Mets scored 13 runs as they routed the Cubs and swept the three-game series, they couldn't have been anything but disappointed as they packed their bags to leave Wrigley and head home. For a team that barely averaged scoring two runs a game for most of the month of June, the Mets averaged ten runs a game during their brief visit to Chicago. While the team as a whole feasted on the Cubs' pitching staff, no one enjoyed himself more then Mike Phillips. Phillips hit for the cycle in the opener, homered in the next two games, and added a bases-loaded single in the second inning of the finale.

Mike Phillips led off the game where he had left off the day before, as he homered in his second consecutive at-bat and his third in the series. The Mets batted around in the second inning as they broke the game wide open, scoring eight runs. It was the Mets' biggest inning in six years, and it began with Del Unser and Wayne Garrett leading the inning off with base hits. After Grote fanned, Cubs starter Rick Reuschel hit Mets starter Craig Swan on the helmet to load the bases. While some of the Mets felt that Swan was being thrown at deliberately, Swan didn't believe so. "I know he wasn't throwing at me," said Swan. "It was a curveball that just dropped on top of me."[39] Mike Phillips, who couldn't be described anything other than unconscious in the series, singled to drive in two runs and put the Mets on top, 3–0. Felix Millan was robbed on a diving catch by the center fielder Joe Wallis, the man who was responsible for breaking up Tom Seaver's last no-hitter bid. A single by Milner scored another run and a double by Kingman plated another two runs. A two-run homer by Kranepool followed, ending Rick Reuschel's afternoon, as his bespectacled brother Paul replaced him on the mound. Del Unser, the first batter to face Paul

Reuschel, greeted him with a double, continued on to third on a wild pitch, and scored on a single by Grote. Jay Kleven, who was recalled from Tidewater when Ron Hodges went on the disabled list with a hand injury and was sent back down after the game when Hodges was activated, drove in the Mets' final two runs with his first and only major league hit for the foreseeable future. Craig Swan, who for most of the season had pitched very well only to suffer from a lack of run support, pitched seven solid innings, allowing only one run while striking out seven as he picked up his fourth win of the year.

Back home to take on the Cardinals, the Mets scored half the amount of runs they averaged per game in Chicago, but they were still enough to beat St. Louis, 5–4. Dave Kingman hit his 26th home run in the fourth inning as the Mets built a 4–1 lead after six innings with Seaver in cruise control. Three straight singles by the Cardinals and a Tom Seaver error cut the Mets' lead to a scant one run and sent Frazier scurrying out to the mound to replace Seaver with Skip Lockwood. Lockwood reached the mound just as a sudden windstorm hit the stadium. Dirt kicked up in the infield, the outfielders were enveloped in a brown mist, and papers whipped out of the stands like confetti at a ticker-tape parade. The wind, however, had no effect on Lockwood as he fanned Hector Cruz, Mike Tyson and Jerry Mumphry while stranding runners on first and third. Lockwood was not as fortunate in the eighth inning. He loaded the bases by walking two batters and surrendering a single before Ron Fairly drove in the tying run with a sacrifice fly.

The Mets scored the go-ahead run in the last of the eighth inning. John Milner led the inning off with a base hit off Cardinals reliever Bill Greif, but was thrown out when he tried to steal second base. Dave Kingman followed with another base hit, and the Cardinals went to their ace of the bullpen, Al Hrabosky, better known as "the Mad Hungarian." Joe Torre was then called upon to pinch-hit for Kranepool and obliged with a single that sent Kingman to third. Mike Vail, another pinch-hitter, failed in his task as he struck out. Hrabosky, only one out from escaping unscarred, tried to be too careful by not hanging a pitch to Wayne Garrett. He instead bounced his first pitch past catcher Ted Simmons, scoring Kingman with what proved to be the winning run.

The middle game of the series saw the Mets go back to the days of scoring two runs a game. However, it didn't matter as the Mets rolled on to their sixth straight win behind the complete game three-hit shutout spun by Mickey Lolich. The Mets scored the only runs they needed in their half of the first inning when with two outs and nobody on, Joe Torre doubled and Dave Kingman followed with his 27th home run of the year, off Cardinals starter Pete Falcone. For Lolich, it was his fourth win in thirteen decisions and his first National League shutout. "I was a little worried about my control," said Lolich after the game. "I hadn't pitched in 10 days."[40]

After completing a three-game sweep over the Cardinals, the Mets hosted the Cubs at Shea Stadium for a weekend four-game series, culminating with a

Sunday afternoon Fourth of July doubleheader. Another overpowering pitching performance sent the Mets to their eighth consecutive win as Jerry Koosman stopped the Cubs on three hits while fanning 12. Koosman's 12 strikeouts matched the National league high for the year set by both John Candelaria and John Montefusco. The Cubs scored their only run off Koosman on an unearned run in the first inning after Ron Hodges allowed a pitch to get by him. The Mets immediately tied the game in their turn at-bat in the last of the first inning. Mike Phillips, still on fire at the plate, led off with a single. Jerry Morales misplayed a drive by Felix Millan for a two-base error and the game was tied.

The Mets took the lead in the sixth inning. Bruce Boisclair led off with a single, stole second, took third on a groundout, and scored when Ron Hodges, atoning for his first-inning miscue, singled Boisclair home.

After the Cubs scored their run in the first inning, Koosman was in total control, not allowing the Cubs another hit until there were two outs in the ninth inning. Madlock and Morales singled, but Koosman was able to induce Manny Trillo to pop up, preserving his pitching masterpiece. "I had good stuff for a change," said Koosman. Referring to his poor performances that saw him lose five consecutive games during the month of June, Koosman said, "I got into a habit of rushing."[41]

The Mets were able to pull off their ninth consecutive win despite the fact that for the second time in less than a week, Tom Seaver was denied his 10th win of the year. A home run off the bat of Jerry Morales in the top of the ninth inning, with the Mets leading 2–1, tied the game. With the game now tied 2–2, Seaver took the mound for the tenth inning, but was removed after allowing a single and a walk. His replacement, Skip Lockwood, was hit hard, but every ball was hit directly at someone, and the tie remained intact as the Mets came to bat in their half of the tenth. Bud Harrelson, not known for his prowess as a power hitter, drilled a pitch off Cubs starter Rick Reuschel against the right field wall and coasted into third with a triple. Rick Reuschel then walked Joe Torre and Mike Phillips intentionally to load the bases, setting up a force at any base, and then departed in favor of left-handed reliever Darold Knowles. After Knowles fanned his first batter, Bruce Boisclair, Mike Vail was called on to pinch-hit for Leon Brown. But before Vail saw a pitch, Knowles threw over to first in an attempt to pick Phillips off. As Phillips dove back to first, the ball struck him and rolled down the right field line, scoring Harrelson with the winning run. With the Mets having won nine consecutive games, they were only two shy of tying the team record of eleven, which was set back in 1969.

More than 25,000 fans showed up to Shea Stadium on a beautiful Fourth of July afternoon. They watched the Mets fall one game short of matching the team record for consecutive wins when they dropped the second game of their doubleheader, 4–2, to the Cubs. After they extended their winning streak to 10 games by scoring nine runs on only six hits and riding the arm of Craig Swan to victory, the Mets gave away the second game when they gave the Cubs two gift runs in the top of the seventh inning. With the Cubs leading by a slim 2–1 margin, Mick Kelleher led off the seventh inning by drawing a walk. Cubs starting pitcher Ray Burris laid down a sacrifice bunt, which Mickey Lolich pounced on, and then heaved it into right field. By the time the ball was retrieved by Kingman, Kelleher was rounding third on his way home. Kingman attempted to throw the ball home, but threw it away, allowing Ray Burris to circle the bases as well. Mickey Lolich picked up his 10th loss of the year in the nightcap, while Craig Swan was credited with his fifth win in 12 decisions in the opener.

Despite the Mets' 10-game winning streak, they were able to pick up only two games on the Phillies and now trailed Philadelphia by a whopping 12½ games. With the Mets carrying only nine pitchers and with the doubleheaders beginning to mount, Frazier elected to go with Bob Apodaca as a spot starter as the Mets hit the road to take on the Astros and Braves before pausing for the All-Star break. While Apodaca was able to keep the Astros off the board for the first three innings, a six-run fourth inning did him in as the Astros trounced the Mets, 7–3.

The recent 10-game winning streak quickly became a distant memory after the Mets lost their third game in a row after being shut out by the Astros and James Rodney Richard, 1–0, despite not lacking scoring opportunities. In fact, the Mets set a record by stranding 15 base runners without scoring a run as the Astros downed the Mets, 1–0, in 10 innings. The Mets came within inches of scoring in the first inning when Bruce Boisclair singled and John Milner followed with a double. On a pitch to Kingman, which he swung on and missed, catcher Skip Jutze allowed the ball to get past him. After hesitating momentarily, Boisclair broke for the plate but was tagged out when Jutze was able to flip the ball to J.R. Richard just in the nick of time. The Mets squandered numerous opportunities, including leaving the bases loaded in both the seventh and eighth innings.

While the Mets were consistently threatening and failing to score, Mets starter Jon Matlack was masterful as he went nine innings without allowing a run on only five hits. The Mets lost the game in the 10th inning as Skip Lockwood took over the pitching. In a play reminiscent of the second game of Sunday's doubleheader, Wilbur Howard attempted a drag bunt. Lockwood picked the ball up and threw it away, allowing Howard to take third. A moment later Jerry DaVanon singled over the drawn-in infield, driving home the game's only run.

Prior to the game, it was announced that Tom Seaver, Jon Matlack and Dave Kingman would represent the Mets on the National League squad in the upcoming All-Star Game.

Reminiscent of their weekend in Chicago, the Mets halted their three-game losing streak and salvaged the finale of the series with the Astros by smacking around Houston pitchers for 12 runs on 20 hits. Koosman, with relief help from Sanders in the ninth inning, picked up his ninth win against seven losses.

On offense Mike Phillips and Jerry Grote had three hits apiece, while Millan, Milner, Torre, Boisclair, Harrelson and Koosman contributed two hits each.

The Mets headed to Atlanta for a final weekend series with the Braves before baseball took a break for its annual All-Star Game. The opener of the series saw four unearned runs do the Mets in as they went down to defeat at the hands of the Braves, 5–3.

The bright side for the Mets was the pitching of Craig Swan, who allowed one earned run on two hits in his five innings of work, and Dave Kingman, who momentarily tied the game in the eighth inning with his 28th home run.

There was no let-up in Dave Kingman's power display as he belted his 29th and 30th home runs of the year to lead the Mets to a 4–2 victory over Andy Messersmith and the Braves in the middle game of the series. After the Braves jumped out in front 2–0 against Mets starter Lolich in the third inning, Kingman responded with the first of his blasts, a solo job, cutting the deficit to one. Ron Hodges' third home run of the year in the sixth inning tied the game 2–2. With Lolich removed from the game in the seventh inning, the Mets came to bat in the eighth inning with the game still tied at 2–2. The tie didn't last much longer, as Kingman led off the inning with a towering drive over the center field fence.

The rubber game of the series saw for the first time in the history of the franchise Jon Matlack, Jerry Koosman and Tom Seaver appear together not only in the same game, but also in the same inning. With the team breaking for the All-Star Game after the contest, manager Frazier had Koosman and Seaver available if the starter, Matlack, should falter. For the most part it seemed that Frazier wouldn't have to go that route as the Mets were coasting along with a 4–1 lead after six innings. Matlack, however, failed in the seventh as he allowed four runs. With Matlack unable to get out of the inning, Frazier called on Koosman, who was no more fortunate than Matlack as he surrendered one run on two hits, and was unable to end the uprising. Frazier then turned to Seaver, who after issuing an intentional walk was able to get the job done.

The Mets came right back, however, scoring four runs in their half of the eighth inning to take an 8–6 lead, with the runs belonging to Seaver. With the Mets now up by a duce, Apodaca took over the pitching for Seaver. Dave May, pinch-hitting, led off with a double, and Jerry Royster followed with a walk. The Mets would've been out of the inning if not for Harrelson booting a double-play grounder. With the bases now loaded and the Braves given new life, Willie Montanez cleared the bases with a double to right field, driving in what proved to be the winning run as the Braves took a 9–8 decision over the Mets.

The game had its share of controversy when a call that went against the Mets enabled the Braves to score their final run in their big five-run inning. The play in question arose when, with Jimmy Wynn at first base, Tom Paciorek hit a ball that appeared to bounce into the stands. The call should've been scored as a ground-rule double that would've sent Wynn to third, where he would've been stranded. However, Braves manager Dave Bristol, after a long discussion with umpire Dutch Rennert, was able to convince the arbiter that fan interference should've been called, and Wynn was waved home. Joe Frazier was livid about the call that may have cost the Mets the ballgame. Frazier's contention was two-fold. First, Mets right fielder Dave Kingman contended that no one touched the ball, which was the umpire's first call. In addition, even if a fan had touched the ball, it would have given the home team an advantage. "They'll have all their fans grabbing balls if it gives their team an extra base."

At any rate the Mets finished the first half of the season three games over .500, with a 45-42 record, but 13 games behind the division-leading Phillies. The reviews on the first half were mixed. On the one hand, the Mets were getting excellent pitching from all five starters, including Lolich, who despite his 10 losses was suffering more from lack of run support than poor pitching performances. The Mets also found a relief ace in the form of Skip Lockwood, who racked up six wins in relief. On the other hand, the Mets offensively were wildly inconsistent. Whereas there were numerous games where the Mets' offense was able to score in double figures, more often than not, run production was a major concern. While Dave Kingman was running away with the league lead in home runs and in hot pursuit of Hack Wilson's National League single-season record for home runs, he was also striking out with tremendous frequency and his batting average left something to be desired. In addition, while the first-base platoon of Ed Kranepool and Joe Torre was batting over .300, and John Milner, when healthy, was providing power, the Mets were sorely lacking in production from their center field position, with Del Unser slacking off from his initial successful season. But the biggest concern had to be the defense, which continued to be a problem as the Mets were committing multiple errors per game on a regular basis. While Tom Seaver, Jon Matlack and Dave Kingman headed off to Philadelphia to partake in the All-Star Game, the rest of the team scattered for a three-day break.

A combination of Jerry Koosman's popping fastball and tantalizing slow curveball kept the Astros off-balance all night as the Mets got the second half of the season off on the right foot, downing the Astros, 3–1. The offense was supplied by Dave Kingman, who continued his assault on Hack Wilson's National League record for home runs with 56, as he belted a two-run homer in the sixth inning, his 31st of the year. The Astros' lone run of the game came in the sixth inning, when Cedeno tripled off Koosman and scored on a passed ball by Grote. For Koosman, it was his 10th win of the year and his fourth straight.

As an added bonus for the just over 20,000 fans who attended the game, they saw Ed Kranepool, one of the many slow-moving vehicles on the team, actually steal a base. Kranepool led off the second inning with a walk, one of seven surrendered by Astros starter J.R. Richard, and took off for second and lumbered into the bag as he beat the throw from Astros catcher Ed Hermann.

Kranepool, in a rare moment of contriteness, admitted to missing a sign. "I missed the sign. I thought it was supposed to be a hit-and-run play."[42]

The Mets' Achilles' heel all season, their defense, did them in again in the middle game of the three-game series. The Astros downed the Mets, 4–3, scoring all their runs in the fourth inning off Jon Matlack. The Astros' fourth started with Rob Andrews leading off the inning with a single. Enos Cabell then grounded a ball to first baseman Ed Kranepool. Kranepool, thinking double play, threw the ball before he fielded it, resulting in the ball going into the outfield, and the Astros had runners on first and third and nobody out. Kranepool, making a habit out of being contrite, explained after the game, "I did everything right fundamentally but catch the ball. I screwed up the inning."[43] After Matlack retired Cedeno, Bob Watson cleared the center field fence for a three-run homer, giving the Astros a 3–1 lead. The Mets' shoddy fielding continued when Wayne Garrett threw away Leon Roberts' grounder for the second error of the inning. A single by Ed Hermann and a wild pitch gave the Astros a 4–1 lead.

When a pitcher holds the opposition to three hits and strikes out eleven, a win could be expected. Not this year. Not with the Mets' Dr. Jekyll-and-Mr. Hyde offense. Joaquin Andujar befuddled the Mets' bats while keeping them off the scoreboard for the second time in a week; the Mets lost a 1–0 decision to the Astros. Tom Seaver, despite being overpowering, made one mistake, which cost him the ballgame. That mistake was a pitch thrown in the first inning to Cesar Cedeno that was redirected over the fence.

Frazier, who had been bickering with the umpires all season, had a run-in with first base umpire Terry Tata in the eighth inning. Leon Brown, pinch-running for Joe Torre at first base, began to retreat to the base after Mike Phillips lifted a pop fly to short left field that was caught by Jose Cruz. With Phillips scampering back to first, Cruz threw wildly to first. As the ball rolled away toward the stands, first baseman Bob Watson fell on Leon Brown as he tried to take second base. With Watson on his back, Brown had no choice but to retreat back to first base. Frazier ineffectually argued that Watson interfered with Brown, and as a result should be awarded second base. Frazier described Tata's response. "Tata told me he thought if Brownie could've made second, he would've given him the base. I said, 'Hell, I knew he couldn't if he was carrying Watson on his shoulders.' The damn umpires, they got all the answers."[44]

The Mets were on the right side of the goose eggs as Mickey Lolich shut out the Braves, 2–0, on a two-hitter at Shea Stadium for a rare Sunday afternoon, Monday evening series. For Lolich it was his fifth win of the year in fifteen decisions. As was the case in so much of the recent past, the Mets' offense was provided in part by Dave Kingman, who hit his 32nd home run of the season. In a break from the recent past, the Mets were helped out by solid defense, including a spectacular diving catch by Mike Vail.

Dave Kingman's 32nd home run of the year would be the last home run he would hit for awhile, and his chase of Hack Wilson's National League record for home runs came to an abrupt halt. Kingman tore ligaments in his left thumb while diving for a ball hit by Braves starting pitcher Phil Niekro in the final game the Mets would play against Atlanta during the season. Kingman's thumb would require surgery, sidelining him for a minimum of six weeks. With the loss of Kingman, the Mets lost the only excitement that was left in their season with the Phillies way ahead of New York in the National League East. Barring a sudden collapse, the likelihood of the Mets catching the Phillies was slim. Aside from losing Kingman, the Mets lost another ballgame as the Braves scored three runs off Craig Swan in the fourth inning, with two runs scoring on an overthrow by right fielder Mike Vail on a sacrifice fly.

11

Kooz: A Dream Realized

The Mets minus Dave Kingman and his booming bat headed off on a road trip that would take them to Cincinnati, Montreal and Philadelphia, before returning home on July 28, to take on the Pirates. With Kingman out of the lineup, it was up to the rest of the Mets' batters to bunch up hits in order to compensate for the loss of their only legitimate power hitter. And bunch up hits they did in the first inning, when Millan, Milner and Kranepool singled for one run and Mike Vail drove home the Mets' second run on a sacrifice fly. Kranepool's RBI single tied him for the club record of 521 with Cleon Jones.

Pete Rose hit Jerry Koosman's first pitch of the evening out of the park, but by that time the Mets had put two on the board, which was enough for the lefthander, who pitched another spectacular game. After Rose's blast, Koosman allowed the Reds just four hits, striking out eight on his way to picking up his 11th victory of the year and his fifth in a row. "I threw Rose a fastball for that homer, but after that, I only used a fastball to fool them with or as a waste pitch. My curve was working real well out there tonight," said Koosman."[1]

After the game the Mets announced a trade, sending Del Unser and Wayne Garrett to the Montreal Expos in exchange for Pepe Mangual and utility out-fielder Jim Dwyer. Unser, who was acquired in exchange for the popular Tug McGraw, was the supposed answer to the Mets' perennial center field problem. He was struggling with a .228 batting average and not performing up to expectations, resulting in the Mets losing patience with him and thus the trade. Unser, who admittedly was shocked by the deal, laid the blame on his poor performance on the incident with Lynn McGlothen earlier in the season, which left Unser playing with a bruised elbow that hampered his swing. Wayne Garrett, who was shipped with Unser to Montreal, was having a sub-par season as well, batting less than .230.

What the Mets liked about Mangual was the added dimension of speed that he brought to the table, a commodity sorely lacking on this team. Mangual, who had been the Expos' starting center fielder, was batting .260 with 18 steals. Unfortunately, Mangual brought along another commodity that the Mets had an over-abundance of, namely poor defensive performance. As Mets beat

In another bad deal the Mets sent Del Unser (left) and Wayne Garrett to the Montreal Expos in exchange for Pepe Mangual and Jim Dwyer (National Baseball Hall of Fame Library).

writer Jack Lang succinctly put it, "Mangual drops everything that he can get to."[2]

After losing the finale in Cincinnati, 4–0, the Mets moved on to Montreal, where Del Unser, whose elbow looked like it was feeling a whole lot better, took immediate revenge on his former teammates. Unser smacked a home run in the 11th inning off Skip Lockwood to send the Mets reeling to defeat. Tom Seaver, the Mets' starter, pitched a solid nine innings, fanning eight batters while allowing only six hits, two of them solo home runs by Barry Foote and Larry Parrish.

The middle game of the weekend series saw the Mets, who were beneficiaries of fourteen bases on balls, walk all over the Expos in a 10–4 rout. The Mets lost the rubber game of the series, however, when Ed Kranepool misjudged a drive by Ellis Valentine in the last of the ninth inning. Jerry Koosman, despite pitching a splendid game, took the loss, ending a personal five-game winning streak.

July 26 saw the Mets pull into Philadelphia to take on the front-running Phillies for a short two-game series. If the first game was any indication of how the rest of the series would play out, the Mets could've shipped their bats to New York straight from Montreal, as they weren't using them anyway. Combined with no offense and poor defensive play, the Mets lost, 4–1, despite a dominating pitching performance by Jon Matlack, who was charged with his fifth loss of the season. Tug McGraw, who picked up his sixth save of the season with three scoreless innings of relief, continued with his biting criticism of his former team. "The Mets scrounge for runs here and there, so a lot of pitchers pitch well against them. They're not known as one of the tougher hitting clubs in baseball."[3] McGraw's reaction to the Unser trade was that the Mets dealt Unser because he was too good for them.

The Mets avenged their 4–1 loss and salvaged the final game of the series with a 4–1 win. The four runs scored by the Mets marked only the second time since Kingman went down that the Mets managed to score more than two runs. The news wasn't all cheerful for the Mets, as Craig Swan had to exit the game after the third inning with pain in his elbow. Bob Myrick, who replaced Swan on the mound and pitched three solid innings, allowing only three hits, picked up his first major league win. Skip Lockwood pitched the final three innings, earning his 10th save of the year. With the win the Mets narrowed their deficit to the Phillies to "only" 16½ games.

Back home for a two-game series against the Pirates, Tom Seaver saw another magnificent pitching performance go to waste. Seaver held the Pirates scoreless for 10 innings, with 10 strikeouts, but came away with another no-decision as the Mets failed to score any runs. Ken Sanders, who replaced Seaver in the 11th inning, pitched two shutout innings before allowing a solo home run to Richie Hebner in the 13th inning. Tom Seaver reflected on his hard luck after the game. "I don't let it bother me as long as I pitch well. All I can really do is pitch well, pitch consistently and let the numbers fall into place."[4]

The second game of the series was a mirror image of the first as the Mets got another great pitching performance from another starter, another dismal output from their offense, and lost another extra-inning game to the Pirates. The Mets, who entered the game without having scored a run in their last 16 innings, went another eight innings before scoring a run in the bottom of the ninth inning to tie the Pirates and send the game into extra innings.

After the Pirates scored a run off Mickey Lolich in the fourth inning to take a 1–0 lead, Lolich stymied the Pirates the rest of the way. Lolich, however, was on the short end as the Mets came to bat in the last of the ninth inning and was three outs away from picking up his 11th loss of the season. Lolich's 11th loss seemed almost assured after Bob Moose retired the first two batters in the inning. Ed Kranepool and Bruce Boisclair then singled and the Mets still had life. John Milner walked, loading the bases, and Joe Torre followed with a single, scoring the tying run, and Lolich was off the hook. With Jerry Grote due up and the Pirates bringing in Kent Tekulve, the Pirates' ace, Frazier turned to his bench and called on Jim Dwyer, hoping the Mets could end the game right then and there. Frazier came in for a lot of second-guessing after Dwyer flied out to right field, ending the rally. At issue was why Frazier called on Dwyer and not Hodges, who was batting .287 compared to Dwyer's .189, and was coming in to catch anyway if the Mets failed to score in the ninth. Frazier received even more questioning after the Pirates scored the go-ahead run in the tenth inning on a questionable defensive alignment. With Skip Lockwood taking over the pitching, Rennie Stennett led off the 10th inning with a base hit and moved to third when Al Oliver followed with a single. Frazier then elected to play his middle infield halfway, instead of playing in and cutting off the go-ahead run at the plate. The next batter, Bill Robinson, did hit the ball on the ground, and the Mets did pull off the double play, but the go-ahead and eventual winning run scored.

Frazier responded to the criticism on both accounts. He elected to go with Dwyer over Hodges because he thought Dwyer was a pinch-hitting specialist, which was why the Mets acquired him in the first place. Frazier defended his positioning of the infield in the tenth inning, saying he wanted to cut off the big inning, a sentiment echoed by none other than Buddy Harrelson. Harrelson argued, "You're at home and you have a chance to come to bat. We come back and score and you forget about it."[5] However, with the way the Mets scored runs, the likelihood of scoring a run was not good.

The first-place Phillies followed the second-place Pirates into Shea for a four-game weekend series. Jerry Koosman, the only pitcher who was winning games despite the Mets' propensity for not scoring runs, came within an out of pitching a shutout and walked off with a 3–2 decision over the Phillies. Again by capably alternating his tantalizing slow curveball with his blazing fastball, Koosman was able to keep the Phillies batters off-balance all night. Koosman took a two-hitter into the ninth inning and then retired the first two batters. Koosman then got himself into trouble by walking Mike Schmidt and lost his shutout when Greg Luzinski doubled, driving home Schmidt. Ollie Brown, a Koosman killer over the years, singled to left, scoring Luzinski, and Koosman's victory was very much in jeopardy. However, he was able to reach back and get Jerry Martin to ground out, ending the game. For Koosman, the team leader in victories, it was his twelfth win of the season. "I wanted that shutout," said Koosman after the game. "Then I started overthrowing and I got wild."[6] The Mets lost the remaining three games of the series by scores of 2–1, 7–6, and 2–0.

Joe Frazier's frustrating rookie season became even more frustrating after the Mets blew a 4–2 lead in the ninth inning when pinch-hitter Jose Morales slammed a three-run homer off Skip Lockwood, sending the Mets down to a shocking 5–4 defeat in the opener of a three-game series against the Expos. Frazier allowed the frustration to get to him, as he began to argue balls and strikes calls by home plate umpire Nick Colosi when the Expos came to bat in the top of the ninth. Frazier continued his taunting when the Mets came to bat in the last of the ninth inning. Having heard too much, Colosi excused Frazier for what was left of the inning and the game. The ejection wasn't taken lightly by Frazier, who emptied the Mets' dugout of chest protectors, shin guards, gloves and whatever else he could get his hands on, much to the approval of the over

50,000 fans who showed up for the Jacket Night giveaway. Tom Seaver, the starter, pitched seven solid innings, but had not won since July 8 despite being among the league leaders in ERA.

Ed Kranepool's 100th career home run with a runner aboard in the last of the eighth inning was the difference as the Mets downed the Expos, 9–8, to capture the middle game of the series. The Mets also won the rubber game of the series as Jerry Koosman continued his dominating pitching, shutting out the Expos on four hits and raising his record to 13–7. After the game, Koosman proudly talked about his pitching of late. "I've been consistent and that's been my goal this year. Last year I walked 98 guys and that was very embarrassing to me because I have better control than that."[7]

The Mets were on the road again, this time to Pittsburgh, where they were able to win three out of four games against the Pirates. Ironically, the only pitcher to perform poorly was none other than Tom Seaver, who surrendered five runs on eight hits in five innings during a 12–3 drubbing. Jon Matlack picked up his 11th win of the year, and his first since July 1, in the opener of the series.

The Mets returned home right after their series with the Pirates to start a homestand with the San Diego Padres. The opener pitted a matchup between the two hottest pitchers in the National League — lefthanders Jerry Koosman and Randy Jones. Randy Jones entered the game as an eighteen-game winner, while Koosman came in with thirteen wins.

Neither starter was particularly sharp in the early going as each team traded four-run innings. The Mets took an early 4–0 lead in the last of the second inning, with Koosman helping his own cause with a two-run single. The Padres tied the game in the third inning, the big blow a three-run blast by Dave Winfield.

Both pitchers then settled into a groove and the game remained tied until the Mets came to bat in the last of the eighth inning. Joe Torre led off the inning with a single and was replaced by pinch-runner Leo Foster. A successful sacrifice by Grote moved Foster to second, and Foster advanced to third on a single by Roy Staiger. John Milner, batting for Harrelson, then drilled a single for the tie-breaking run. Koosman, who easily retired the Padres in the ninth inning, picked up his 14th win of the year and had won eight out of his last nine starts while completing his last six outings.

The Mets fine play in general and pitching in particular continued the next night as they downed the Padres in a tightly pitched, hard-fought battle, 2–1. With the win the Mets moved to within 2½ games of the second-place Pirates. The Mets scored their two runs in the last of the first inning and then held off the Padres behind the stellar pitching of Jon Matlack, who picked up his 12th win, and Skip Lockwood, who picked up his 13th save of the year. The game also featured a near brawl in the last of the first inning after the Mets had already scored their two runs courtesy of a bases-loaded double by Mike Vail.

Vail, who pulled into second, believed that Padres second baseman Tito Fuentes made a hard tag after he was already safely on the base. Vail took exception and the benches cleared. Despite a lot of milling around, no punches were thrown and the game continued without incident.

The Padres were able to salvage the final game of the series as Tom Seaver's winless streak continued. The Padres bunched their only five hits together in the second inning as they scored the only three runs of the game. Padres starter Rick Sawyer scattered eight hits but induced Mets batters to ground into three double plays, keeping the Mets off the scoreboard.

With their bats stifled once again, the only noise emanating from the Mets came from the front office, where the team announced that manager Joe Frazier's contract had been extended through the 1977 season. "We're satisfied with Joe and he's satisfied with us," said board chairman M. Donald Grant. Joe Frazier echoed Grant's sentiments. "Naturally I'm pleased, as I feel I've accomplished as much as I could here so far."[8]

After splitting the first two games of a weekend series with the Reds, the Mets took the rubber game. Jerry Koosman just kept on rolling along, scattering five hits in shutting out the Reds, 1–0. For Koosman it was his ninth win in his last ten starts and seventh straight complete game as he picked up his fifteenth win. Koosman fanned 11 batters as well, bringing his strikeout total to 130, the most for a left-hander in the National League. Koosman was untouchable as he deftly kept the Reds off-balance by mixing his off-speed breaking ball with an occasional overpowering fastball. Koosman was helped out by his defense, which came up with numerous sparkling defensive plays. The first came in the fourth inning when Ed Armbrister led the inning off with a two-base hit. With Concepcion at the plate, Armbrister took off for third as Concepcion swung and grounded the ball right at Staiger, who tagged out a sliding Armbrister and then threw to first to complete the double play. In addition to Koosman's artistic mound work, the pitcher was right in the middle of the lone run scored in the game. Roy Staiger, who led off the fifth inning with a base hit, was subsequently forced at second on a fielder's choice by Harrelson. Koosman then sacrificed Harrelson over to second, where he scored on a base hit by Bruce Boisclair.

With the homestand complete, the Mets boarded a flight that would take them out to the West Coast for their second and final trip of the season. After three heart-breaking one-run losses to the Dodgers at Dodger Stadium, it was Jerry Koosman who picked up a deflated team as the Mets opened up a weekend series in San Diego. Jerry Koosman gave the Mets an immediate lift as he continued his dominating pitching, leading New York to a 7–1 decision with another complete game, his eighth in a row.

While the 7–1 score appeared to be a rout, the game was actually tightly pitched through the first six innings. A 2–0 Mets lead was cut in half when Tito Fuentes homered off Koosman in the last of the sixth inning. The Mets, however, struck back, scoring four runs in their half of the seventh inning, putting the game out of reach. Koosman, with 16 wins and more than a month left to the season, was the closest that he's ever been to having a chance at winning 20 games. Koosman had won 19 games in his rookie season of 1968 and 17 in 1969, hasn't won more than 15 since then.

After the middle game of the series, Met fans must have been scratching their brows, wondering how many wins the Mets would have if they had any semblance of an offense to go with the pitching they were receiving. The latest was a 1–0 masterpiece turned in by Jon Matlack, who out-dueled Randy Jones as the Padres' left-hander took the mound in search of his 20th win.

The lone run scored by the Mets came with an abundance of assistance from first base umpire Jim Quick, who called Joe Torre safe leading off the seventh inning on a ground ball to third baseman Ted Kubiak, who threw wide to first baseman Mike Ivie. While the throw pulled Ivie off the bag, the replay showed Ivie making the swipe tag on Torre as he passed by. With Torre being given a free pass to first, Frazier sent Mangual in to run for Torre. A moment later Mangual was dispatched to second when Quick called a balk on Randy Jones. Jerry Grote followed with a double, scoring Mangual. An enraged Padres manager John McNamara stormed the field but accomplished nothing except for getting himself tossed out of the game.

With Koosman winning the night before and Jones losing, the dynamics of the Cy Young Award race was beginning to take on a new twist. While at the All-Star break Jones appeared to be a shoo-in to win the prestigious award with an eye-popping 16-3 record, he had dropped six of his last nine starts. Koosman, on the other hand, had won nine out of his 10 last starts with eight straight complete games to put serious pressure on the front-runner.

A shutout against the Giants by Tom Seaver extended the string of outstanding performances by a Mets starter to three. The string, however, came to an end when the Mets sent Lolich to the mound to take on Ed Halicki and the Giants. For Halicki, it marked exactly a year and a day since he no-hit the Mets. While Halicki was more liberal on this day in the hits department, allowing eight, he was just as efficient in the runs allowed department, limiting the Mets to only one. While Lolich pitched well, allowing the Giants only one run, he removed himself from the game after the fourth inning upon complaining he wasn't feeling well. Frazier then turned to rookie Nino Espinosa, who after keeping the Giants off the board in the fifth inning, made the mistake of allowing the Giant batters to hit the ball to Mike Vail in right field. Confounded by the Candlestick Park wind and sun, Vail misplayed two balls for doubles and committed a throwing error. The Giants put up a six spot in the inning as the Mets went down to a 7–1 defeat.

Dave Kingman, after a six-week absence, was reactivated. The Mets hoped that the return of their only legitimate power hitter would give their offense a much-needed boost as the Mets opened up a homestand against the Dodgers and Giants. To make room for Kingman, the Mets designated a disappointing Jim Dwyer for assignment.

The opener featured a pitching matchup between sixteen-game winner Jerry Koosman and Don Sutton, a fifteen-game winner. Koosman, in search of his 17th win, was instead saddled with his eighth loss of the season after a Dodgers' three-run eighth inning snapped a 2–2 tie.

The final two games of the series saw each team win a 2–1 decision, with the Mets winning the middle game of the series behind Jon Matlack's 14th win. Tom Seaver, who must have felt bewitched, surrendered a two-run homer to Reggie Smith in the top of the first inning. That was enough to do him in, as the Mets could muster no more than one run.

An anguished Seaver let his feelings be known after the game. "Some more of the same. It's frustrating for sure."[9] Seaver, by the way, had a 2.50 ERA, the lowest for any starter in the National League. After losing the finale of the series with the Dodgers, the Mets ended the month of August with a 6–2 victory over the Giants.

While September 1 marks the unofficial start of the pennant race, for the Mets pennant fever in 1976 couldn't even be categorized as a 24-hour virus; the lead the first-place Phillies carried over the Mets appeared insurmountable. However, despite all that had transpired over the course of the long season, the Mets found that finishing second for their rookie manager was a very real possibility.

There was also excitement on a personal level, where Jerry Koosman moved one step closer to realizing his dream as a sixteen-year-old to win 20 games. Koosman whitewashed the Giants in a brilliant pitching duel with New Jersey native John "the Count" Montefusco. The crafty left-hander and the cocky right-hander traded zeroes until the Mets came to bat in the last of the eighth inning, when Felix Millan and John Milner stroked back-to-back doubles to score the only run of the game. Koosman, after allowing a first-inning walk, two hits in the second inning and another in the third, was in total command thereafter, not allowing a single batter to reach base.

With the rosters expanded to 40, the Mets called up reliever Rick Baldwin and outfielder Billy Baldwin. Billy Baldwin was acquired with Lolich in the Rusty Staub trade.

Another personal milestone was reached by Tom Seaver two days later when Tommy Hutton became his 200th strikeout, as the Mets beat the Phillies, 1–0. For Seaver, it was the ninth consecutive season he had reached the coveted plateau of 200 strikeouts in a season. Seaver, who allowed just four hits, fanned eight batters and picked up his 11th win in a tough-luck season, bewitched by a lack of offense. "I had good stuff tonight," said Seaver. "I just went out and challenged their hitters, mostly with fastballs."[10]

Jerry Koosman's 18th win came on September 6 in a game against the Cubs in Wrigley Field. After belting the Cubs for 30 runs in three games during their last visit to Chicago at the end of June, the Mets wasted no time familiarizing themselves with the friendly confines of the ivy-covered relic known as Wrigley Field. Dave Kingman was the first to do the reacquainting when he blasted a tremendous two-run homer in the top of the first. With the home run, Kingman reestablished himself as the league leader in home runs. "It was good to see the guys hitting today," said Koosman. "They were really swinging their bats, especially Kingman."[11]

The hitting barrage continued in the second game of the series as well, with the Mets pounding out another 16 hits in an 11–0 rout of the Cubs. Mike Phillips, who served as a one-man wrecking crew in the Mets' last visit to Chicago, was apparently thrilled to return. Phillips homered in the top of the first and gave the Mets a 2–0 lead two batters into the game. But offensively the day belonged to Leo Foster, who drove in five runs, including his first home run of the year. Jon Matlack was the beneficiary of this uncharacteristic offensive support and picked up his 15th win. Despite hurling a shutout, his league-leading sixth, Matlack admitted he didn't have his best stuff. "It was definitely not one of my best efforts. I had good stuff, but it was a continual struggle."[12]

Making his major league debut for the Mets was Lee Mazzilli, a handsome 21-year-old from Brooklyn, just called up from the Mets' Jackson affiliate in the Texas League. Mazzilli, who entered the game in the seventh inning, made one appearance at the plate and grounded out.

Lee Mazzilli got another turn at bat in the finale of the series and made the most of his opportunity by drilling a three-run pinch-hit home run off Cubs reliever Darold Knowles in the top of the ninth inning. That capped a six-run inning, as once again the Mets trounced the Cubs, 11–5. "It's the best feeling in the world," was Mazzilli's reply to the question of how he felt after hitting his first major league home run.[13]

With the win the Mets swept the series and beat the Cubs seven out of nine games in the Cubs' home park. For the Mets it was a real letdown to leave the Windy City, as they compiled 118 hits, 78 runs and 16 home runs, and averaged a little over 8½ runs per game during the nine games played at Wrigley Field. By comparison, the Mets averaged only 3½ runs in all other parks. Tom Seaver was the starter and winner for the Mets. Seaver's only troubles were trying to solve Rick Monday, who had four hits, including his seventh career homer off the Mets' right-hander.

Two games later, win number 19 came for Koosman in St. Louis. "I've been dreaming about winning 20 games ever since I was a 16-year-old kid." The speaker was Jerry Koosman, talking to reporters after notching his 19th victory in dominating fashion, stopping the Cardinals on only two hits, while allowing only one unearned run. "I had an excellent curveball and good stuff on my fastball," said Koosman.[14] The Mets scored two runs in the fourth, while adding single runs in the sixth and ninth innings in support of Koosman.

After taking two out of three from St. Louis, the Mets headed on to Pittsburgh, the only team still in contention for the National League East Division title. For the Mets, whose only role in the pennant race was that of spoiler, played their role extremely well. After earlier taking two out of three from the first-place Phillies, the Mets turned their attention to the Pittsburgh Pirates, with the intent to inflict as much pain as possible.

Tom Seaver was in peak form by striking out 12 in the opener while allowing the Pirates only five hits in the shutout. The Mets continued their punishment of the contenders after beating the Pirates for the second consecutive day. The Pirates' loss extended their deficit to six games behind the Phillies. More frustrating for the Pirates was the fact that they took a 3–2 lead into the ninth inning and had one out with nobody on before Dave Kingman singled. Stearns followed with a base hit, sending Kingman to third. On came the Pirates' relief ace Kent Tekulve to face the Mets' elite pinch-hitter Ed Kranepool. Kranepool got the better of the duel by singling to center to tie the game and send Stearns, the go-ahead run, to third. A fielder's choice by Harrelson gave the Mets the ball game. Skip Lockwood, who was on the hook for his eighth loss of the year, instead picked up his eighth win.

After splitting a doubleheader with the Cardinals, Jerry Koosman's longtime dream of becoming a 20-game winner turned into reality after beating the Cardinals. It was also Koosman's most overpowering performance of a very

Jerry Koosman is congratulated by teammates after winning 20 games for the first time in his career (AP Images).

overpowering season, as he fanned 13 batters, the most for a National League pitcher on the year. The popular left-hander with both players and fans alike was mobbed by his teammates after striking out Hector Cruz for the final out of the game. After coming out for a curtain call when the cheering crowd refused to disappear into the night, Koosman returned to sip champagne with his family and teammates and meet with the press. "This was the night I was waiting for," said Koosman. "The pressure has been building ever since I reached No. 17 and people constantly asked me if I thought I could win 20."[15]

The pennant race gained steam as the Pirates came into Shea Stadium for a four-game series and took the opener behind the superb pitching of ex–Yankee Doc Medich. The Pirates, who on August 24 trailed the Phillies by a whopping 15½ games, with the win had won 18 out of their last 22 games, and reduced the deficit to three games.

Jon Matlack, despite a decent performance, allowing the Pirates three runs over eight innings while fanning seven, received no offensive support from his teammates and suffered his ninth defeat of the year.

Jerry Koosman celebrates his 20th win with a toast of champagne (AP Images).

After a one-day respite, the Mets continued their role as spoilers, beating the surging Pirates, 6–2. Dave Kingman's lead-off home run in the bottom of the second was his 35th home run, retying Mike Schmidt for the league lead. Tom Seaver, who earlier in the season went two months without a victory, picked up his fourth consecutive win and 14th overall with his complete game five-hitter. "Seaver may not win 20 games this year, but he's still a super pitcher," said Joe Frazier. "He'll have three more starts, so he might wind up with 17 victories the way he's throwing now."[16]

The Pirates continued to blow opportunities to move up on the Phillies, who lost to the Cubs, after the Mets beat the Pirates for the second consecutive day. This loss was particularly painful to the Pirates after blowing a 6–2 lead.

The Pirates took a 2–0 lead by scoring two runs off Mets starter Craig Swan in the first inning. Dave Kingman's 36th home run in the second inning cut the Pirates' lead to 2–1, and his sacrifice fly in the third inning tied it. But the Pirates regained what seemed to be a comfortable lead when Omar Moreno and Willie Stargell hit two-run homers in the fifth inning, giving the Pirates a 6–2 lead. Dave Kingman got right back to work, however, blasting his 37th home run off the year with two runners on to reduce the Mets' deficit to one. With the home run, Kingman broke the record for most home runs by a Met, a record he had set a year ago, when he hit 36. "There is no stadium that can hold this guy," said a frustrated Stargell. "He's got power and he's got a great stroke."[17]

John Stearns tied the game when he led off the sixth inning with a home run. Bruce Boisclair then followed with a triple, and a pinch-hit single by Eddie Kranepool drove home what proved to be the deciding run. The lead stood up thanks to a dominating performance by Skip Lockwood, who struck out seven in his three innings of work as he picked up his 17th save of the year.

The Mets continued to punish the Pirates, beating them in heartbreaking fashion after Lee Mazzilli's two-out, two-run homer in the last of the ninth inning beat Pittsburgh, 5–4. Mazzilli's blast practically hammered home the final nail in the coffin of the Pirates' pennant hopes. "I guess I'll remember this for a long time," said an exuberant Mazzilli in the Mets' clubhouse after the game. "I was waiting for a fastball, and it came in belt high."[18]

The Mets had taken a 3–0 lead after they scored three runs in the last of the third inning in support of Mickey Lolich. But the Pirates began to claw back, scoring a run in the fifth and then tying the game in the seventh inning. The Pirates finally crept out in front in the eighth inning when Willie Stargell homered off Lolich.

The Pirates appeared to have the game wrapped after Kent Tekulve retired the first two Mets in the last of the ninth inning. But John Milner, pinch-hitting for winning pitcher Bob Apodaca, singled to center field, bringing Mazzilli to the plate.

With the homestand concluded, the Mets headed out of the country to Montreal where they would play their last series ever in Jarry Park. If the Mets could brag about spoiling the Pirates' pennant hopes, then the Expos could take credit for damaging Jerry Koosman's bid for the Cy Young Award after defeating Koosman and the Mets, 4–0. Koosman and the Expos' starter, rookie left-hander Dan Warthen, exchanged zeros for the first 5½ innings. But after Koosman retired the first two Expos in the last of the sixth inning, Ellis Valentine and Earl Williams went deep back-to-back, giving the Expos a 2–0 lead.

The Expos scored two more unearned runs off Koosman in the eighth. The Mets in the meantime could do nothing with Dan Warthen, who held the Mets hitless for the first 5⅔ innings until the new rookie sensation, Lee Mazzilli, broke up the no-hitter with a clean single. Mazzilli had the only other hit allowed by Warthen, another clean single, this one coming in the eighth inning.

"I have no excuses," said Koosman after the game. "I was just out-pitched and I give him lots of credit."[19]

The Mets were able to split the series with the Expos. Mazzilli had another big game with three hits, including a double. "I think I can safely say he'll be on our roster when the 1977 season gets under way," said manager Frazier. "He's made a few throwing mistakes in the field since joining us, but he's one fine fielder."[20]

Jon Matlack, with last-out help from Skip Lockwood, picked up his 16th win of the year; Lockwood notched his 18th save. For the Mets it was their 81st win of the year, and with 11 games left, both 90 wins and second place were still in reach.

The Mets returned home to take on the Chicago Cubs for a three-game weekend series, a team the Mets manhandled all year long. The Mets, in the opener, continued their abuse of the Cubbies, coming away with a 4–3 win. Billy Baldwin, who came to the Mets along with Mickey Lolich in the Rusty Staub trade, smacked a home run in the last of the ninth inning and snapped a 3–3 tie.

The middle game of the series saw the Mets keep right on rolling as they won their 16th game out of their last 22 by once again beating the hapless Cubs. Again Billy Baldwin played a key role in the victory with three hits, including a first-inning triple that brought home two Met runs.

For the Mets it was their 83rd win, tying their second-highest win total in their history. Craig Swan picked up his sixth win of the year, while Skip Lockwood earned his 19th save.

The Mets completed the series sweep of the Cubs behind the pitching of Jerry Koosman and Bob Apodaca. The win was momentous for both Koosman individually and for the Mets as a whole. For Koosman it increased his career-high season win total to 21, enhancing his chance at winning the Cy Young Award. For the Mets it was their 84th win of the year, marking their second-highest win total ever. More importantly, it left the Mets only three games behind the fading Pirates in the battle for second place. "We've got a shot at second and we'll keep going," said Frazier. "The 84 victories don't mean much to me."[21]

With the Mets leading 2–0 and Koosman holding the Cubs hitless through the first six innings with nine strikeouts, it appeared the game would be a cakewalk for the veteran left-hander. But in the seventh inning, the Cubs touched Koosman for four consecutive hits, scoring one run and loading the bases to chase Koosman. In came Apodaca, who pulled a Houdini act by escaping the jam without any further damage. Larry Biittner, Apodaca's first batter, grounded to first, where Dave Kingman threw home for the force. Champ Summers then popped to first while Pete LaCock grounded to Millan.

John Milner, who entered the season with an undefined role and already was guaranteed to finish with his most successful season to date, crushed two home runs, including a grand slam, to power the Mets to a 10–3 victory over the Expos, the next visitors into Shea. For the Mets it was their fifth win in a row and their 85th overall. For Milner it was his 14th and 15th home runs of the year, but more importantly he was batting .271, a career high, as well as 78 runs batted in, also a career high. Jon Matlack, the winning pitcher, set a career high for victories, picking up his 17th.

The series with the Expos concluded as a twilight doubleheader. Ed Kranepool, who had the distinction of being the only Met who had been around since the day the franchise opened its doors, was the hero in the opener of the doubleheader as the Mets won their sixth straight. With the Expos leading the Mets 4–3, Kranepool slammed his 10th home run of the year, thus tying the game. With the game still tied in the last of the ninth inning, and after Expos reliever Joe Kerrigan retired the first two Mets batters, Bruce Boisclair and Jim Dwyer singled. The previous day's hero, John Milner, followed with a walk to load the bases, bringing Kranepool up to the plate. Kranepool came through with a game-winning single, sending the Mets to their sixth straight win.

The nightcap saw two rookies, Bob Myrick, who spent most of the season toiling in the Mets' bullpen, take the hill for the Mets, while Gerald Hannahs, a 20-game winner in the Expos' minor league system, toed the rubber for Montreal. Myrick struggled, allowing the Expos four runs, including Larry Parrish's 10th home run of the year, as the Mets saw their six-game win streak snapped.

While Del Unser got instant payback against the Mets only one day after being dealt to the Expos, when he hit a game-winning home run against his former teammates, Wayne Garrett waited until the final Mets' home game to get his revenge. Garrett did it in grand fashion by smacking his first career grand slam, leading the Expos to a 7–2 triumph over Tom Seaver and the Mets.

Seaver, who was searching for his 15th win of the year, had a perfect game going with one out in the fourth before he walked another ex–Met, Mike Jorgensen. A single by Ellis Valentine and a subsequent walk to Larry Parrish loaded the bases, and Garrett followed with his clout.

The Mets moved on to Philadelphia, closing out the season with a weekend series against the National League East champion Phillies. Jerry Koosman, in search of his 22nd victory of the season, pitched a magnificent game, striking out 11 and taking a 1–1 tie into the last of the ninth. With one out, Koosman took on an obscure career journeyman, John Vukovich. In a season where few players had won confrontations with Koosman, it was Vukovich who got the better of this confrontation as he took Koosman deep.

A win by Koosman would've in all likelihood clinched the Cy Young Award for him. The 11 strikeouts for Koosman gave him 200 for the season, a career high.

In the middle game of the series, Jon Matlack failed in his bid to win a career-high 18th game, despite being furnished with an early 3–0 lead as the Phillies roughed up the left-hander, touching him for seven runs. The win for the Phillies was their 100th, marking the first time since the Mets in 19 that a National League East had won 100 games.

Steve Carlton pushed himself into the Cy Young Award battle, along with Jerry Koosman and Randy Jones, after winning his 20th game on the final day of the season as the Phillies downed the slumping Mets, who lost their final five games of the year. J.R. Richard and Don Sutton won 20 games as well and also had to be considered candidates for the lofty award.

In another contest lost by the Mets, Mike Schmidt ended up winning the home run title, edging Dave Kingman by one, with Schmidt hitting a total of 38. Kingman, who had 32 in mid–July and was threatening Hack Wilson for the National League record for home runs in a single season, missed 33 games after tearing a ligament in his left thumb on an ill-advised dive while trying to catch a ball by Braves pitcher Phil Niekro. Pepe Mangual, who overall turned out to be a disappointment, both offensively and defensively, accounted for the Mets' lone run.

Thus ended a season with mixed emotions. On the one hand, the Mets with their 86 victories accomplished their second-highest win total with 86. The starting rotation with Seaver, Koosman, Matlack and Lolich accounted for 61 wins, by far the highest total for any starting rotation. On the other hand, the Mets were never in contention as the Phillies ran away early with the division. The Mets' biggest problem was their lack of offense. Dave Kingman was the only legitimate power threat, but he also struck out far too much.

The Mets also got nice production from their elder-statesman platoon at first base of Joe Torre and Ed Kranepool and surprising output from John Milner. Roy Staiger, despite displaying flashes of brilliance with the glove, was carrying too light a bat to handle third base, known as a power position. Rusty Staub's replacement, Mike Vail, never fully recovered from his ankle injury sustained in an off-season pickup basketball game and struggled both offensively and defensively. In addition, there were too many holes on defense, where injuries and age had taken a toll on the former dependable keystone tandem of Harrelson and Millan.

However, there was reason for optimism as the Mets and their fans looked toward 1977. Aside from the dominating pitching staff, the power of Dave Kingman, and the fine play of youngsters John Stearns and Lee Mazzilli, who appeared to be primed to give the Mets solid defense, offense and speed behind the plate and in center field, respectively, winds of change were blowing in baseball. The offseason would mark the first free agent draft in which teams could bid on the services of players with six years of service whose contracts had run out. With stars on the market, such as Reggie Jackson, Gary Matthews, Bob Grich, and Joe Rudi, with the Mets presumably being one of the wealthiest teams while playing in the large New York market with its lucrative radio and TV contracts, both fans and players alike were confident that the Mets' management would be very proactive in pursuing those players that would have a major positive impact on the team.

12

The Massacre

All was not well in Metsville as the ball club gathered in Chicago to open up the 1977 season against the Cubs. Despite a desperate need for another big bat in the lineup, an aging double-play combination, and a .220 hitting third baseman, the Mets' hierarchy elected to stand pat over the winter. With baseball holding its first free-agent re-entry draft in November, the Mets selected the rights to negotiate with Gary Matthews, Joe Rudi, Bobby Grich, Don Baylor, Don Gullett, Reggie Jackson, Sal Bando and Bert Campaneris. While the Mets made a serious offer to Matthews, ultimately the Mets failed to sign a single free agent. The Mets' attitude regarding free agents was expressed by Donald Grant on the day of the draft. "The most important factor is what effect it will have on our other players," said Grant. "We will try to run our business in a sensible way. Nobody is going to plan to spend a lot of money for players and lose money at the park. I am also concerned for the fans. In the end it is they who are going to have to pay. Baseball is still a family game. That is still one of our selling points. But when a man can no longer afford to take his family to a game on any given day, it ceases to be a family game and we are in trouble. I will continue to fight against rising ticket prices."[1]

General manager Joe McDonald echoed Grant's sentiments. "We made a substantial seven-digit offer to Jackson and Grich, but it doesn't seem to be enough. To increase the offer seems senseless. I can't tell other clubs what to do. But in talking to people in baseball, I find that many feel it is ridiculous. Some clubs are over-extending themselves. That's their business, not mine."[2]

In addition to being shutout in the free-agent market, the Mets came away empty in the trading market as well. To add insult to injury, Mickey Lolich, for whom the Mets dealt away their most prolific run producer, announced his retirement after the 1976 season, deciding he wasn't interested in playing away from his hometown of Detroit.

The new fiscal realties of baseball were causing internal dissension as well. Tom Seaver, who last spring after bitter and contentious negotiations signed a new three-year contract at $225,000, was no longer the highest-paid pitcher in baseball and as a result was looking to renegotiate his contract. Dave Kingman, who came into spring training unsigned, was looking for a contract similar to the one signed by Reggie Jackson of the Yankees. With the Mets refusing to come close to those terms, Kingman announced he would play out his option and become a free agent at the end of the season.

With this as a backdrop, Tom Seaver went to the mound for his 10th consecutive Opening Day assignment, and for the sixth time walked away victorious, as the Mets downed the Cubs, 5–3. While the Mets spotted the Cubs an early 2–0 lead, a four-run fifth inning put the Mets ahead to stay. An outfield collision between Bobby Murcer, acquired by the Cubs in a trade with the Giants over the offseason for Bill Madlock, and center fielder Jerry Morales opened the gates for the Mets' big inning.

Jerry Koosman, deprived of a Cy Young Award over the winter when Randy Jones was named the winner, was deprived of a victory in the second game of the season after the bullpen failed to hold a 6–3 lead for him. Only a two-run double by Joe Torre in the top of the ninth inning saved the day for the Mets, who came away with an 8–6 win.

The Cubs were able to salvage the series finale with a 5–2 win. A three-run homer by Cubs rookie shortstop Ivan DeJesus off Jon Matlack in the fifth inning did the Mets in. The series with the Cubs complete, the Mets returned home for their home opener against the St. Louis Cardinals. Tom Seaver was on the mound again and was in top form as he shut out the Cardinals on five hits and drove home two runs as the Mets downed the Cardinals, 4–0. John Stearns, who took over as the number one catcher, and John Milner both hit solo home runs to account for the other two Mets runs. The Cardinals were able to take the remaining two games of the series despite another fine pitching performance by Jerry Koosman in the series finale. The Mets lost their third consecutive game when the Cubs, in for a weekend series, scored seven runs in the top of the eighth inning off Jon Matlack and Skip Lockwood, eclipsing a 4–1 Mets lead. The Mets recovered, however, to win the next two games behind Nino Espinosa and Tom Seaver. It was a fifth-inning base hit by Steve Ontiveros, acquired with Bobby Murcer in the Bill Madlock deal, that ruined Seaver's bid for the first no-hitter thrown by a Mets pitcher. The one-hitter was the fifth of Seaver's career.

The Mets, one game over .500 in the early going, headed to St. Louis for a three-game rendezvous with the Cardinals before returning home to face the always-tough Pittsburgh Pirates. After the Mets lost two out of three to the Cardinals, the Mets left St. Louis a .500 ball club. Jerry Koosman won his first game of the season in the middle game of the series, as the Mets beat the Cardinals, 5–2. "I enjoyed the way it turned out, but I didn't enjoy my performance," said Koosman. "Out of my three starts this year, this was my worst."[3]

The Mets returned home to take on the Pirates and for two consecutive games, the Pirates scored ninth-inning runs to beat the Mets by one run and sweep a rain-shortened series. The inclement weather continued as the Expos followed the Pirates into Shea Stadium, and rain allowed only one of the scheduled games to be played. Jerry Koosman, not blessed with much luck in the early season, saw his luckless streak continue. Despite a masterful performance, Koosman had only his second loss of the season to show for his efforts. With the Mets carrying a 1–0 lead in the top of the third inning, and Andre Dawson on third with two outs, Expos shortstop Pepe Frias bounced the ball back to Koosman. With the easiest of plays in front of him, Koosman threw to Kingman for what seemed certain to be the third out of the inning. But Kingman inexplicably dropped the throw, allowing the tying run to score. The Expos continued to make the Mets pay for the miscue after the next batter, Ellis Valentine, cleared the fence for a two-run blast, giving the Expos an insurmountable 3–1 lead. Koosman in his typically classy manner refused to blame Kingman but rather shouldered the blame himself. "Mental mistakes bother you, but anyone can make a physical mistake. This time I fielded the ball and threw it to first base so hard that the ball tailed and I handcuffed Kingman with it."[4] The Mets did score a ninth-inning run to make it close, but Expos ace Steve Rogers was able to strikeout Joe Torre in a pinch-hitting role to end the game, sending Koosman to his third loss.

With the Mets' offense in dire need of some additional punch, the Mets signed Lenny Randle, whose best punch to date was the one he threw at his former manager, Frank Lucchesi, during a spring training altercation, which earned Randle his unconditional release. Randle, however, was eager to put the incident behind him. "It's something that happened, and it's over, and I just hope people would let me forget," said Randle. "I wish it hadn't happened, and I would hate to have some kid think of me as an example and hit his coach."[5]

Off to California went the Mets, where their first stop was San Diego. The Mets' offense, led by Dave Kingman's two home runs and sixth overall, pounded the Padres in the opener, 9–2, as Jon Matlack picked up his first win of the season. Tom Seaver continued to roll as the Mets beat the Padres and Cy Young Award winner Randy Jones, 4–1, in the middle game of the series. With the win Seaver improved his undefeated record to 4–0. Lenny Randle made his first appearance in a game as a Met and made a spectacular diving catch in left field after he came in for Dave Kingman as a defensive replacement. The Mets completed their first sweep of the season the next afternoon, raking the Padres, 8–2. Lenny Randle started his first game as a Met and tripled in his first Mets at-bat.

The Mets traveled on to Los Angeles for a four-game series with the Dodgers where the contrast in the starting lineups couldn't be more startling. Whereas the Dodgers' starting lineup featured heavy hitters such as Davey Lopes, Reggie Smith, Steve Garvey, Ron Cey, Dusty Baker and Rick Monday, the only legitimate power threat emanating from the Mets' lineup was a disgruntled Dave Kingman. In the opener Jerry Koosman, despite another outstanding performance, suffered his third loss of the season, as the Mets were able to muster no more than one run, a second-inning home run by Mike Vail. Good defensive plays by the Dodgers deprived the Mets of additional scoring, and Koosman took the mound in the last of the eighth inning with the game tied 1–1. Lenny Randle, installed in left field for Dave Kingman as a defensive replacement, was unable to duplicate his feat from two games earlier, as his attempt to make a diving catch on a ball hit by Davey Lopes was unsuccessful, and Lopes ended up at second credited with a double. A "seeing eye" base hit off the bat of Bill Russell scored Lopes with the go-ahead run. Russell was able to move onto third base when Mike Vail made a wild and ill-advised throw home, and scored on an infield hit by Steve Garvey.

The Mets didn't have much better luck in the remaining three games of their series with the Dodgers while going down to defeat in each game. The Mets' losing streak reached five games after they lost the opener of a weekend series with the Giants at Candlestick Park. Jerry Koosman snapped the losing streak with a three-hit shutout as the Mets beat the Giants, 6–0. But the Mets' losing ways continued the next day when they were swept by the Giants, 4–2 and 10–0, in a Sunday afternoon doubleheader. With rain falling all afternoon, the Mets played the second game under protest, contending that due to the terrible field conditions, the contest should've never been played. The protest had little chance to be upheld. That ended a disastrous road trip that started off so promisingly after the Mets swept the Padres.

The Padres came into Shea to start the homestand and avenged their recent sweep by the Mets with a three-game sweep of their own. The series started with a twilight doubleheader after rain forced the postponement of the originally scheduled game. One inning into the opener, the Padres already had a 2–0 lead after Dave Winfield drilled a Tom Seaver pitch over the fence. Seaver was chased in the third inning, which was his earliest forced departure of the season, as the Padres went on to win the opener, 6–3. The Padres won the second game as well, 4–3, at the expense of Craig Swan. Jerry Koosman surrendered a first-inning run in the series finale when he walked Gene Tenace with the bases loaded and a home run to the opposing pitcher, Tom Griffin, in the seventh inning, before being removed from the game for a pinch-hitter, trailing 2–0. While a two-run homer by John Milner was able to get Koosman the two runs back, it was too late to save him from a loss after his replacement, Bob Myrick, allowed three Padres runs in the top of the eighth. Despite allowing just five hits and striking out ten, Koosman saw his record drop to 2-4. For the Mets, it was their 10th loss in 11 games.

Jon Matlack's seven-hit shutout and home runs by Dave Kingman, his eighth of the season, and Lenny Randle gave the Mets a momentary respite from the daily losses that were beginning to pile up on the dispirited franchise as the Mets beat the Dodgers, 3–0, to open a three-game weekend series. By the time the weekend ended, two more games were added to the loss column, and the grumbling by Tom Seaver in particular grew louder after the Mets lost another one-run game, 4–3, in 12 innings. "When you think that just a few months ago with our pitching, management could really have helped us. They had a golden opportunity and did nothing."[6]

The Mets' offense finally showed some life late in the opener of a three-game series with the Giants. After Jerry Koosman and John Montefusco hooked up in a scoreless pitching duel through the first five innings, the Giants touched Koosman for a run in the sixth inning. The Giants' lead was short-lived, however, as Ed Kranepool homered in the last of the sixth with a runner on board to give the Mets a 2–1 lead. However, it wasn't until the last of the seventh inning that the Mets had their most prolific inning of the short season. The outburst began with the first pitch delivered by Montefusco, which his counterpart, Jerry Koosman, rerouted over the left field fence for his second career home run and the first since his rookie season of 1968. Base hits by Randle, Staiger and Boisclair loaded the bases. Two runs scored on a botched double play, and after Jerry Grote was intentionally walked, Bud Harrelson cleared the bases with a double, putting the cap on a six-run inning. Koosman finished strongly, allowing only four hits all evening and picking up his third win of the season.

The Mets were able to take the second game of the series as well behind Jon Matlack's second consecutive shutout and the continued inspired play of Lenny Randle. After doubling with two outs in the third inning, Randle on a heads-up play took third when Darrell Evans threw behind the runner. The extra base allowed Randle to score the Mets' first run when Giants starter Jim Barr threw a wild pitch. Randle was equally impressive on defense, making three nice plays in aiding Matlack to keep the Giants off the scoreboard, as the Mets beat the Giants, 2–0.

The Mets completed a sweep of the Giants the next afternoon with the bat of Lenny Randle again being the big story. Randle, who had hit in six consecutive games, added his second home run and a single, raising his average to .420. But the biggest story of the day was the pitching of Jackson Todd, who picked up his first major league win in his first major league start. More significant than the win for Todd was the fact that he was still alive and able to take his start since a little more than two years earlier he was diagnosed with cancer and given a 10 percent chance for survival. Todd, whose only blemish on this day was an eighth-inning three-run homer off the bat Terry Whitfield, took pride in assisting people going through the same travails that he did. "It gives me a warm spot inside to answer people who write me and tell them how I beat cancer, giving them hope. I like to encourage other people who have the disease."[7]

The Mets were not feeling very good themselves after heading to Cincinnati for a four-game series and just barely managed to escape with one victory after beating the Reds, 4–3, in 11 innings in the final game of the series. Jackson Todd picked up his second win in less than a week after pitching two solid innings of relief, including escaping with a one-out, bases-loaded threat.

After another week of dismal play in which the Mets lost a game to the Pirates, three to the Phillies, and then were swept by the Expos in a Memorial Day doubleheader, Joe Frazier became the fall guy for the dispirited and disenchanted sorry state of affairs of the franchise and was relieved of his duties. In his stead the Mets named Joe Torre, long mentioned as a managerial candidate, as player-manager. While the players believed Torre would be an upgrade, they also believed his installation wouldn't resolve the core issues which brought the team to its pathetic state in the first place. Tom Seaver's dispute was with the management and not with the manager. One criticism of Frazier, which Torre quickly promised to end, was the consistent juggling act by Frazier. In the 45 games played by the Mets thus far in the season, Frazier used 34 different lineups. Felix Millan, who had been shuttling between second, third and the bench, was returned to second base, Lenny Randle to third base, Dave Kingman was given the regular left field job, and John Milner became the regular first baseman. One other change instituted by Torre was to catch Grote on days the kids were starting.

The immediate effect on the club was positive as the Mets decisively beat the Expos in Torre's first game, 6–2, behind Craig Swan. A grand slam home run by John Stearns made a winner out of Tom Seaver in Torre's second game. When Torre went to the mound to remove Seaver, an unusual scene ensued. First, Seaver held out the ball for Torre to take. Then as he started off the mound, Seaver slapped the manager on the butt and then they clasped hands. "Don't forget," said Torre, "I'm still one of the guys."[8] Jerry Koosman became the next beneficiary of the Mets' new and improved play, as the Mets completed a two-game sweep of the Expos in their new ball park, Olympic Stadium. It was a game that saw the Mets steal a season-high four bases as well as pull off their first suicide squeeze of the season when Koosman bunted Bud Harrelson home in the fourth inning. Lee Mazzilli, installed as the starting center fielder based solely on his

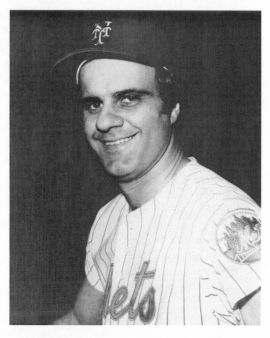

With the team sown with dissension and playing poorly, the Mets replaced Joe Frazier as manager with the popular Joe Torre (National Baseball Hall of Fame Library).

impressive September from the previous season, and was struggling mightily at the plate, added his first home run of the season.

June 3 saw the Phillies come in to Shea for a big four-game weekend series. In the opener, Torre sustained his first loss as manager, a game the Mets lost, 1–0, when a ninth-inning rally fizzled. Despite the loss, a new attitude had taken hold of the moribund franchise. The Mets bounced back the next day as Nino Espinosa and Skip Lockwood combined to shut out Steve Carlton and the Phillies, 2–0. The Mets' record under Torre improved to 6-1 after the Mets swept a Sunday afternoon doubleheader from the Phillies to take three out of four. Joe Torre made his first appearance as a player since being named manager when he inserted himself as a pinch-hitter in the 10th inning of the first game. After the Mets had jumped out to a 5–4 lead in the last of the seventh inning, Tim McCarver's two-out home run off Bob Apodaca in the top of the ninth inning sent the game into extra innings. With the game still tied 5–5 in the last of the 10th inning, John Milner singled with one out and Dave Kingman followed with a single of his own, sending Milner to third. But with the Mets' new aggressive style, Kingman headed for second, where he slid in safely, breaking the nose of Phillies second baseman Davey Johnson in the process. With runners now on second and third, Torre appeared out of the dugout with a bat, hitting for the left-handed batting Bruce Boisclair. Torre's appearance was greeted by a rousing applause from the over 30,000 fans in attendance, which quickly changed to boos after the Phillies intentionally walked Torre. But it was all academic after the first pitch thrown by Phillies reliever Tom Underwood took off and nicked the glove of catcher Bob Boone as John Milner scampered home with the winning run.

Dave Kingman's ninth home run of the year, a three-run job off Jim Kaat in the last of the fourth inning, was enough as the Mets held off a ninth-inning Phillies' rally for a 3–2 win and a sweep of the doubleheader.

The Mets made it seven wins out of eight games for Torre after the Cincinnati Reds came into Shea and were greeted to an 8–0 whitewashing by Tom Seaver and the newly resurgent Mets. Aside from pitching his 42nd shutout of his career, Seaver reached an additional milestone when Dan Driessen became Seaver's 2,397th strikeout victim, moving him into 13th place among all-time strikeout leaders and ahead of Sandy Koufax. An unforgiving Reds team avenged their being shut out when Jack Billingham shut the Mets out, 5–0. A three-run homer by George Foster off Jerry Koosman in the first inning put the Mets in a hole they couldn't crawl out of. For Mets fans the only excitement on this night consisted off seeing their new manager being ejected from his first game despite being on the job for a little over a week. The play in question evolved in the eighth inning on a ground ball hit by Dan Driessen, fielded by Millan and thrown to Milner at first, but ruled safe by first base umpire Ed Montague, causing Torre to rush out of the dugout to argue the call. After an emphatic argument, Torre was given the good old heave-ho to the delight of the crowd of just under 20,000.

For the time since Torre took over the managerial reins, the Mets lost two games in a row as the Mets headed out to Houston for a weekend four-game series against the Astros, and lost the opener, 4–1. The Mets returned to the win column when they split a Saturday afternoon doubleheader, losing the first game, 4–1, but salvaging the nightcap, 6–4, scoring two runs in the ninth inning to tie the game and then adding two runs in the tenth to win the contest and snap Torre's longest losing streak at three games. With Jose Cruz having driven in all four of Houston's runs in the second game of the doubleheader, the Mets came to bat in the top of the ninth inning trailing, 4–2, and only three outs away from losing their fourth consecutive game. After the first of those outs were recorded, Astros reliever Joe Sambito walked both Felix Millan and Lenny Randle. Sambito was relieved in favor of Ken Forsch, who induced Stearns to hit into a fielder's choice, putting runners at the corners, but the Mets were down to their last out. That last out appeared to be easy in coming when John Milner bounced a grounder to the first baseman, Bob Watson, who threw wildly to Ken Forsch, allowing Millan to score. Dave Kingman, who had already struck out six times over the course of the doubleheader, finally made contact, but again just enough to apparently end the game, when he sent a ground ball to Enos Cabell, who booted the ball, allowing John Stearns to score the tying run.

After Skip Lockwood was able to hold the Astros off the board in the ninth inning, Bruce Boisclair led off the Mets' tenth with a double. Jerry Grote followed with a sacrifice bunt, which catcher Ed Hermann, in an attempt to nail the lead runner Boisclair, threw wildly down the third base line, allowing Boisclair to score the go-ahead run. A double by Millan brought home an insurance run.

A five-hitter by Seaver allowed the Mets to split the series, but the big news item on this day was Tom Seaver's refusal to speak to the press after the game, telling reporters to "leave me alone please." Seaver sat with his head bowed, his eyes fixed on the floor. Known only to Mets beat reporter Jack Lang, on June 10, Seaver asked the Mets to trade him, as his long-standing dispute with Donald Grant reached a climax. While Donald Grant accused Seaver of being a greedy ingrate, who wanted to renegotiate his contract after the new realities of the free-agent market set in, Seaver begged to differ. "My unhappiness started long before the free agent bit," said Seaver. "It began during my contract negotiations. They charged me with a lot of things and even threatened to trade me. All of a sudden, nine years of performance and loyalty was being thrown out the window. I kept it inside me for a year, but then it all came out. I realized I could no longer work for Mr. Grant. The situation was impossible. I asked them to trade me if conditions remained the same. "One of the conditions Seaver was referring to was the Mets' adamant refusal to enter the free-agent market and pursue the solid hitter they were so desperately lacking. "They expect us to be aggressive on the field, but they remain passive in the front office," charged Seaver.[9]

When the Mets reached Atlanta, Seaver ate dinner with his two buddies, Jerry Koosman and Bud Harrelson, and confided to them as well that he had pitched his last game as a Met. The Seaver drama kept unfolding as the series against the Braves opened. The Mets, behind Jerry Koosman, took the opener, beating the Braves, 7–1, with Koosman striking out 10 batters. The usual press gathering around the winning pitcher was nonexistent as media members instead made their way over to Tom Seaver to get a reaction on the team's statement concerning the possibility of an impending trade. Naturally, Seaver had no comment.

As the deadline neared, Seaver began to have misgivings about his decision to move on. On the advice of Mets beat reporter Jack Lang, Seaver went over the head of Donald Grant and went directly to the team president, Mrs. Lorinda de Roulet, to try and resolve his differences with his employer. While Mrs. De Roulet as a rule didn't interfere in the operation of the ball club, for once she agreed to intercede. After four phone conversations on June 14, Mrs. De Roulet agreed to extend Seaver's contract for two more years, and Seaver's future as a Met appeared to be salvaged. Yet on the morning of June 15, Tom Seaver learned of an article written in the *New York Daily News* by Dick Young. Young wrote that the reason Seaver wanted to renegotiate his contract was because his wife, Nancy, was jealous of her friend Ruth Ryan, because her husband, Nolan Ryan, was making more money than Seaver. After the impact of the words set in, Seaver got on the phone with the team's PR director, Arthur Richman. "Get me out of here," yelled Seaver. "Tell Joe McDonald everything I said last night is forgotten. I want out. The attack on my family is just something I can't take."[10]

At the conclusion of the Mets-Braves game, which incidentally the Mets won, 6–5, came the dreaded announcement that Met fans were hoping they would never hear, as the following statement was issued from the Mets' board of directors:

> Last night Tom Seaver talked to Joe McDonald with strong suggestions regarding his remaining with the Mets. While the owners and directors were considering those suggestions this morning, a message came from Tom Seaver that he had a change of heart. He said: "Forget what I told Joe McDonald last night. I want out." Therefore the board felt an obligation to consider the deal at hand and have decided to accept Cincinnati's offer. It is with sincere regret that we have accepted Tom Seaver's request and traded him to Cincinnati for the following players: Doug Flynn, Pat Zachry, Steve Henderson and Dan Norman.

But the bloodletting didn't end there. Shortly after announcing the Seaver trade, the Mets announced that they had taken care of their second problem by sending the most prolific home run hitter the team ever had, Dave Kingman, over to the San Diego Padres, in return for Bobby Valentine, a utility infielder, and Paul Siebert, a minor league pitcher.

With the trading of the pitcher affectionately known as "The Franchise" and the exiling of Kingman on the same evening, this night would always sadly be recorded in the annals of Mets history as "the Midnight Massacre."

13

Into the Abyss

A deflated and depleted Mets team returned home to a stadium now aptly called Grant's Tomb by the disgruntled Met fans that besieged the Shea Stadium switchboard in the days preceding the trade, hoping to avert the cataclysmic event.

The reactions by the veteran Met players were decidedly mixed with distress and confusion. They had this to say in the June 16, 1977, edition of the *New York Times*:

JERRY KOOSMAN: "What it will take is to win, win and keep winning, to make us forget the loss of Seaver."

ED KRANEPOOL: "I just hope that our scouts did their homework in who we got for Seaver. Tom Seaver forced the Mets to rebuild."

JON MATLACK: "I don't want to get into trouble, so I want to be careful of what I say. But I don't think this deal was made, per se, to help this ball club. It was a deal that had to be made."

BUD HARRELSON: "I'm selfish. Who we got for Tom is trivia as far as I'm concerned. I lost my friend."

The only one who expressed any kind of optimism at all was not, surprisingly, manager Joe Torre. "I hope the fans won't overreact. I hope they'll wait and see. We made a hell of a lot better deal than we had last week with Cincinnati. (The Reds originally refused to part with Steve Henderson). We've added speed and we've added youth. We've got a deeper ball club and we won't strike out as much."

A crowd of just fewer than 9,000 showed up to Shea Stadium as the Mets played their first game in nine years without Tom Seaver on the Mets' roster. Yet despite the new realities, the Mets continued the exciting and scrappy style of play they had exhibited since Torre took over the managerial reigns, as the Mets scored two runs in the last of the seventh inning and held off the Houston Astros, 4–3, as Torre improved his record as manager to 12-5.

The next night saw three of the new Mets in the starting lineup as Pat Zachry took Seaver's spot in the starting rotation, Steve Henderson was inserted as the regular left fielder, and Doug Flynn started at shortstop in place of Bud

Despite aggressive play by young players such as Steve Henderson (right) and John Stearns, the Mets often found themselves outmatched by the rest of the league (National Baseball Hall of Fame Library).

Harrelson, who was feeling ill. The crowd of 15,201 was not as docile as they were the previous evening, chanting "We want Tom! We want Tom!" for most of the evening. The evening for the Mets ended as a lost cause as they were defeated by the Astros, 7–1. Despite the lopsided score, Pat Zachry in his Mets debut was actually impressive, allowing only one earned run in his six innings of work. An error by Lenny Randle in the fifth inning opened the gates for three unearned runs to score to give the Astros a 4–1 lead.

While Tom Seaver, in his new role as a starting pitcher for the Cincinnati Reds, was busy shutting out the Expos on a three-hitter, Jerry Koosman's defense was busy falling apart behind him, as the Mets let a 3–0 lead evaporate on their way to a 4–3 loss. It was a solo home run by John Milner in the second inning and a two-run job by Kranepool in the fourth inning that gave the Mets their 3–0 lead as Houston came to bat in the top of the sixth inning. Koosman may have been getting weary due to the fact that he was on base twice with two base hits on a hot, muggy New York June afternoon. Enos Cabell had a base hit that dropped in front of the not fleet-footed right fielder Ed Kranepool. After a double steal, Jose Cruz lifted a fly ball that Ed Kranepool allowed to bounce over his head, scoring both base runners. A moment later Cruz scored the tying run on a base hit by Bob Watson. In the seventh inning, a drive by Julio Gonzalez, which got in between Steve Henderson and Lee Mazzilli, went for a triple, and the go-ahead run scored on a sacrifice fly by Cesar Cedeno. An 8–2 rout allowed the Mets to split the series with the Astros.

The Braves followed the Astros into Shea Stadium and Steve Henderson's 10th major league at-bat resulted in his first career home run, a three-run blast in the last of the 11th inning off Don Collins to give the Mets a 5–2 extra-inning win. In a game in which the Braves took a 2–0 lead in the top of the first inning when Willie Montanez hit a two-run homer off Jon Matlack, it took until the last of the ninth inning, when starting left fielder Ed Kranepool homered, for the Mets to be able to draw even. In the top of the 11th inning, Torre replaced Kranepool with Henderson for defensive purposes. With one out in the last of the 11th inning, John Stearns doubled and Felix Millan was intentionally walked to get to the rookie Henderson. Two pitches later the game was over as Henderson deposited an 0–1 pitch into the left field stands. "It makes you kinda mad because they don't have no respect for me. In the major leagues, they don't have no respect for a rookie. I just want some respect," said Henderson.[1] Yet Henderson admitted to being nervous before his at-bat, but was calmed down by his manager. "He stopped me and told me it's just a game, relax," said Henderson. "If he hadn't done that, I mighta gone up there and swung at bad balls. After the game, I went to his office and thanked him personally."[2]

Despite the early success of Torre as manager and the inspired and aggressive play of the new Mets, it became painfully but increasingly clear that when it came time to play the more elite teams of the league, they were clearly overmatched. By the middle of July the Mets were firmly entrenched in the cellar of the National League East. The downward spiral began with a trip to Chicago on June 24 for a three-game weekend series with the surprising Cubs, residing atop the National League East. The Cubs promptly swept the three-game series, including a shocking 5–4 victory in the middle game of the series, despite trailing 4–1 as they came to bat in the last of the ninth inning. "That was the toughest loss we've had since I took over," said Torre.[3]

Pat Zachry, who pitched well in his second consecutive start, was just three outs away from picking up his first win as a Met with relief ace Skip Lockwood on the mound to close it out. Steve Swisher led off the inning with a double, and after the first out of the inning was recorded, Ivan DeJesus and Larry Biittner followed with doubles, cutting the Mets' lead to a single run, 4–3. With Lockwood replaced by Bob Apodaca, Bill Buckner followed with a drive to deep left-center field, where Steve Henderson camped under the ball ready to put it away for the second out when Lee Mazzilli came drifting in from center field and speared the ball. Just as he did, Mazzilli bumped into Henderson and dropped the ball, allowing the tying run to score. An intentional walk and then an unintentional walk loaded the bases. Manny Trillo followed with a grounder to third, where Doug Flynn, who entered the game as a defensive replacement, bobbled the ball momentarily, precluding any possibility of a double play as the winning run scored.

After being swept by the Cubs, the Mets headed home for three with the Phillies. The Mets lost the first two games of the series and their sixth straight before a fine pitching effort by Jerry Koosman and a big offensive night from Bobby Valentine snapped the losing streak as the Mets beat the Phillies, 5–3. The Mets got off to a quick start after scoring two runs in the last of the first inning. Lenny Randle led off with a double and Bobby Valentine followed with his first hit as a Met, putting runners at the corners with nobody out. Steve Henderson followed with a double off the top of the center field fence, scoring both Randle and Valentine. The next batter, Ed Kranepool, was thrown out of the game after arguing balls and strikes with home plate umpire Frank Pulli. Bud Harrelson, on the bench, was called on to take Kranepool's spot in the lineup, and defensively took over the shortstop position. Bobby Valentine, who was the game's starting shortstop, moved over to first base to take the position vacated by Kranepool. Valentine homered in the fifth inning to increase the Mets' lead to 4–0. With the losing streak behind them, the Mets hit the road again for a trip that would see them play five games in Montreal, then move on to Philadelphia for four, including a Fourth of July game, before returning home to take on the Expos.

After scoring a ninth-inning run in the opener for a 4–3 win against the Expos, the Mets fell short in the remaining four games. The closest the Mets came to winning one of the four was the opener of the Friday evening double-header. Despite the Expos touching up Jon Matlack for six runs in the first five innings to open up a 6–1 lead, the Mets fought back to score four runs in the eighth inning but fell one run short.

Jon Matlack, suffering his worst season in his career and had not won a game since May 18, saw his record drop to 3–9. "I'll kick myself in the butt to see if I can get turned around," said Matlack. "We've filmed my moves in prac-tice. We've filmed them during a game. We've gone through old films of my winning games. I've asked everybody and anybody what they thought I was doing wrong. When the answers overlapped, I considered them seriously. If anything eventually works, I'll do handsprings."[4]

The Mets fared no better in Philadelphia as they were swept by the Phillies. A crowd of better than 63,000, the largest in Veterans Stadium history, showed up for the Fourth of July game. The large crowd was not only treated to a fire-works display after the game, but there were almost fireworks during the game as well when John Stearns came crashing into Phillies catcher Bob Boone on a play at the plate. While Boone and Stearns faced off against each other and both dugouts cleared, no punches were thrown and order was quickly restored. Jerry Koosman, the Mets' starter, was once again done in by a lack of offense and poor defense as he watched his record fall to 6–9 as the Mets dropped a 3–1 decision. The Phillies, who scored all their runs in the third inning, were assisted when Ed Kranepool, the left fielder, couldn't locate a ball hit by Mike Schmidt that eventually fell in for a double. A moment later, two runs came home to score when long-time Koosman nemesis, Ollie Brown, tripled off the center field fence. A single by Garry Maddox brought home Brown to account for the Phillies' scoring. On the other hand, solid defense by the Phillies, including a great diving catch by Jerry Martin off a ball hit by Ron Hodges, was able to hold the Mets to a single run.

The Phillies thrashed Mets pitching the next night, belting four home runs and chasing starter Pat Zachry before the right-hander could get out of the third inning, as the Phillies romped, 12–1.

Jon Matlack started the third game of the series but fared no better than his predecessors as he came away with his 10th loss of the season. The loss for the Mets was their seventh in a row.

The losing was extended to eight games before the Mets returned home for a weekend series with the Expos. By the time the evening was over, the streak stood at nine games when a late rally fell just short as the Mets went down to defeat one more time, 5–4. Jerry Koosman put in another strong effort, allowing the Expos only three of their five runs. Koosman, bedeviled all season by poor defensive play behind him, for once was guilty himself when he threw the ball away on a pickoff attempt with the bases loaded, allowing two runs to score. With the score tied 2–2, the Expos were able to scratch another run off Koosman to go ahead, 3–2. The Expos scored a couple more runs off Bob Apodaca to give them a 5–2 advantage as the Mets came to bat in the last of the ninth inning. The Mets refused to go down to their ninth straight loss quietly. There were two outs and nobody on before the Mets began to mount their comeback. Doug Flynn started the rally with a base hit, which appeared to be meaningless at the time. But Bruce Boisclair, pinch-hitting for Rick Baldwin, homered into the Mets bullpen to cut the Expos' lead to one run. At that point Expos manager Dick Williams replaced his pitcher, Joe Kerrigan, with Santo Alcala. Alcala was intent on making the game interesting, as he walked the next two batters, Lenny Randle and Bobby Valentine, on eight pitches. After throwing his ninth consecutive ball, and ball one to Steve Henderson, Alcala was excused in favor of Bill Atkinson. While Atkinson was able to break the streak of consecutive balls by getting his first pitch over, his next three deliveries were balls, and suddenly the Mets had the bases loaded and their most productive hitter, John Stearns, at the plate. But Stearns flied out to left field to end the game and extend the losing streak. Despite the losing, it was an upbeat Torre who met with the press after the game. "These guys don't know how to quit. Losing streak and all, they're all trying. Nobody has quit on me."[5]

It took another 17 innings, but the Mets finally snapped their losing streak when Lenny Randle's 17th-inning home run broke a 5–5 tie, as the Mets were finally able to beat the Expos. The game appeared early on to have loss written all over it as the Expos jumped on Craig Swan for three runs in the top of the fifth inning. The Mets, however, came right back to score four runs of their own, with the big blow a bases-loaded pinch-hit double by Bruce Boisclair,

Lenny Randle celebrates after his 17th-inning home run snapped a 5–5 tie and the Mets' nine-game losing streak (AP Images).

clearing the bases. While the Expos were able to immediately tie the game in their half of the sixth inning, there was no more scoring until the Expos scored a run in the top of the 11th inning to go ahead, 5–4. With the Mets now down to their last three outs before the losing streak reached 10 games, Steve Henderson stepped to the plate to lead off the inning. A moment later, Henderson was on the ground as Joe Kerrigan decked him with a fastball directed to his head. Unperturbed, Henderson dusted himself off, stepped back to the plate and deposited the next pitch over the left field fence to once again tie the game. The game remained tied until the last of the 17th inning when Lenny Randle hit his home run with the winning pitcher, Paul Siebert, acquired in the Kingman trade, on base.

The Mets were able to win the rubber game of the series as well, as Pat Zachry, nearly a month after being acquired by the Mets, won his first game in a New York uniform. While once again it was the Expos who jumped out to the early lead by scoring a run in the fifth inning, a double by Mike Vail in the last of the seventh inning gave the Mets the only runs they would need on their way to an impressive 2–1 victory.

The Cubs were next into town for a three-game series, and the opener saw the Mets extend their miniscule winning streak to three games. Jon Matlack was able to snap his losing streak as the Mets in dramatic fashion beat the Cubs, 4–2, when the new wonder kid, Steve Henderson, hit a two-run homer in the last of the eighth inning off Cubs relief ace Bruce Sutter to snap a 2–2 tie.

While figuratively speaking the lights went out on the franchise on the evening of June 15, the night of "the Midnight Massacre," the lights literally went out on the Mets on the evening of July 13. With the Cubs taking a 2–0 lead in the second inning of the middle game of the series on a two-run homer by Steve Ontiveros off Jerry Koosman, the veteran left-hander, angry with himself, began to overpower the Cubs. Koosman fired extreme heat, fanning 11 batters by the time the Cubs finished batting in the top of the sixth inning. A home run by Mike Vail in the last of the fifth inning off the Cubs' starter Ray Burris gave the Mets their first run of the evening, and they came to bat in the last of the sixth inning trailing by only run. Jerry Koosman led off the Mets' sixth inning with a groundout, and up to the plate stepped Lenny Randle. Burris went into his windup, and lo and behold, the lights went out. "I thought 'God, I'm gone,'" said Randle. "I thought for sure He was calling me. I thought it was my last at-bat."[6] It was 9:31 P.M. on the Shea scoreboard clock when the power failed. Emergency power in the stadium allowed for auxiliary lights in the exit areas as well as the public address system and the organ to keep functioning. With the hope of power being restored shortly, Jane Jarvis, the Mets' organist, kept the over 22,000 fans in attendance entertained by playing ("I'm Dreaming of a) White Christmas" on a sweltering 90-degree July evening. By 10:52 it became obviously and painfully clear that the power wouldn't be coming on any time soon, as the power outage wasn't restricted to Shea Stadium and its environs. Rather, it was a massive power outage that affected a good portion of New York state and would long be remembered by New Yorkers as the "Blackout of '77." As a result, the game became a suspended game, to be completed on September 16, when the Cubs would return to Shea Stadium. By the next afternoon, power was not yet restored, forcing the postponement of the finale of the series as well, which again was rescheduled as part of a September 17 doubleheader.

With power finally restored late on July 14, the Mets began a big weekend five-game series with the Pittsburgh Pirates that would carry the Mets into the All-Star Game break. The series saw the Mets take three out of five from the powerful Pirates as the two clubs split the doubleheaders played on Friday evening and Sunday afternoon. Again the big story of the series was Steve Henderson, whose two-run homer won the Saturday afternoon Old-Timers Day game with a two-run homer. Henderson then blasted a grand slam in the nightcap of the Sunday afternoon doubleheader to pace Jerry Koosman to his seventh win of the season.

With the first half of the season in the books, the Mets found themselves languishing in the cellar of the National League East, but there was yet a glimmer of light penetrating through the gloom of the basement. Despite being 18 games out of first only halfway through the season and already having given

Steve Henderson is congratulated by teammates after hitting his first major league grand slam (AP Images).

up on the 1977 season, the play of some of the youngsters on the roster gave rise to hope for the future. Despite the trade of Seaver, the Mets still had a solid five-man rotation, starting with Jerry Koosman and Jon Matlack and rounding out with three promising youngsters in Pat Zachry, Nino Espinosa and Craig Swan. "I like my pitching for the future," said Torre. "And what I like about it is that except for Koosman, all the arms are young."[7]

The second half of the season saw the Mets head off to California for a trip that would have them play three with the Padres and two games each with the Dodgers and Giants. While the Mets continued to play tough and aggressive ball, they were only able to win one of the three games with the Padres. Despite getting excellent pitching from the starters, only Jon Matlack, who scattered seven hits in a 5–0 Mets shutout, walked away with a win. Despite impressive performances by Zachry and Koosman, neither one was involved in the decision as Skip Lockwood was the loser in the two remaining games with the Padres.

Sunday afternoon, July 22, saw the Mets move on to Los Angeles and seemed to have the first game won. With the Mets leading 3–2 in the last of the ninth inning, two Dodgers were on base with two outs when Davey Lopes hit a long foul fly ball that Bruce Boisclair got under, put his glove on it, and then dropped the ball. Given second life, Lopes crashed a three-run homer, sending the Mets to a crushing 5–3 defeat. Had Boisclair held onto the ball, the Mets could've avenged their sweep at the hands of the Dodgers in early May with a sweep of their own, after Craig Swan stopped the Dodgers on three hits as the Mets took the finale of the series, 1–0.

The Mets were able to return from California with a winning record after sweeping the Giants handily in a short two-game series. However, the Mets returned home concerned about the health of Jon Matlack, who despite being the winning pitcher in the final game of the road trip, had to leave the game after five innings with a stiff shoulder.

Dave Kingman made his first appearance in Shea Stadium since being dealt to the Padres during a three-game weekend series that would close out the month of July for the Mets. Kingman was greeted by the Shea faithful with a loud round of boos. "I expected that," said Kingman. "I'm a villain around here. But now I can sit back the next two games and not have to listen to it. The Padres don't play me against right-handers." The left-hander Kingman was referring to was Jerry Koosman, who held the Padres to only three hits as the Mets beat the Padres, 4–1. New York scored three runs in the seventh inning and added a fourth run in the eighth inning as Koosman picked up his eighth win of the year.

A slugfest ended the Mets' four-game winning streak as the Padres outscored the Mets, 8–6. Joe Torre was ejected for the third time since becoming manager when he argued too loudly after Felix Millan was called out on a play at the plate in the fourth inning. But the Mets were able to win the series by outscoring the Padres in the rubber game of the series, 10–9.

The Dodgers followed the Padres into Shea and the Mets continued their feisty play by again winning two out of three from the Dodgers. New York won the opener in 12 innings, 8–7, with Steve Henderson hitting his seventh homer in the short period that he had been with the ball club. The Mets won the finale as well, a 14-inning rain-drenched affair that saw the Mets score two runs in the last of the ninth inning to tie the game, 3–3, despite trailing since the first inning. The Mets were able to scratch out the winning run in the last of the 14th inning thanks to Joel Youngblood, who also was acquired on the night of "the Midnight Massacre" in a deal that received little attention, as the Mets sent Mike Phillips to the Cardinals in return. After the Dodgers' pitcher, Mike Garman, balked Youngblood to second, Flynn advanced him to third with a sacrifice. Lee Mazzilli, nursing a sore left hand that he hurt sliding into the plate with the winning run in the first game of the series, was then called on to pinch-hit. Mazzilli singled past Steve Garvey to drive home Youngblood with the winning run. Paul Siebert won his second game as a Met without a loss. The only blemish for the Mets in the series was the middle game, where the Mets' classy left-hander Jerry Koosman hooked up against the Dodgers' own classy left-hander, Tommy John. The two left-handers were locked in a 2–2 duel as the game headed to the seventh inning. But the Dodgers loaded the bases in the inning, when with one out Reggie Smith singled and Ron Cey doubled. Garvey, who had homered earlier off Koosman, was then walked intentionally. Then perhaps pitching too carefully to Dusty Baker, Koosman walked him as the go-ahead run scored. Koosman then nearly escaped the inning without any further damage when Steve Yeager drilled a ball to right-center field that Youngblood dived for and grabbed, only to see the ball roll out of his glove as two more runs scored. The Mets were unable to do any further damage to Tommy John, who ended the evening with 10 strikeouts and his 12th win of the year.

The San Francisco Giants were the next club in to Shea and the Mets opened the series with a 3–2 victory when they scored a run in the eighth inning. With the win, the Mets had won eight of their last ten games to the delight of their manager. "These kids aren't selfish the way a lot of young ballplayers are, the way I was when I was a young player," said Torre. "They don't go yelling and screaming one minute and then quieting down the next minute. They have a kind of quiet confidence. They go right at them. They're playing good ball." Torre may have put his foot in his mouth as the Giants beat the Mets decisively in the final two games of the series.

With the Mets finished with the California clubs for the season, it was back to playing Eastern Division teams for awhile, and it was the St. Louis Cardinals who came rolling into Shea Stadium for a three-game series. Jerry Koosman took the start for the Mets and a 1–1 tie into the ninth inning. But after the Cardinals had a single and walk, Ken Reitz sent a tantalizing slow curve over the left field fence to give the Cardinals a 4–1 lead. Again the offense abandoned Koosman as the Mets were only able to add on a single run in the last of the ninth inning, and Koosman was charged with his 12th loss of the season. While the Mets were able to win the middle game of the series behind Espinosa, they lost the rubber game and then headed off to Pittsburgh to take on the Pirates for a big five-game series.

After the Pirates routed the Mets and Pat Zachry in the opener of the series, the Mets played the Pirates tough in a Friday evening doubleheader, but came up short in both games as they lost, 3–2 and 6–5, the latter in 12 innings. In the opener, Jerry Koosman limited the powerful Pirates' offense to three runs, but had nothing to show for it except for his 13th loss of the season, as the Mets' offense could only muster two first-inning runs. This marked the third consecutive outing for Koosman in which the Mets scored only two runs for the snake-bitten left-hander. In the second game the Mets lost more than just a game. They lost their second baseman, Felix Millan, for the remainder of the season when he broke his collarbone in a fight with Pirates catcher Ed Ott. With the Pirates leading 3–1 as they came to bat in the last of the sixth inning, Joe Torre brought Millan into the game to play second when he changed his infield. With Ott on first base, Mario Mendoza bounced a grounder to short. Millan took the throw at second for a force out. Before Millan could get out of the way of the hard-charging runner, Ott crashed into Millan, knocking him to the ground. An enraged Millan got up from the ground and punched Ott in the jaw. In retaliation, Ott lifted Millan over his head and slammed him on his back. Millan, with a broken collarbone, was removed on a stretcher, while Ott was ejected from the game. "I was just trying to break up that double play," said Ott, "when he came up to me and without saying a word hit me in the mouth with the baseball still in his hand. I just picked him up and hurled him to the ground. It's unfortunate that he broke his collarbone, but I can't see what else I could do. I can't stand there and say, 'Hey, you just punched me in the mouth,' and not do anything."[8] Ironically, it was Ott's replacement, Duffy Dyer, that drove home the game-winning run in the 12th inning after once again the Mets fought back to the tie game and force extra innings.

The Mets lost their fourth consecutive game to the Pirates, and fifth in a row overall, despite getting another excellent performance from a starter. This time it was Matlack, who allowed the Pirates a first-inning run and nothing more in his seven innings of work. But the Mets' bats remained dormant, as Jerry Reuss shut the Mets out while scattering seven hits. By the time the Mets gleefully left Pittsburgh, they were riding a six-game losing streak as they headed on to St. Louis.

The Mets' offense broke out in a manner not seen in a while as they scored seven runs in support of Craig Swan. The Mets snapped their six-game losing streak in a 7–4 win over the Cardinals. The win also snapped a personal six-game losing streak for Swan, who saw his record improve to 8-7. The Mets followed through with a 5–1 victory the next day as Zachry picked up his first complete-game victory as a Met. But the Mets' offense that seemingly overexerted themselves in the first two games of the series had nothing left for Jerry Koosman in the finale of the series as he suffered his 14th defeat of the season. While Koosman allowed the Cardinals only two runs in another outstanding performance, his mound opponent, Bob Forsch, allowed the Mets only two hits.

For the first time in his career, Tom Seaver showed up at Shea Stadium not wearing a New York uniform as the Cincinnati Reds came into town to take on the Mets for a weekend series, starting with a Friday evening twilight doubleheader. After the Reds handily took the Mets in the first three games of the series, it was Tom Seaver's turn to face his old teammates for the first time. Even though it was Pat Zachry's turn in the rotation, Jerry Koosman requested and received permission from Joe Torre to take the start against his long-time friend. The second largest crowd of the season, over 46,000 fans, attended to pay homage to their long-time hero.

It was an obviously tense Koosman who took the mound in the first inning, and was immediately greeted by a Pete Rose double down the right field line. Two outs later a single by George Foster brought home Rose, and the Reds ended the top of the first inning with a 1–0 lead. From the moment Seaver leapt out of the dugout to take the mound in the last of the first inning, the fans gave him a tumultuous ovation that lasted throughout his warm-ups. In response

Tom Seaver, in his first return to Shea Stadium after being exiled, pitches to his former teammate and friend Jerry Koosman (© Bettmann/Corbis).

Seaver tipped his cap to the fans in appreciation. "If I have given them any thrills over the years," said Seaver, "they have returned it to me tenfold."[9] But once the Mets' leadoff batter, Lenny Randle, stepped into the batter's box, it was the same old Seaver pitching with the same intensity that had earned him the title of "the Franchise" in his nine years with the Mets. Koosman settled down after his shaky first inning, and the two buddies then hooked into a classic pitching duel, with neither team scoring until the top of the fifth inning, when Seaver doubled and scored on a base hit by Pete Rose. It wasn't until the sixth inning that the Mets were able to score against Seaver. Bud Harrelson and Steve Henderson singled, and then Ed Kranepool, after hitting a foul home run that would've put the Mets ahead, hit a sacrifice fly, scoring Harrelson. With the Mets trailing, 2–1, in the eighth inning, the defense fell apart behind Koosman, leading to the Reds scoring three unearned runs and coming away with a 5–1 win. "If Kooz is pitching for us today," said Sparky Anderson, manager of the Reds, "he wins. They were both that good."[10]

After the game both Seaver and Koosman spoke to the press about the emotional reunion that saw the two star pitchers face off against each other. Tom Seaver said "It's awfully nice to come home. But this was no fun. It would've been fun if this was spring training, but it was too emotional. I was aware that they were up there at bat, but I tried to block it out of my mind. And now I'm awfully glad that it's over." According to Jerry Koosman, "I think the best man came out on top. I really don't think I can put myself in Tom's class. But I told Joe Torre in the dugout that I wished every game could be like this one — it was the highlight. And now Seaver can pick on me for 20 years about that double he hit off me."[11]

While Seaver came away with his 14th win of the season and also moved ahead of Don Drysdale into 11th place on the all-time strikeout list, for Koosman all his excellent work earned him was his 15th loss of the year. He appeared on the way to losing 20 games after winning 20 games the previous season. Only three other pitchers in the recent past shared the dubious distinction of losing 20 games after winning 20 games the preceding season: Mel Stottlemyre, who went 20-9 in 1965, but then went 12-20 in 1966; Steve Carlton, 27-10 in 1972, but 13-20 in 1973; and, Wilbur Wood, who was 20-19 in 1974, but then slipped to 16-20 in 1975. "I'm right up among the leaders with a 3.17 ERA," bemoaned Koosman. "I don't know how much better I could pitch. I can just go out and pitch every game the best I can and hope they get enough runs for me."[12] Koosman was also second in the league in strikeouts with 163 and was headed for his second consecutive season of 200 strikeouts or more. With any other team Koosman may have been gunning for his second consecutive 20-win season. But not with the Mets and their puny offense. In Koosman's 15 losses, the Mets scored a total of 22 runs for him. "Jerry has had a super year," said his manager Joe Torre, "but unfortunately he has not had the kind of support deserving of the way he pitched."[13]

The Mets were able to snap their five-game losing streak at the hands of the Houston Astros, who followed the Reds for a short two-game series. The Mets swept the series by identical scores of 2–1, keyed by clutch hits off the bats of Bruce Boisclair and Ed Kranepool in pinch-hitting roles. While Kranepool was getting his fair share of playing time in the first half of the season, with the team in a rebuilding mode, Torre wanted to see what he had in his younger players, namely Steve Henderson, Lee Mazzilli, Mike Vail and Bruce Boisclair. Kranepool, thus, was relegated to a pinch-hitting role. "There's no point in screaming and complaining," said Kranepool, who had been with the team since its inception in 1962. "You bet I'd rather play every day than pinch-hit some of the time. But they've talked about trading me a lot of times. But I stopped worrying about being traded 10 years ago and now I'm resigned to pinch-hitting or whatever they want me to do."[14]

By the time the Mets won another ball game, the calendar had turned from August to September, they were in the midst of a seven-game losing streak, and mathematically eliminated from the pennant race, 30½ games behind the division-leading Phillies with 29 games left.

By the time the season ended, the Mets found themselves firmly entrenched in the cellar, the doormat of major league baseball. Jerry Koosman, the proud left-hander whose ERA and strikeout numbers were equivalent to twenty-game

Lee Mazzilli was one of the few bright spots left on a franchise that had self-destructed (AP Images).

winners Rick Reuschel and John Candelaria, ended the season with 20 losses. "I didn't deserve to lose 20 this year," said Koosman. "I was behind 1–0 or 2–0 in the sixth and I'd wind up with the big L. If you don't get runs to keep you in the game, they have to pinch-hit for you, and you wind up with the loss. I think I pitched well enough in maybe 16 of those 20 defeats. I got pasted in about four of those, but 16 I deserved to win."[15]

But in the eyes of the Mets' fans, who stayed away from Shea in record numbers, the real loser was Donald Grant, who refused to accept the new realities of the times. He believed that baseball was a family game, and the key was to keep ticket prices down, even if it meant refusing to take part in the serious pursuit of free agents, or trading off both the team's best pitcher and its leading home run hitter. What Grant actually succeeded in doing was bringing the once-proud franchise into the abyss, making them the laughingstock and doormat of baseball, while the cross-town Yankees heavily invested in the free agent market and were reaping the benefits, both in attendance numbers and in the standings.

Notes

Chapter 1

1. *New York Times*, April 7, 1973.
2. *Sporting News*, May 5, 1973.
3. *New York Times*, April 19, 1973.
4. *New York Times*, April 20, 1973.
5. *Sporting News*, May 19, 1973.
6. Ibid.
7. *New York Times*, May 12, 1973.
8. *New York Times*, May 15, 1973.
9. *New York Times*, May 26, 1973.
10. *New York Times*, June 12, 1973.
11. *New York Times*, June 14, 1973.
12. *New York Times*, June 22, 1973.
13. *New York Times*, July 1, 1973.
14. Golenbock, *Amazin,'* 303.
15. Ibid., 299.
16. *New York Times*, July 12, 1973.
17. *Sporting News*, Aug. 4, 1973.

Chapter 2

1. *Sporting News*, Aug. 18, 1973.
2. *New York Times*, Aug. 12, 1973.
3. *New York Times*, Aug. 13, 1973.
4. *New York Times*, Aug. 18, 1973.
5. *New York Times*, Aug. 19, 1973.
6. *New York Times*, Aug. 20, 1973.
7. *New York Times*, Aug. 25, 1973.
8. *New York Times*, Aug. 29, 1973.

Chapter 3

1. *Sporting News*, Sept. 8, 1973.
2. *New York Times*, Sept. 4, 1973.
3. *New York Times*, Sept. 22, 1973.
4. *Sporting News*, Oct. 13, 1973.
5. *New York Times*, Sept. 27, 1973.

Chapter 4

1. *New York Times*, Oct. 7, 1973.
2. *New York Times*, Oct. 8, 1973.
3. *New York Times*, Oct. 9, 1973.
4. *New York Times*, Oct. 10, 1973.
5. *New York Times*, Oct. 14, 1973.
6. *New York Times*, Oct. 18, 1973.
7. *New York Times*, Oct. 19, 1973.
8. *New York Times*, Oct. 23, 1973.

Chapter 5

1. *Sporting News*, Oct. 10, 1973.
2. *Sporting News*, March 3, 1974.
3. Ibid.
4. *Sporting News*, Jan. 26, 1974.
5. *Sporting News*, April 6, 1974.
6. *Sporting News*, March 23, 1974.
7. *Sporting News*, May 4, 1974.
8. Ibid.
9. *New York Times*, April 22, 1974.
10. *New York Times*, April 27, 1974.
11. *New York Times*, April 28, 1974.
12. Jacobson, *The Pitching Staff*, 103.
13. *Sporting News*, March 23, 1974.
14. Jacobson, *The Pitching Staff*, 105.
15. Ibid.
16. *New York Times*, May 9, 1974.
17. *Sporting News*, June 1, 1974.
18. *Sporting News*, June 8, 1974.
19. *New York Times*, June 4, 1974.
20. *New York Times*, June 7, 1974.
21. Jacobson, *The Pitching Staff*, 150.
22. *Sporting News*, July 20, 1974.
23. *New York Times*, July 5, 1974.
24. *New York Times*, July 6, 1974.
25. *New York Times*, July 8, 1974.
26. *Sporting News*, Aug. 3, 1974.

Chapter 6

1. Jacobson, *The Pitching Staff*, 161.
2. Ibid.
3. *New York Times*, Aug. 6, 1974.
4. Jacobson, *The Pitching Staff*, 180.
5. *New York Times*, Aug. 21, 1974.
6. *New York Times*, Aug. 26, 1974.
7. Jacobson, *The Pitching Staff*, 192.
8. While it was widely believed that Aaron would retire at year's end, Aaron would not rule out coming back for another year. Eventually, Aaron did return, not to the Braves, but to the city where he first started his career, Milwaukee, as a member of the Brewers.
9. *New York Times*, Sept. 2, 1974.
10. *Sporting News*, Sept. 21, 1974.
11. *Sporting News*, Sept. 28, 1974.
12. Ibid.
13. Jacobson, *The Pitching Staff*.
14. *New York Times*, Sept. 13, 1974.
15. *New York Times*, Sept. 22, 1974.
16. *Sporting News*, Oct. 19, 1974.

Chapter 7

1. *Sporting News*, Dec. 7, 1974.
2. Ibid.
3. *Sporting News*, Nov. 30, 1974.
4. *New York Times*, Dec. 4, 1974.
5. *Sporting News*, Dec. 21, 1974.
6. *New York Times*, April 12, 1975.
7. *New York Times*, April 14, 1975.
8. *Sporting News*, May 3, 1975.
9. *New York Times*, May 3, 1975.
10. Mike Phillips was just acquired in a cash deal from the San Francisco Giants to backup Buddy Harrelson, who began having trouble with his knees.
11. *New York Times*, May 12, 1975.
12. *Sporting News*, May 31, 1975.
13. *New York Times*, May 13, 1975.
14. *Sporting News*, June 7, 1975.
15. *Sporting News*, June 21, 1975.
16. *New York Times*, June 5, 1975.
17. *New York Times*, June 6, 1975.
18. *Sporting News*, June 28, 1975.
19. *Sporting News*, July 5, 1975.
20. *New York Times*, June 20, 1975.
21. *New York Times*, June 23, 1975.
22. *New York Times*, June 28, 1975.
23. *New York Times*, June 29, 1975. (Sadly, this would be Stengel's last Old-Timers Day Game, as he would pass away at the end of the season.)

24. *New York Times*, June 30, 1975.
25. *Sporting News*, July 19, 1975.
26. Ibid.
27. *New York Times*, July 2, 1975.
28. *New York Times*, July 4, 1975.
29. *New York Times*, July 5, 1975.
30. *New York Times*, July 7, 1975.
31. *New York Times*, July 9, 1975.
32. *New York Times*, July 13, 1975.
33. *Sporting News*, Aug. 2, 1975.

Chapter 8

1. *New York Times*, July 18, 1975.
2. *Sporting News*, Aug. 2, 1975.
3. *New York Times*, July 22, 1975.
4. Associated Press, July 23, 1975.
5. *New York Times*, July 23, 1975.
6. *New York Times*, July 24, 1975.
7. *Sporting News*.
8. *New York Times*, July 30, 1975.
9. *New York Times*, Aug. 1, 1975.
10. *New York Times*, Aug. 2, 1975.
11. *New York Times*, Aug. 4, 1975.
12. *New York Times*, Aug. 5, 1975.
13. *New York Times*, Aug. 6, 1975.
14. Five days previously the Yankees fired their manager Bill Virdon, who was replaced by Billy Martin.
15. Golenbock, *Amazin'*.
16. Associated Press, Aug. 8, 1975.
17. Ibid.
18. Associated Press, Aug. 7, 1975.
19. *New York Times*, Aug. 8, 1975.
20. *New York Times*, Aug. 11, 1975.
21. *Sporting News*, Sept. 6, 1975.
22. *New York Times*, Aug. 20, 1975.
23. *New York Times*, Aug. 25, 1975.

Chapter 9

1. *New York Times*, Sept. 2, 1975.
2. *New York Times*, Sept. 3, 1975.
3. *New York Times*, Sept. 4, 1975.
4. *New York Times*, Sept. 7, 1975.
5. *New York Times*, Sept. 8, 1975.
6. *New York Times*, Sept. 11, 1975.
7. *New York Times*, Sept. 12, 1975.
8. *New York Times*, Sept. 16, 1975.
9. *New York Times*, Sept. 19, 1975.
10. *New York Times*, Sept. 22, 1975.

Chapter 10

1. *Sporting News*, Dec. 27, 1975.
2. Ibid.
3. *New York Times*, April 10, 1976.
4. *New York Times*, April 11, 1976.
5. *New York Times*, April 12, 1976.
6. *New York Times*, April 14, 1976.
7. *New York Times*, April 15, 1976.
8. *New York Times*, April 16, 1976.
9. *New York Times*, April 18, 1976.
10. *New York Times*, April 21, 1976.
11. *New York Times*, April 26, 1976.
12. *New York Times*, April 27, 1976.
13. *New York Times*, April 28, 1976.
14. *New York Times*, April 30, 1976.
15. *New York Times*, May 8, 1976.
16. *New York Times*, May 9, 1976.
17. *New York Times*, May 10, 1976.
18. *New York Times*, May 15, 1976.
19. Ibid.
20. *New York Times*, May 16, 1976.
21. *New York Times*, May 20, 1976.
22. *New York Times*, May 21, 1976.
23. *New York Times*, May 22, 1976.
24. *New York Times*, May 26, 1976.
25. *New York Times*, May 27, 1976.
26. *New York Times*, May 31, 1976.
27. *New York Times*, June 1, 1976.
28. *New York Times*, June 3, 1976.
29. *New York Times*, June 8, 1976.
30. *New York Times*, June 9, 1976.
31. *New York Times*, June 10, 1976.
32. *New York Times*, June 11, 1976.
33. *New York Times*, June 14, 1976.
34. *New York Times*, June 16, 1976.
35. *New York Times*, June 18, 1976.
36. *New York Times*, June 23, 1976.
37. *New York Times*, June 26, 1976.
38. *New York Times*, June 27, 1976.
39. *New York Times*, June 29, 1976.
40. *New York Times*, June 30, 1976.
41. *New York Times*, July 3, 1976.
42. *New York Times*, July 16, 1976.
43. *New York Times*, July 17, 1976.
44. *New York Times*, July 18, 1976.

Chapter 11

1. *New York Times*, July 21, 1976.
2. Lang, *The New York Mets: 25 Years of Baseball Magic.*

3. *New York Times*, July 27, 1976.
4. *New York Times*, July 29, 1976.
5. *New York Times*, July 30, 1976.
6. *New York Times*, July 31, 1976.
7. *New York Times*, Aug. 5, 1976.
8. *New York Times*, Aug. 13, 1976.
9. *New York Times*, Aug. 30, 1976.
10. *New York Times*, Sept. 4, 1976.
11. *New York Times*, Sept. 7, 1976.
12. *New York Times*, Sept. 8, 1976.
13. *New York Times*, Sept. 9, 1976.
14. *New York Times*, Sept. 12, 1976.
15. *New York Times*, Sept. 17, 1976.
16. *New York Times*, Sept. 19, 1976.
17. *New York Times*, Sept. 20, 1976.
18. *New York Times*, Sept. 21, 1976.
19. *New York Times*, Sept. 22, 1976.
20. *New York Times*, Sept. 23, 1976.
21. *New York Times*, Sept. 27, 1976.

Chapter 12

1. *Sporting News*, Nov. 27, 1976.
2. Ibid.
3. *New York Times*, April 20, 1977.
4. *New York Times*, April 28, 1977.
5. *New York Times*, April 30, 1977.
6. *New York Times*, May 16, 1977.
7. *New York Times*, May 20, 1977.
8. *New York Times*, June 2, 1977.
9. *Sporting News*, July 2, 1977.
10. *Sporting News*, July 9, 1977.

Chapter 13

1. *New York Times*, June 22, 1977.
2. Ibid.
3. *New York Times*, June 26, 1977.
4. *New York Times*, July 2, 1977.
5. *New York Times*, July 9, 1977.
6. *New York Times*, July 15, 1977.
7. *Sporting News*, Aug. 13, 1977.
8. *New York Times*, Aug. 13, 1977.
9. *Sporting News*, Sept. 3, 1977.
10. *New York Times*, Aug. 22, 1977.
11. Ibid.
12. *Sporting News*, Sept. 10, 1977.
13. Ibid.
14. *New York Times*, Aug. 24, 1977.
15. *Sporting News*, Oct. 8, 1977.

Bibliography

Adell, Ross, and Ken Samelson. *Amazing Mets Trivia*. Lanham, MA: Taylor Trade Publishing, 2004.

Angell, Roger. *Five Seasons: A Baseball Companion*. New York: Simon and Schuster, 1977.

Ballew, Bill. *The Pastime in the Seventies: Oral Histories of 16 Major Leaguers*. Jefferson, NC: McFarland, 2002.

Bjarkman, Peter. *The New York Mets Encyclopedia*. Champaign, IL: Sports Publishing, 2001.

Blatt, Howard. *Amazin' Met Memories: Four Decades of Unforgettable Moments*. Tampa, FL: Albion Press, 2002.

D'Agostino, Dennis. *This Date in New York Mets History: 20 Amazin' Years*. Briarcliff Manor, NY: Stein and Day, 2001.

Fishman, Lew. *New York's Mets: Miracle at Shea*. Englewood, NJ: Prentice Hall, 1974.

Golenbock, Peter. *Amazin': The Miraculous History of New York's Most Beloved Baseball Team*. New York: St Martin's Press, 2002.

Honig, Donald. *The New York Mets: The First Quarter Century*. New York: Crown, 1986.

Jacobson, Steve. *The Pitching Staff*. New York: Crowell, 1975.

Kalinsky, George. *The New York Mets: A Photographic History*. New York: Macmillan, 1995.

Kiner, Ralph. *Kiner's Korner: At Bat and on the Air — My 40 Years in Baseball*. New York: Arbor House, 1987.

Lang, Jack. *The New York Mets: 25 Years of Baseball Magic*. New York: Henry Holt, 1986.

Markusen, Bruce. *Tales from the Mets Dugout*. Champaign, IL: Sports Publishing, LLC, 2005.

Parker, Kathryn. *We Won Today: My Season with the Mets*. Garden City, NY: Doubleday, 1977.

Silverman, Matthew. *Mets Essential: Everything You Need to Know to Be a Real Fan*. Chicago, IL: Triumph Books, 2007.

Index